KEROUAC
AND FRIENDS

KEROUAC AND FRIENDS

A BEAT GENERATION ALBUM

Fred W. McDarrah

WILLIAM MORROW AND COMPANY
NEW YORK

The author is grateful to the following publishers, literary agents, and writers for use of previously copyrighted material:

Kerouac quotation on origin of "beat," from *Encounter*, August 1959. Copyright 1959 by Jack Kerouac. Reprinted by permission of the Sterling Lord Agency Inc.

"This Is the Beat Generation" by John Clellon Holmes, from the *New York Times Magazine*, November 16, 1952. Copyright 1959 by John Clellon Holmes. Reprinted by permission of the Sterling Lord Agency Inc.

"Youth Will Serve Itself" by Lawrence Lipton, from *The Nation*, November 19, 1956. Reprinted by permission of *The Nation*.

On the Road book review by Gilbert Millstein, from the *New York Times*, September 5, 1957. Copyright 1957 by the New York Times Company. Reprinted by permission.

"In Pursuit of Kicks" by David Dempsey, from the *New York Times Book Review*, September 8, 1957. Copyright 1957 by the New York Times Company. Reprinted by permission.

"Back to the Village—but Still on the Road" by Jerry Tallmer, from the *Village Voice*, September 18, 1957. Reprinted by permission of the author and the *Village Voice*.

"Jazz and Poetry" by Kenneth Rexroth, from *Esquire*, May 1958. Copyright 1958, 1984. Used by permission of Bradford Morrow for the Kenneth Rexroth Trust.

"Kerouac at the Village Vanguard" by Dan Wakefield, from *The Nation*, January 4, 1958. Reprinted by permission of the author and *The Nation*.

"Off the Road, into the Vanguard, and Out" by Howard Smith, from the *Village Voice*, December 25, 1957. Reprinted by permission of the author and the *Village Voice*.

"King of the Beats" by Seymour Krim, from *Commonweal*, January 2, 1959. Reprinted by permission of the author and *Commonweal*.

"The Beats Debated—Is It or Is It Not?" by Marc D. Schleifer, from the *Village Voice*, November 19, 1958. Reprinted by permission of the author and the *Village Voice*.

"The Roaming Beatniks" by Jack Kerouac, from *Holiday* magazine, October 1959. Copyright 1959 by Jack Kerouac. Reprinted by permission of the Sterling Lord Agency Inc.

"The Upbeat Beatnik" by Art Buchwald, from the *New York Herald Tribune*, January 4, 1960. Copyright by Art Buchwald. Reprinted by permission.

Preface

K *erouac and Friends* is more than a collection of photos and articles from the 1950s; it's a loving memoir of the wonderful carefree days when I had nothing to do except go to poetry readings, the Artist's Club, the Living Theatre, and the Cedar Street Tavern. I stayed out all night with friends and with Gloria.

This book is about me and Gloria and a specific time in our lives in New York's Greenwich Village. Those were happy-go-lucky days for all of us who wanted to have fun and be beat.

Kerouac and Friends is about the vintage years of the beat generation when everything seemed to happen and everyone who was anybody was in New York writing, reading, acting, painting, drinking, talking, playing.

Rents were cheap. I lived at 304 West 14th Street on the edge of the Village and paid $46.68 a month. In 1960 I moved to 64 Thompson Street near Broome in what is now fashionable Soho. I paid $55.57 per month for five rooms and a bath. I earned about $50 a week but we could eat out for two bucks and entertainment was cheap.

On weekends everybody from the neighborhood went to Washington Square Park to be part of the action—Norman Mailer, Anatole Broyard, Tuli Kupferberg, Sylvia Topp, Nat Hentoff, Mark Sufrin, Danny List, Harriet Sohmers, Bill Ward, Gil Millstein, Howard Smith, Millie Brower, Jack Micheline, Lenny Horowitz, and of course Ted Joans. Everybody knew everybody and it was like a family get-together. In those years the park was positively quaint with the Shanty Boys playing their homemade instruments and folk dancing around the foot of the arch.

Painting, poetry, avant-garde, and off-Broadway theater were in full swing; abstract painters threw globs of paint on canvases; poets shouted beat words at enthralled café crowds. Everybody was "creating" something and nobody deliberately did things to get their names in the papers. The beat scene was exciting, stimulating, inspirational. Gloria and I were authentic beatniks.

I was a groupie at heart. In the mid-1950s I went regularly to the Poetry Center of the YMHA on 92nd Street and heard the established writers and poets, so when the beat generation arrived I was prepared for the onslaught. I admired their work, collected it, read it, and followed in their footsteps, going everywhere and taking little snapshots along the way with an ancient Rolleicord, then later with a beat-up 35 mm Nikon S2.

I wanted to be part of the action. My camera was my diary, my ticket of admission, my way of remembering, preserving, proving that I had been there when it all happened.

But what really set me apart from the others was that I had a daytime job on the *Village Voice,* a savvy underground weekly that thumbed its nose at the establishment and told its small world all about the radical, crazed beat generation.

In the 1950s the paper usually ran twelve pages per week and, since I had once worked on Madison Avenue, I became the space salesman, selling one-inch ads to little shops along 8th Street. At night and on weekends I turned into a demon beatnik with a camera, eventually publishing my photos in the *Voice.* Later, the editor Dan Wolf made me the staff photographer.

While the daytime hours were occupied with the awesome task of peddling ads, my other life was far more interesting. Here is an example from my yearbook of what I did on March 16, 1959, a typical day: "Met Gloria at Lester Johnson's show at Zabriskie then went to Dody Müller's exhibit at The Hansa Gallery. Kerouac, Ginsberg, Corso, Frank, Amram, everybody was there. It was an exciting opening and I took 2 rolls of pictures. Spoke to Robert Frank about showing the Kerouac film [*Pull My Daisy*] at the Artist's Club but no reaction. Later Gloria and I had a sandwich at my house and then we went to the Living Theatre to hear Kenneth Patchen read to the jazz of Charlie Mingus. A nice crowd showed up and I took pictures as usual. Spoke to Howard Hart and some other poets and then G and I went to the Cedar Street Tavern and sat in a booth with Ted Joans, Lenny Horowitz, Jack Micheline and William Morris. We drank beer and goofed until 2 A.M. and then went home to bed."

As the months rolled by I accumulated a lot of photos; some were out of focus, blurred, overexposed, underexposed. As a novice photographer I actually threw away some of the negatives that didn't look good, a practice I wouldn't recommend today. But I had enough for a book and started to collect poems from everybody. In 1960 Ted Wilentz of the 8th Street Bookshop then published *The Beat Scene,* my first book.

Unlike the artists of the same period whose goal was to get an uptown show, the poets seemed more interested in reading their prose or poems to anyone who would listen, on the streets, in the parks, in the cafés, nightclubs, small theaters, anywhere. They wanted to be visible, admired, heard, and loved. They all had something to say, because they were the first of the postwar generation that rebelled against society.

Most of them grew up during the Depression, some under good family conditions. Many had gone to college, served in World War II, and found nothing had changed when they came home. Finally in the 1950s they believed they were chosen to engage in the holy crusade to raise the public conscience, to "tell the truth," to espouse the philosophy of living to their true feelings, stripping the mask of hypocrisy from a culture long weighed down by the traditional dogma of family, church, and state.

When the private lives of the beats were exposed, the public was outraged. Fearing these wild beasts had been turned loose to undermine and destroy the public morals, the media, especially *Time* and *Life* magazines, developed an unprecedented blitz against the beat generation, each week alerting the public to the menace.

Although very tame, this is one typical example of *Time* in one issue: "The bearded, sandaled beat likes to be with his own kind, to riffle through his quarterlies, write craggy poetry, paint crusty pictures and pursue his never ending quest for the ultimate in sex and protest. When deterred from such pleasures by the goggle-eyed from Squaresville, the beatnik packs his pot (marijuana), shorts and bongo drums, grabs his blackhosed pony-tailed beatchick and cuts out."

The public believed that a beatnik was anybody who looked

scruffy, carried a sheaf of rumpled papers, and read a kooky poem that included a few four-letter words. The public believed that beats slept on floors on dirty mattresses and were no different from Bowery bums.

The public never did take the beat generation seriously but the beats in fact paved the way for the quick acceptance of the New Journalism of Tom Wolfe, Pete Hamill, Jack Newfield, Hunter Thompson, Joe Flaherty, which was to emerge a decade later. And now after twenty-five years it is obvious that life in America has changed because of them.

Today, as an example, famous Hollywood male and female stars sell and sniff cocaine, have numerous illegitimate children, tell the world they have had an abortion or vasectomy, appear naked in films, say "fuck," "shit," "piss" on screen without batting an eye, and their exploits guarantee them a five-page spread in the weekly tabloids, numerous radio and TV appearances on talk shows, and a six-figure book contract.

It is mind boggling to think that in 1959 William Morris was thrown into jail for reading poetry in Washington Square Park, and I was thrown into jail when I was accused of throwing a snowball at a cop's car.

In New York the beat movement lasted only a couple of years. By 1961 the cafés began to feature folk music; the bars were jammed with tourists searching for beatniks; the writers and poets moved back to the West Coast. Some went back to school, some went to prison, some gave up the fight and disappeared.

My days as a beatnik were ended and I went on to other things. I opened up a bank account, and even bought insurance. Gloria and I got married and raised two sons, both now in college. We traveled to Europe, produced a half dozen books, bought a little cottage in the country, and I settled down at the *Village Voice* where I have now worked steadily for more than twenty-five years. Figure that out.

It was also twenty-five years ago that Jack Kerouac's *On the Road* was published. Numerous friends and my sons Timothy and Patrick said it was now time for me to pull out all my old photos, some never before published, and do a book because they wanted to find out what the beat generation was all about.

I read hundreds of articles and picked those that were significant—for their ideas, their style, their authors. Some of these writers loved the beats; others hated them. But all the articles make important points about a significant literary period in America.

Contacting all the writers, poets, and friends was a formidable task. I wanted to find out where they were now, what they had been doing all these years. Some I have kept in touch with over the years—Krim, Ginsberg, Mailer, Wilentz, Baraka, Joans, Koch, Kupferberg, Topp, Romney, Murnaghan—but all the others I had lost track of completely. Finding them twenty-five years later meant numerous long-distance phone calls and letters to friends of friends.

The remarkable thing is that everybody I found acted as though we had seen and talked to each other the day before; there seemed to be no distance imposed by the intervening years. Conversations just resumed where they left off. The thing that really changed is the way we now look. I was trim and muscular. Now I am flabby and overweight.

In my 1959 version here, everybody is young, proud, and beautiful; we are all frozen in time. But twenty-five years later we now emerge in a new skin, older, wiser perhaps, completely reborn.

In Arthur and Kit Knight's *The Beat Road* (Box 439, California, PA 15419), there are new snapshots of heroes from the beat vagabond days. In Knight's updated version, Burroughs is going bald. Corso is grizzlier, seedier, puffier. Ginsberg looks like Joe Gould, the famous Greenwich Village character who wrote the oral history of the world. Holmes has a double chin. Micheline looks like a white-haired hardware merchant. Ferlinghetti has a beard and looks like a sea captain on a book jacket. McClure looks like Timothy Leary, Julius Caesar, and Marlon Brando all rolled into one. Bremser is thin-faced and bearded, resembling Bernard Shaw. Only Bremser has jailhouse wisdom in his eyes. Diane DiPrima is ageless, oval-faced, like the picture of the cook on an Italian tomato paste can. And David Amram is now an uncanny, frightening double for Jack Kerouac.

The King lives!

—Fred W. McDarrah
May 1984

ACKNOWLEDGMENTS

The author wishes to acknowledge with gratitude and appreciation the willing and invaluable editorial assistance of Timothy S. McDarrah through this entire project.

CONTENTS

Contents

That wild eager picture of me on the cover of *On the Road* where I look so Beat goes back much further than 1948 when John Clellon Holmes (author of *Go* and *The Horn*) and I were sitting around trying to think up the meaning of the Lost Generation and the subsequent Existentialism and I said "You know, this is really a beat generation" and he leapt up and said "That's it, that's right!"

Jack Kerouac

THIS IS THE BEAT GENERATION

by John Clellon Holmes

New York Times Magazine, November 16, 1952

Several months ago, a national magazine ran a story under the heading "Youth" and the subhead "Mother Is Bugged at Me." It concerned an 18-year-old California girl who had been picked up for smoking marijuana and wanted to talk about it. While a reporter took down her ideas in the uptempo language of "tea," someone snapped a picture. In view of her contention that she was part of a whole new culture where one out of every five people you meet is a user, it was an arresting photograph. In the pale, attentive face, with its soft eyes and intelligent mouth, there was no hint of corruption. It was a face which could only be deemed criminal through an enormous effort of righteousness. Its only complaint seemed to be "Why don't people leave us alone?" It was the face of a Beat Generation.

That clean young face has been making the newspapers steadily since the war. Standing before a judge in a Bronx court house, being arraigned for stealing a car, it looked up into the camera with curious laughter and no guilt. The same face, with a more serious bent, stared from the pages of *Life* magazine, representing a graduating class of ex-G.I.'s, and said that as it believed small business to be dead, it intended to become a comfortable cog in the largest corporation it could find. A little younger, a little more bewildered, it was this same face that the photographers caught in Illinois when the first non-virgin club was uncovered. The young copywriter, leaning down the bar on Third Avenue, quietly drinking himself into relaxation, and the energetic hot-rod driver of Los Angeles, who plays Russian roulette with a jalopy, are separated only by a continent and a few years. They are the extremes. In between them fall the secretaries wondering whether to sleep with their boyfriends now or wait; the mechanics, beering up with the guys and driving off to Detroit on a whim; the models studiously name-dropping at a cocktail party. But the face is the same. Bright, level, realistic, challenging.

Any attempt to label an entire generation is unrewarding, and yet the generation which went through the last war, or at least could get a drink easily once it was over, seems to possess a uniform, general quality which demands an adjective. It was John Kerouac, the author of a fine, neglected novel *The Town and the City*, who finally came up with it. It was several years ago, when the face was harder to recognize, but he has a sharp, sympathetic eye, and one day he said, "You know, this is really a *beat* generation." The origins of the word "beat" are obscure, but the meaning is only too clear to most Americans. More than mere weariness, it implies the feeling of having been used, of being raw. It involves a sort of nakedness of mind, and, ultimately, of soul; a feeling of being reduced to the bedrock of consciousness. In short, it means being undramatically pushed up against the wall of oneself. A man is beat whenever he goes for broke and wagers the sum of his resources on a single number; and the young generation has done that continually from early youth.

Its members have an instinctive individuality, needing no bohemianism or imposed eccentricity to express it. Brought up during the collective bad circumstances of a dreary depression, weaned during the collective uprooting of a global war, they distrust collectivity. But they have never been able to keep the world out of their dreams. The fancies of their childhood inhabited the half-light of Munich, the Nazi-Soviet pact and the eventual blackout. Their adolescence was spent in a topsy-turvy world of war bonds, swing shifts and troop movements. They grew to independent mind on beachheads, in ginmills and U. S. O.'s, in past-midnight arrivals and pre-dawn departures. Their brothers, husbands, fathers or boy friends turned up dead one day at the other end of a telegram. At the four trembling corners of the world, or in the home town invaded by factories and lonely servicemen, they had intimate experience with the nadir and the zenith of human conduct, and little time for much that came between. The peace they inherited was only as secure as the next headline. It was a cold peace. Their own lust for freedom, and their ability to live at a pace that kills, to which war had adjusted them, led to black markets, bebop, narcotics, sexual promiscuity, hucksterism and Jean-Paul Sartre. The beatness set in later.

It is a postwar generation, and, in a world which seems to mark its cycles by its wars, it is already being compared to that other postwar generation, which dubbed itself "lost." The Roaring Twenties, and the generation that made them roar, are going through a sentimental revival, and the comparison is valuable. The Lost Generation was discovered in a roadster, laughing hysterically because nothing meant anything any more. It migrated to Europe, unsure whether it was looking for the "orgiastic future" or escaping from the "puritanical past." Its symbols were the flapper, the flask of bootleg whisky, and an attitude of desperate frivolity best expressed by Noel Coward's line: "Tennis, anyone?" It was caught up in the romance of disillusionment, until even that became an illusion. Every act in its drama of lostness was a tragic or an ironic third act, and T. S. Eliot's *The Wasteland* was more than the dead-end statement of a perceptive poet. The pervading atmosphere was an almost objectless sense of loss, through which the reader felt immediately that the cohesion of things had disappeared. It was, for an entire generation, an image which expressed, with dreadful accuracy, its own spiritual condition.

But the wild boys of today are not lost. Their flushed, often scoffing, always intent faces elude the word, and it would sound phony to them. For this generation conspicuously lacks that eloquent air of bereavement which made so many of the exploits of the Lost Generation symbolic actions. Furthermore, the repeated inventory of shattered ideals, and the laments about the mud in moral currents, which so obsessed the Lost Generation, does not concern young people today. They take it frighteningly for granted. They were brought up in these ruins and no longer notice them. They drink to "come down" or to "get high," not to illustrate anything. Their excursions into drugs or promiscuity come out of curiosity, not disillusionment.

Only the most bitter among them would call their reality a nightmare and protest that they have indeed lost something, the future. But ever since they were old enough to imagine one, that has been in jeopardy anyway. The absence of personal and social values is to them, not a revelation shaking the ground beneath them, but a problem demanding a day-to-day solution. *How* to live seems to them much more crucial than *why*. And it is precisely at this point that the copywriter and the hot-rod driver meet, and their identical beatness becomes significant, for, unlike the Lost Generation, which was occupied with the loss of faith, the Beat Generation is becoming more and more occupied with the need for it. As such, it is a disturbing illustration of Voltaire's reliable old joke: "If there were no God, it would be necessary to invent Him." Not content to bemoan His absence, they are busily and haphazardly inventing totems for Him on all sides.

For the giggling nihilist, eating up the highway at ninety miles an hour, and steering with his feet, is no Harry Crosby, the poet of the Lost Generation who flew his plane into the sun one day because he could no longer accept the modern world. On the contrary, the hot-rod driver invites death only to outwit it. He is affirming the life within him in the only way he knows how, at the extreme. The eager-faced girl, picked up on a dope charge, is not one of those "women and girls carried screaming with drink or drugs from public places," of whom Fitzgerald wrote. Instead, with persuasive seriousness, she describes the sense of community she has found in marijuana, which society never gave her. The copywriter, just as drunk by midnight as his Lost Generation counterpart, probably reads *God and Man at Yale* during his Sunday afternoon hangover. The difference is this almost exaggerated will to believe in something, if only in themselves. It is a *will* to believe, even in the face of an inability to do so in conventional terms. And that is bound to lead to excesses in one direction or another.

The shock that older people feel at the sight of this Beat Generation is, at its deepest level, not so much repugnance at the facts, as it is distress at the attitudes which move it. Though worried by this distress, they most often argue or legislate in terms of the facts rather than the attitudes. The newspaper reader, studying the eyes of young dope addicts, can only find an outlet for his horror and bewilderment in demands that passers be given the electric chair. Sociologists, with a more academic concern, are just as troubled by the legions of young men whose topmost ambition seems to be to find a secure berth in a monolithic corporation. Contemporary historians express mild surprise at the lack of organized movements, political, religious or otherwise, among the young. The articles they write remind us that being one's own boss and being a natural joiner are two of our most cherished national traits. Everywhere, people with tidy moralities shake their heads and wonder what is happening to the younger generation.

Perhaps they have not noticed that, behind the excess on the one hand, and the conformity on the other, lies that wait-and-see detachment that results from having to fall back for support more on one's human endurance than on one's philosophy of life. Not that the Beat Generation is immune to ideas: they fascinate it. Its wars, both past and future, were and will be wars of ideas. It knows, however, that in the final, private moment of conflict a man is really fighting another man, and not an idea. And that the same goes for love. So it is a generation with a greater facility for entertaining ideas than for believing in them. But it is also the first generation in several centuries for which the act of faith has been an obsessive problem, quite aside from the reasons for having a particular faith or not having it. It exhibits on every side, and in a bewildering number of facets, a perfect craving to believe. Though it is certainly a generation of extremes, including both the hipster and the "radical" young Republican in its ranks, it renders unto Caesar (i.e., society) what is Caesar's, and unto God what is God's. For in the wildest hipster, making a mystique of bop, drugs and the night life, there is no desire to shatter the "square" society in which he lives, only to elude it. To get on a soapbox or write a manifesto would seem to him absurd. Looking out at the normal world, where most everything is a "drag" for him, he nevertheless says: "Well, that's the Forest of Arden after all. And even it jumps if you look at it right." Equally, the young Republican, though often seeming to hold up Babbitt as the culture hero, is neither vulgar nor materialistic, as Babbitt was. He conforms because he believes it is socially practical, not necessarily virtuous. Both positions, however, are the result of more or less the same conviction—namely that the valueless abyss of modern life is unbearable.

A generation can sometimes be better understood by the books it reads, than by those it writes. The literary hero of the

Lost Generation should have been Bazarov, the nihilist in Turgenev's *Fathers and Sons*. Bazarov sat around, usually in the homes of the people he professed to loathe, smashing every icon within his reach. He was a man stunned into irony and rage by the collapse of the moral and intellectual structure of his world.

But he did nothing. The literary hero of the Beat Generation, on the other hand, might be Stavrogin, that most enigmatic character in *The Possessed* by Dostoevski. He is also a nihilist, or at least intimately associated with them.

But there is a difference, for Stavrogin, behind a facade very much like Bazarov's, is possessed by a passion for faith, almost any faith. His very atheism, at its extreme, is metaphysical. But he knows that disbelief is fatal, and when he has failed in every way to overcome it, he commits suicide because he does not have what he calls "greatness of soul." The ground yawned beneath Bazarov, revealing a pit into which he fell: while Stavrogin struggled at the bottom of that pit, trying feverishly to get out. In so far as it resembled Stavrogin, there have been few generations with as natural and profound a craving for convictions as this one, nor have there been many generations as ill-equipped to find them.

For beneath the excess and the conformity, there is something other than detachment. There are the stirrings of a quest. What the hipster is looking for in his "coolness" (withdrawal) or "flipness" (ecstasy) is, after all, a feeling of somewhereness, not just another diversion. The young Republican feels that there is a point beyond which change becomes chaos, and what he wants is not simply privilege or wealth, but a stable position from which to operate. Both have had enough of homelessness, valuelessness, faithlessness.

The variety and the extremity of their solutions is only a final indication that for today's young people there is not as yet a single external pivot around which they can, as a generation, group their observations and their aspirations. There is no single philosophy, no single party, no single attitude. The failure of most orthodox moral and social concepts to reflect fully the life they have known is probably the reason, but because of it each person becomes a walking, self-contained unit, compelled to meet the problem of being young in a seemingly helpless world in his own way, or at least to endure.

More than anything else, this is what is responsible for the generation's reluctance to name itself, its reluctance to discuss itself as a group, sometimes its reluctance to be itself. For invented gods invariably disappoint those who worship them. Only the need for them goes on, and it is this need, exhausting one object after another, which projects the Beat Generation forward into the future and will one day deprive it of its beatness.

Dostoevski wrote in the early 1880s, "Young Russia is talking of nothing but the eternal questions now." With appropriate changes, something very like this is beginning to happen in America, in an American way; a reevaluation of which the exploits and attitudes of this generation are only symptoms. No simple comparison of one generation against another can accurately measure effects, but it seems obvious that a Lost Generation, occupied with disillusionment and trying to keep busy among the broken stones, is poetically moving, not very dangerous. But a Beat Generation, driven by a desperate craving for belief and as yet unable to accept the moderations which are offered it, is quite another matter. Thirty years later, after all, the generation of which Dostoevski wrote, was meeting in cellars and making bombs.

This generation may make no bombs; it will probably be asked to drop some, and have some dropped on it, however, and this fact is never far from its mind. It is one of the pressures which created it and will play a large part in what will happen to it. There are those who believe that in generations such as this there is always the constant possibility of a great new moral idea, conceived in desperation, coming to life. Others note the self-indulgence, the waste, the apparent social irresponsibility, and disagree.

But its ability to keep its eyes open, and yet avoid cynicism; its ever-increasing conviction that the problem of modern life is essentially a spiritual problem; and that capacity for sudden wisdom which people who live hard and go far, possess, are assets and bear watching. And, anyway, the clear, challenging faces are worth it.

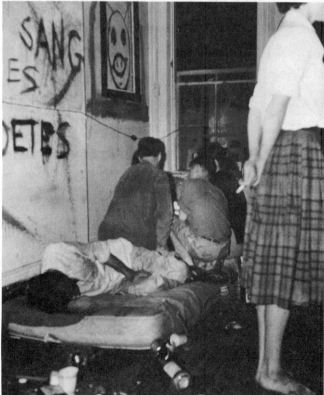

Guests at Ted Joans's beatnik birthday party sit on floor of storefront railroad flat under wall graffito, "The Blood of the Poets." July 25, 1959.

Beatnik birthday party at Ted Joans's railroad flat, St. Mark's Place, July 25, 1959.

Village Voice auto columnist Dan List inspects lost shoe at Ted Joans's beatnik birthday party, July 25, 1959. Filmmaker Frank Simon in background.

Bongo drums and aluminum pots make music at Ted Joans's beatnik birthday party, July 25, 1959. Robert Smithson, rear center.

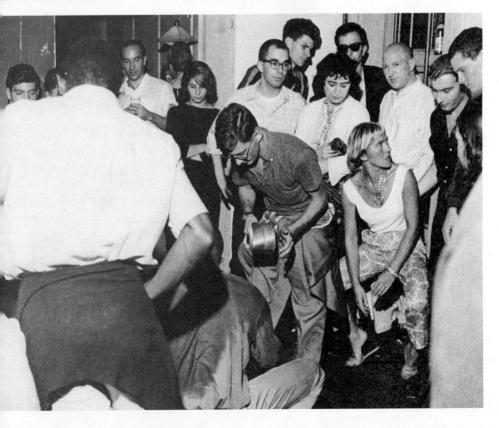

YOUTH WILL SERVE ITSELF

by Lawrence Lipton

The Nation, November 19, 1956

Youth will be served. We hear the old adage repeated more than ever today, when everybody is trying to keep looking young in order to avoid being tossed out on the industrial scrap heap. But the adage—it was never even half true—brings a wry smile to most of our youth. They know that in the past it has meant that youth will be served—with a draft summons. And those who were not careful to keep their mouths shut might be served once more—with subpoenas and contempt citations. Five years ago somebody coined the phrase, The Silent Generation, and on many the label seemed to fit. Today there are indications that, in some quarters at least, youth is beginning to realize that if it is to be served anything it really needs or really wants it will have to serve itself.

When *Time* surveyed The Younger Generation (Nov. 5, 1951) it reported that the youth from eighteen to twenty-eight was grave and fatalistic, conventional and gregarious. Intellectually, *Time* reported, the young seemed "a bit stodgy." Their mental adventures were apt to be "mild and safe," and their literature ran to "querulous and self-protective introspection." There were "precocious technicians" like Truman Capote, William Styron and Frederick Buechner, but their books had "the air of suspecting that life is long on treachery, short on rewards," that disappointment is life's only certainty, and their work was "a by-product of their neuroses." Either through "fear of being tagged 'subversive'" (*Time* was still putting it in quotation marks in 1951) through "passivity or conviction," youth was "ready to conform." Marxism seemed "dead" among them, democracy "strong but inarticulate" and "the movement" was "what Poet-Professor Peter Viereck calls the revolt against revolt." It was significant that "increasing numbers" of the youth were "seeking their faith not in secular panaceas but in God." In short it was The Silent Generation.

That was the picture *Time* painted in 1951. Thereafter its news columns reported the more spectacular tidbits from the juvenile crime file, and an occasional story on drug addiction, draft evasion, army desertions, conscientious objectors, and now and then a running gag like young Davis, self-styled Citizen of the World. But it did not then, and does not now, consider "Timeworthy" such items as the appearance of a new little magazine (unless it has rich and/or eccentric sponsors), or a new literary trend or change of reading tastes among the youth, or the emergence of a new type of student publication. Otherwise it might have found, even in 1951, more in the literature of the young than bogus youths who are merely failures to mature or college boys flirting with gilded bohemias. Today youth is beginning to serve itself, in ways that are, I think, newsworthy if not Timeworthy, on campus as well as off campus.

Thumbing their noses at the *Time* and *Life* literary directives and without waiting for permission from the faculty, some Harvard undergraduates have brought out during the last two years six issues of *i.e. The Cambridge Review*. A few quotes will suffice to give the reader some idea of its direction and tone: "The great lament now is student apathy. This is the most inarticulate form of opposition, and it has come to exist because there is very little place for articulate response"—a place that the *Review* was designed to provide. "At the time of their greatest independence the universities . . . were guilds of masters and students. . . . A power [against official meddling] that arose, oddly enough, from their very poverty. Unhampered . . . by physical apparatus, great libraries, worldly goods, and substantial college foundations, they could and on occasion did migrate, taking with them their large numbers of students and profitable trade." So Black Mountain College was founded by a migration in the early 1930s, a footnote adds. "Few things are more beautiful to see than good teaching . . . even so, the scene of the same aging grown-ups hanging around while generations of youth pass by, has something in it that stinks in the nostrils. As for colleagues, the company of the like-minded is both stimulating and comforting, but to be immured with the like-minded is like—living at Princeton."

> The struggle of this magazine has been the struggle to assume the critical position which dissatisfaction with the University necessitated. There is, it has been our conviction, much that is drastically wrong with Harvard's system. *i.e.* itself was started partly to give some of the content which we felt was lacking in University courses, and partly because the only other possible outlet, *The Harvard Advocate*, was a hotel for intellectual stuffed shirts.

Paul Goodman is prominent in its pages. One finds translations from Simone Weil; "Eros and Culture" by Herbert Marcuse is a notable contribution; and jazz plays in *i.e.* something like the role it plays in the lives of the young today. No. 3 leads off with a poem, "Requiem for 'Bird' Parker," by Gregory Corso, and No. 5 contains a piece on Gerry Mulligan by Glenn Coulter. In June the *Review* published a hundred-page issue, "Harvard 1956," subjecting the whole Harvard educational system to examination and criticism. "We care as much as we dare," say the four editors who wrote the whole issue themselves. "We want fights because only then can there be a type of peace— what seems like peace now is only fitful boredom."

This, I submit, is something new and far from apathetic in campus publications.

Or take the case of the *Chicago Review*, published at the University of Chicago. Here, too, editorial policy has during the last two or three years taken on the tone of iconoclastic inquiry. The Young Idea is infectiously potent even in the language of such a caption as "Jazz and the Intellectuals: Somebody Goofed," by Nat Hentoff. And the content is constantly provocative. "America's native musical voice (jazz) is an alien tongue to most of the country's intellectuals. . . . During the past half-century (while jazz has evolved from New Orleans brass bands to Brubeck polytonality), the American intellectual-artist has continued to search restlessly and often profoundly for the roots of his culture. . . ." But he has overlooked jazz, "both as a musical language and as a way of life."

Youth Will Serve Itself

The Spring 1953 issue attempts to evaluate and assimilate the influence of Robert M. Hutchins. A young writer takes a look at the Hemingway of *The Old Man and the Sea* and turns away. What is needed is a new White Hope of American fiction, he says, "someone like Ernest Hemingway, 1926 version . . . dissolute perhaps, perhaps drunk, . . . [but] roaring mad with the excitement of truth." The off-beat note is everywhere in these pages. Walt Kelly, the creator of Pogo, turns up in the Fall 1955 issue with a parable that packs some effective but gentle irony: "We have faults which we have hardly used yet. But we are getting around to them." Student articles, stories and poems, both here and in *The Cambridge Review,* hold up well alongside such professionals as Selden Rodman, Bernard Berenson, E. E. Cummings, Mark Van Doren and Henry Miller. There is room for Russell Kirk's New Conservatism and also for my own "disaffiliation" and dedicated poverty. The *Chicago Review* augments its university subsidy with public poetry readings. Its articles of opinion are widely commented on by magazines of larger circulation and often reprinted.

This is a far cry from the cute capers of student mags which made news only on the intellectual level of goldfish swallowing and panty raids. Perhaps the schooling provisions of the G.I. bill had something to do with it. The new campus magazines are drawing much of their editorial talent, material and readership from "vets" in their late twenties. Lachlan MacDonald of the *Chicago Review* is a good example of the type. "Form? Yes. Technique? Of course. But the first thing I look for is content," I heard him tell a group of young writers recently. And Angus Stewart Fletcher of *i.e. The Cambridge Review* wrote to me, "We have been thinking of devoting a whole issue of *i.e.* to the undermining effects of American business upon American thought and art."

Off campus the same ferment is brewing. Unsubsidized, never more than a jump ahead of the printer, financed for the most part out of the editor's weekly paycheck (and often also his wife's), the little Davids do battle with the Goliaths of middle class complacency and the "engineers of public acceptance." From the monthly newsprint *Intro Bulletin* in New York to the quarterly *Coastlines,* in Los Angeles the accent is on youth, but a youth that demands answers, and none of the old, easy answers, whether they come from the Right or from the Left. Everything is "at the crossroads." Whether it is an article on modern dance by Leighton Kerner, on jazz by George H. Moorse; or Storm De Hirsch, F. N. Karmatz or Lawrence Ferlinghetti reporting on public poetry readings in New York, Chicago and San Francisco (in *Intro Bulletin*), Mel Weisburd on science fiction in *Coastlines*, or Jay Pell or Leslie Woolf Hedley taking the New Criticism apart in *Whetstone*, the question is always "What went wrong, what do you know that's new, and where do we go from here?"

In magazines like the new *Liberation* it takes social and political form. The first (March 1956) issue started right off with a "Tract for the Times," searching for "roots" in four "root traditions from which we derive our values and standards": the Judeo-Christian prophetic tradition; the American tradition as exemplified in Jefferson, Paine, Emerson, Debs, the Utopian community experiments, the Abolition movement, the Underground Railway (to name a few); the libertarian democratic, antiwar, socialist, anarchist and labor movements in Europe and the United States, and the tradition of pacifism or nonviolence as exemplified for instance in Gandhi and Vinoba Bhave. A heritage, a guide, but not an answer. The answers are still to be explored, by discussion, but also and more importantly by experience, by action. Past and forthcoming contributors include veterans—Waldo Frank, A. J. Muste, Lewis Mumford, Dorothy Day, Pitrim Sorokin, Kenneth Rexroth and Kenneth Patchen—but the editors are nearly all young men and some of the most thoughtful and penetrating material in the magazine is coming from their hands.

Michael Harrington, who is one of its younger contributors, takes the editors to task for downgrading Karl Marx's analysis of capitalism as a guide to present-day world trends: "Some of its [Marx's analysis] specific predictions were wrong; some were amazingly exact; but as a living instrument of knowledge it is still the finest tool the radical has. This is especially true with regard to themes that *Liberation* clearly intends to make its own: of the alienation of man in modern society, of his de-spiritualization." It is strikingly characteristic of the younger generation today that Harrington, a politically active writer, should also be the author of "Art: Philosophy or the God-Like Image?" in the *Chicago Review*.

The same versatility of interests—and abilities—is discovered even in more popular, satirical media like *Mad* magazine, which are edited and read by young people for the most part. In *Mad*, everything in American life comes in for critical comment, in text, cartoons and captions: politics, radio-tv, Hollywood, newspapers, advertising, sports, comics, manners and mores. And it is good, solid, cogent comment, not despite but because of its burlesque tone, which it describes as "humor in a jugular vein." Newsstands cannot keep up with the demand as huge stacks of *Mad* are snatched up by young people eager to read things like—

TENSE TYCOONS
AND LUCKY BUCKS

Mad's own Business Novel 'Crash
McCool' Reaffirms Spiritual
Values of Cool Cash

The shrewd parody of *Cash McCall* that follows is as good literary criticism in its way as any review of the book in the radical or liberal magazines.

What is most significant about this new trend in the literature of the younger generation is the unanimity of its attitudes on so many things. Simultaneously you will find a cartoon strip in *Mad*, an editorial in *Liberation*, an article in the *Chicago Review*, a short story in *Coastlines*, a poem in *Whetstone*, an essay in *The Cambridge Review*, and an interview in *Intro Bulletin*, all focused on the same subject or the same book or the same recent event, and all from pretty much the same point of view. Clearly something is "in the air."

Noisiest of all, paradoxically, are the privately—well, all but privately—published, and the as yet unpublished. The sound they are putting down, to fall in with their own lingo, is deafening, but it is audible only to those who know what doors to open. They might be called the underground of contemporary American literature. Here jazz is very nearly the language and the way of life that Hentoff says it should be. Their literary models appear to be Walt Whitman, Ezra Pound (the *early* Pound, and the Pound of the Letters), Henry Miller, William Carlos Williams, Robinson Jeffers, and, here again, the two

Kenneths, Patchen and Rexroth. Richard Eberhart described their West Coast scene—he thinks it is unique, but I doubt it— in the Sept. 2 [1956] *N. Y. Times Book Review*. If you are living in the San Francisco area, he says, you might receive a card:

CELEBRATED GOOD TIME
POETRY NIGHT

Either you go home bugged or completely en-lightened. Allen Ginsberg blowing hot; Gary Snyder blowing cool; Philip Whalen puffing the laconic tuba; Mike McClure his hip high notes; Rexroth on the big bass drum. Small collec-tion for wine and postcards . . . abandon, noise, strange pictures on walls, oriental music, lurid poetry. Extremely serious. Town Hall theatre. One and only final appearance of this apocalypse. Admission free.

Eberhart reported a recent visit: "Hundreds from about sixteen to thirty may show up and engage in an enthusiastic, free-wheeling celebration of poetry, an analogue of which was jazz thirty years ago . . . shouting, stamping, interrupting, applaud-ing. Poetry here has become a tangible social force . . . through spoken, even shouted verse. . . ."

In the Seattle area it is more of a beer joint affair, centering on the off-campus curriculum sparked by Theodore Roethke and Stanley Kunitz at the University of Washington. In the Los Angeles area it is, like the city itself, less centralized and more varied in literary influences and group behavior. There is the group that gathers at the *Coastlines* fund-raising parties. Thomas McGrath is perhaps the best known example of the type. A poetry workshop meets in the home of poet-fictionist Curtis Zahn in Malibu for beef stew and explication. There are the student groups around U.C. and U.C.L.A. There is the *California Quarterly* group. Gil Orlovitz is convivial and vocal enough to be a movement all by himself. James Boyer May's house is on the visiting list of almost everyone in the little magazine world; his "circle," although it is chiefly a mail corre-spondence circle, is worldwide. The ocean front group, finally, centers on Stuart Z. Perkoff whose book of poems, *The Suicide Room*, is scheduled for early publication by Jonathan Williams. (The Williams list includes Patchen, Robert Creeley, Charles Olson and his own poetry with prefaces by Louis Zukofsky and Robert Duncan.)

The counterparts of most of these will doubtless be found in New York, Boston, Baltimore, Chicago, St. Louis, New Orleans and other cities, grouped around small presses, little magazines and influential literary personalities. They are closed circles, but highly vocal within their own groups. Their members work, preferably, at jobs like nightwatchman or shipping clerk—six months punching a time-clock and six months with the Muse— on Unemployment Insurance. They are not joiners, either socially or politically. They regard trade unions as labor agencies whose pie-card bosses "sell labor" at the bargaining table. They are not Orwells or Isherwoods "discovering" poverty and being shocked by it. They accept it. All they ask of the state is to deliver water at the tap, pick up garbage, keep their Unemployment Insurance files straight, and leave them alone. "Our prime value," one of them told me, "is 'making it', by which we mean taking your reality and not being destroyed by it." To "make it" is to make a living on the minimum subsistence level and still do your writing. They live from day to day. "We try not to think about the future. There isn't any future. You have to live as if there isn't any future." Not a few of them are marijuana users. "It heightens the sense of the immediate present," one of them explained to me. "Pot enables me to live in the immediate present, and take it." The motto of the apoliticals among them is "Keep cool (in the jazz sense), get what you can, keep out of trouble. Mistrust everything." What you will hear from them most frequently is "Why don't they leave us alone?" "They" are the "squares," the respectables who sooner or later turn out to be the cop, "the man with the gun on his hip." Or the man who hands you a rifle and orders you to kill.

The Silent Generation? Yes, and No, depending on where you look and whom you listen to. If you have ears to hear, even the silence has an ominous sound.

San Francisco writer
Lawrence Lipton, author
of The Holy Barbarians,
photographed in New
York.

Gregory Corso making a
phone call, February 22,
1959, in the White Horse,
567 Hudson Street, a
writers' beer tavern (half
'n' half) during the 1950s.

Poet and novelist Marvin
Cohen at the Living
Theatre, November 13,
1959. One of Cohen's
popular prose poems
begins, "I woke up
feeling too good to be
true. That was my first
mistake . . ."

Washington poet-editor-
publisher Bill Walker
in the 8th Street
Bookshop.

Allen Ginsberg in his 170
East 2nd Street
apartment, January 9,
1960.

Poet-editor Bill Berkson
on Washington Square
North, October 9, 1959.
The bronze lions were
stolen in 1983.

Gary Snyder, West Coast poet, in New York. His poems written in Japan—"Higashi Hongwanji," "A Stone Garden," "Kyoto: March," "Toji"—appeared in Riprap, Snyder's 1959 book of poetry.

George Nelson Preston in the Artist's Studio, where he ran poetry readings and jazz sessions.

Barbara Guest waiting for a train at the old Pennsylvania Station, which was torn down in the early 1960s, October 16, 1959.

West Coast poet John Wieners, January 5, 1960, in New York. In The Hotel Wentley Poems, Wieners begins "A Poem for Suckers" with "Well we can go in the queer bars w/ our long hair reaching down to the ground and we can sing our songs of love like the black mama on the juke box after all what have we got left . . ."

Seymour Krim, *author of* Views of a Nearsighted Cannoneer, *in the garden of the Jumel mansion, West 160th Street, October 12, 1960.*

West Coast poet Robert Duncan in the 8th Street Bookshop, May 2, 1960. His entertaining play Faust Foutu *was given a dramatic reading at The SIX Gallery, 3119 Fillmore, San Francisco, in January 1955 with a cast that included Duncan, Jack Spicer, Mike McClure, Helen Adam, and others.*

Kenneth Koch in Sheridan Square, September 29, 1959.

Poet-novelist Gilbert Sorrentino with Jesse and Delia at 4812 Foster Avenue, Brooklyn, October 10, 1959.

Novelist and short-story writer Grace Paley at Ted Wilentz's party, October 9, 1959.

John Clellon Holmes, who did the first major article on the beat generation, photographed at his house in Milford, Connecticut, August 4, 1962.

Kirby Doyle in Dave Lambert's apartment, 24 Cornelia Street, writing notes in his diary for Happiness Bastard, *a novel. Dian Doyle, a jazz singer, appears in one of McClure's early novels and is the "Dido" referred to in many of Doyle's love poems in* Sapphobones.

Philip Lamantia and Stella Pittelli in Dave Lambert's 24 Cornelia Street apartment, December 5, 1959. Lamantia's Narcotica *and* Ekstasis *were both published in 1959.*

Ted Joans in his Astor Place loft, November 4, 1959.

Poet-playright-lyricist Kenward Elmslie at 48 West 10th Street, October 19, 1959.

Denise Levertov at the Living Theatre reception for Jonathan Williams's publication of two new books, November 13, 1959.

Margaret Randall on East 10th Street, September 13, 1959. She lived in Latin America for 23 years before returning to America in 1984.

Paul Blackburn in his 322 West 15th Street flat, September 20, 1959.

Anthologist and poet Stanley Fisher, who published Beat Coast East, *October 18, 1959, 340 East 18th Street.*

Bruce Fearing in front of 8th Street Bookshop, October 9, 1959. His father, Kenneth Fearing, was also a writer.

Frank O'Hara with Auguste Rodin's St. John the Baptist Preaching *in the Museum of Modern Art Sculpture Garden, January 20, 1960.*

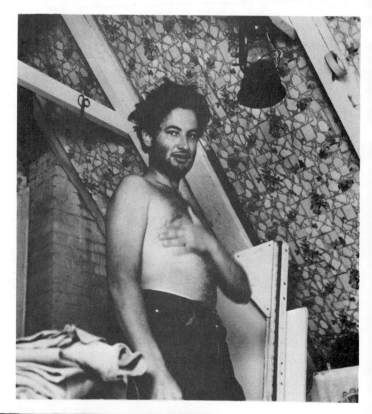

Beatnik artist Leonard Horowitz vacationing in Provincetown, July 4, 1959.

Poet and writer Fielding Dawson, artist for Jargon and Totem Press, in Provincetown, July 4, 1959.

William S. Burroughs at a Grove Press book party. In Kerouac's novels Burroughs is identified as Will Dennison, Will Hubbard, and Frank Carmody and in On the Road as Old Bull Lee.

Carl Solomon at a book party in Ted Wilentz's apartment over the 8th Street Bookshop, September 17, 1960. Allen Ginsberg dedicated Howl to Solomon.

REVIEW OF *ON THE ROAD*

by Gilbert Millstein

New York Times, September 5, 1957

O*n the Road* is the second novel by Jack Kerouac, and its publication is a historic occasion in so far as the exposure of an authentic work of art is of any great moment in an age in which the attention is fragmented and the sensibilities are blunted by the superlatives of fashion (multiplied a million-fold by the speed and pound of communications).

This book requires exegesis and a detailing of background. It is possible that it will be condescended to by, or make uneasy, the neo-academicians and the "official" avant-garde critics, and that it will be dealt with superficially elsewhere as merely "absorbing" or "intriguing" or "picaresque" or any of a dozen convenient banalities, not excluding "off-beat." But the fact is that *On the Road* is the most beautifully executed, the clearest and the most important utterance yet made by the generation Kerouac himself named years ago as "beat," and whose principal avatar he is.

Just as, more than any other novel of the Twenties, *The Sun Also Rises* came to be regarded as the testament of the "Lost Generation," so it seems certain that *On the Road* will come to be known as that of the "Beat Generation." There is, otherwise, no similarity between the two; technically and philosophically, Hemingway and Kerouac are, at the very least, a depression and a world war apart.

THE "BEAT" BEAR STIGMATA

Much has been made of the phenomenon that a good deal of the writing, the poetry and the painting of this generation (to say nothing of its deep interest in modern jazz) has emerged in the so-called "San Francisco Renaissance," which, while true, is irrelevant. It cannot be localized. (Many of the San Francisco group, a highly mobile lot in any case, are no longer resident in that benign city, or only intermittently.) The "Beat Generation" and its artists display readily recognizable stigmata.

Outwardly, these may be summed up as the frenzied pursuit of every possible sensory impression, an extreme exacerbation of the nerves, a constant outraging of the body. (One gets "kicks"; one "digs" everything, whether it be drink, drugs, sexual promiscuity, driving at high speeds or absorbing Zen Buddhism.)

Inwardly, these excesses are made to serve a spiritual purpose, the purpose of an affirmation still unfocused, still to be defined, unsystematic. It is markedly distinct from the protest of the "Lost Generation" or the political protest of the "Depression Generation."

The "Beat Generation" was born disillusioned; it takes for granted the imminence of war, the barrenness of politics and the hostility of the rest of society. It is not even impressed by (although it never pretends to scorn) material well-being (as distinguished from materialism). It does not know what refuge it is seeking, but it is seeking.

As John Aldridge has put it in his critical work, *After the Lost Generation,* there were four choices open to the post-war writer: novelistic journalism or journalistic novel-writing; what little subject-matter that had not been fully exploited already (homosexuality, racial conflict), pure technique (for lack of something to say), or the course I feel Kerouac has taken— assertion "of the need for belief even though it is upon a background in which belief is impossible and in which the symbols are lacking for a genuine affirmation in genuine terms."

Five years ago, in the Sunday magazine of this newspaper, a young novelist, Clellon Holmes, the author of a book called *Go,* and a friend of Kerouac's, attempted to define the generation Kerouac had labeled. In doing so, he carried Aldridge's premise further. He said, among many other pertinent things, that to his kind "the absence of personal and social values . . . is not a revelation shaking the ground beneath them, but a problem demanding a day-to-day solution. *How* to live seems to them much more crucial than *why.*" He added that the difference between the "Lost" and the "Beat" may lie in the latter's "will to believe even in the face of an inability to do so in conventional terms"; that they exhibited "on every side and in a bewildering number of facets a perfect craving to believe."

THOSE WHO BURN, BURN, BURN

That is the meaning of *On the Road*. What does its narrator, Sal Paradise, say? ". . . The only people for me are the mad ones, the ones who are mad to live, mad to talk, mad to be saved, desirous of everything at the same time, the ones who never yawn or say a commonplace thing, but burn, burn, burn like fabulous yellow roman candles. . . ."

And what does Dean Moriarty, Sal's American hero-saint say? "And of course no one can tell us that there is no God. We've passed through all forms. . . . Everything is fine, God exists, we know time. . . . God exists without qualms. As we roll along this way I am positive beyond doubt that everything will be taken care of for us—that even you, as you drive, fearful of the wheel . . . the thing will go along of itself and you won't go off the road and I can sleep."

This search for affirmation takes Sal on the road to Denver and San Francisco; Los Angeles and Texas and Mexico; sometimes with Dean, sometimes without; sometimes in the company of other beat individuals whose ties vary, but whose search is very much the same (not infrequently ending in death or derangement; the search for belief is very likely the most violent known to man).

There are sections of *On the Road* in which the writing is of a beauty almost breathtaking. There is a description of a cross-country automobile ride fully the equal, for example, of the train ride told by Thomas Wolfe in *Of Time and the River*. There are the details of a trip to Mexico (and an interlude in a Mexican bordello) that are, by turns, awesome, tender and funny. And, finally, there is some writing on jazz that has never been equaled in American fiction, either for insight, style or technical virtuosity. *On the Road* is a major novel.

Kerouac at 304 West 14th Street, December 10, 1959.

IN PURSUIT OF KICKS

by David Dempsey

New York Times Book Review, September 8, 1957

Thirty years ago it was fashionable for the young and the weary—creatures of Hemingway and F. Scott Fitzgerald—simply to be "lost." Today, one depression and two wars later, in order to remain uncommitted one must at least flirt with depravity. *On the Road* belongs to the new Bohemianism in American fiction in which an experimental style is combined with eccentric characters and a morally neutral point of view. It is not so much a novel as a long affectionate lark inspired by the so-called "beat" generation, and an example of the degree to which some of the most original work being done in this country has come to depend upon the bizarre and the offbeat for its creative stimulus. Jack Kerouac has written an enormously readable and entertaining book but one reads it in the same mood that he might visit a sideshow—the freaks are fascinating although they are hardly part of our lives.

The story is told—with great relish—by Sal Paradise, a young college student who satisfies, through his association with a character named Dean Moriarty, his restlessness and search for "kicks." Moriarty, a good-natured and slap-happy reform-school alumnus, is pathologically given to aimless travel, women, car stealing, reefers, bop jazz, liquor and pseudo-intellectual talk, as though life were just one long joyride that can't be stopped. He is Mr. Kerouac's answer to the age of anxiety—and one of the author's real accomplishments is to make him both agreeable and sympathetic.

Through Moriarty we meet his three wives. We are also introduced to a dope addict, a poet—and an assortment of migratory decadents whose playground is the vast American subcontinent of cheap lodgings, saloons, broken-down cars, cross-country buses and all night restaurants. Moriarty's continual roaming is interrupted only by a halfhearted attempt to find his alcoholic father. The incessant and frenetic moving around is the chief dynamic of *On the Road,* partly because this is one of the symptoms of "beatness" but partly, too, because the hot pursuit of pleasure enables Mr. Kerouac to serve up the great, raw slices of America that give his book a descriptive excitement unmatched since the days of Thomas Wolfe.

Unlike Wolfe, Nelson Algren or Saul Bellow (there are trace elements of all three writers here), Mr. Kerouac throws his characters away, as it were. His people are not developed but simply presented; they perform, take their bows and do a handspring into the wings. It is the difference between a vaudeville act and a play. The hedonism, the exquisite pointlessness of Moriarty's way of life is not so much the subject of *On the Road* as a sightseeing device.

The non sequiturs of the beat generation become the author's own plotless and themeless technique—having absolved his characters of all responsibility, he can absolve himself of the writer's customary attention to motivation and credibility. As a portrait of a disjointed segment of society acting out of its own neurotic necessity, *On the Road* is a stunning achievement. But it is a road, as far as the characters are concerned, that leads nowhere and which the novelist himself cannot afford to travel more than once.

Kerouac at 304 West 14th
Street, December 10,
1959.

Cult hero Neal Cassady
appeared on national
television to discuss his
San Quentin experience
from July 4, 1958, to June
3, 1960. He was the
character Dean Moriarty in
On the Road, and Cody
Pomeray in four other
Kerouac books.

JACK KEROUAC: BACK TO THE VILLAGE— BUT STILL ON THE ROAD

by Jerry Tallmer

Village Voice, September 18, 1957

Jack Kerouac, the Greenwich Village writer who (with Allen Ginsberg and Gregory Corso) had to go to San Francisco to become a San Francisco writer and get famous, sat in Goody's Bar, off 10th Street, the other night, in a battered royal-blue polo shirt, his white T shirt showing beneath, the bright red top of a cigarette package projecting from the pocket on his chest, his strong arms reaching perpetually for the bottle of Schlitz before him on the table, his dark rakish face and glistening black hair more handsome than Cary Grant's or Wally Reid's. "Man," he said, "I can't make it. I'm cutting out."

He was talking about the whirl of TV and radio and cocktail parties they've had him in, the Viking people, ever since he returned from Europe and Tangiers just a few days ago. He was talking about the publicity, the success, the rave reviews, the terrifying half-hour with Wingate on "Nightbeat," the girls, the bars, the lionhunters, the whole bit.

"Someday," he said, "if I can write it. If anyone could write it. They have a little girl there, sitting by you, while you wait to go on the TV."

"Just to keep you happy?"

"Just to keep you happy. One of those cute little uptown chicks. If I could write it . . ." He muzzily flagged the waitress for another beer and told how he and Wingate had gone out on the town after the show. The show itself had come as quite a shock to many of his friends and the general public. Kerouac had clammed up almost totally, giving terse, noncommunicative answers and looking like nothing so much as a scared rabbit. One of the few young authors of (inversely) the Big Yes, he had sat there like a stump, saying no.

"What was it? Were you scared?"

"Yeah, man, plenty scared. One of my friends told me don't say anything, nothing that'll get you in trouble. So I just kept saying no, like a kid dragged in by a cop. That's the way I thought of it—a kid dragged up before the cops."

The conversation switched to poetry readings. Could Kerouac go on stage to read some of the San Francisco poetry, his own and Corso's and Ginsberg's? "No, not me. I can't go that. I get stage fright. Wait till Allen comes back—he's great. He loves that."

To what did Kerouac attribute his sudden recognition on the West Coast, after years of the opposite here in the East? "One thing," he said. "Rexroth. A great man. A great critic. Interested in young people, interested in everything." But presently, when the subject had drifted to jazz—its decline and fall this past half-decade—Kerouac talked of a California jazz concert which Kenneth Rexroth hadn't dug at all. "What a square!" Kerouac cheerfully hooted. *"What* a square!" And then it emerged that, some time since, Rexroth had kicked Kerouac out of his house as an objectionable loafer—just to be an artist, he had said, wasn't enough. As Kerouac recalled the incident he seemed to derive great pleasure from it, and to hold no grudge against his mentor.

About *On the Road,* the novel now making such a splash everywhere, Kerouac insists on dismissing it as "my potboiler." He wrote it six years ago, in 1951, allegedly "to amuse my wife"—the wife he had then, anyway. "I'm a serious artist," he said, lightly but intently, downing the beer without a break, "a serious artist . . . like James Joyce. I've written eight books since *On the Road.* Viking's going to start bringing them out."

"What's your best one?"

"A book called *Dr. Sax,* a kind of Gothic fairy tale, a myth of puberty, about some kids in New England playing around in this empty place when a shadow suddenly comes out at them, a real shadow. A *real* shadow," he said, stressing the image, his black eyes flashing. "Then there's *The Subterraneans.* That's about an affair with a colored girl. And then there's . . ." But he let it drop as something weird popped back into his head and he said: "Man, man, on that TV they make you *up!*"

"And what's happening to you next? Beside the TV and all that?"

"I'm cutting out. They don't know it, but I'm cutting out. I'm going down to my mother's in Orlando. Always go back to my mother. Always." He grinned widely, dangerously, but not altogether freely.

"And if we want to get in touch with you tomorrow? For a picture or something?"

"Call this chick. Wonderful kid—really important. She'll know where I am." He gave a telephone number and a name which for our purposes here can be Elizabeth Jones. We did in fact want to get him for a picture later, and when I called that number the next day, a girl answered, but she drew a blank. "I'm not Elizabeth Jones," she said, doubtfully.

"Oh? Is there any Elizabeth Jones at this number?"

Long pause. "No," she said, "but maybe it's me. I'm Harriet Jones."

Jack Kerouac clutching doll as he leaves the Artist's Club after New Year's Eve party, December 31, 1958. The Club, on 10th Street and Fourth Avenue, had weekly art discussions and frequent parties in its huge unheated loft. Gregory Corso, hidden from view, is in white shirt.

Jack Kerouac jamming with band at Artist's Club New Year's Eve party, 1958.

JAZZ AND POETRY

by *Kenneth Rexroth*

Esquire, May 1958

Things are beginning to get out of hand. The other day Ralph Gleason, the jazz critic, said to me that he expected any day to see ads in the trade papers: "JAZZ POET: blues, ballad, upbeat, free verse or rhyme. Have tux. Will travel." And T.S. Eliot touring the kerosene circuit with Little Richard and the Harlem Globetrotters. Crazes are usually pretty empty, sterile things. It would be a pity if incompetents looking for a fast buck turned this into a temporary social disease like pee-wee golf or swallowing goldfish.

I, for one, take it very seriously indeed. I started doing it long ago in the Green Mask in Chicago to Frankie Melrose's piano and anybody else who wandered in to blow. The music was pretty gut-bucket usually, sort of paleo-funky, if you dig, and much of the poetry was Service, Sandburg, even Swinburne, but some of it wasn't. *The Waste Land* was read to jazz, all of it, shortly after it appeared. Bert Williams and Bert Savoy were both in the audience and thought it was a gasser . . . the cat's whiskers it was then.

I read poetry to jazz because I like to. I like poetry. I like to read to people. I like jazz. The people like the combination. But there's more to it than that. Poetry and jazz gain new and different dimensions in association. Poetry has always gained by association with music . . . ancient China, Japan, India, Greece, the troubadours and minnesingers and scalds. Not just as lyrics for songs, but also as recitation. The Homeric poems were recited in this way. There was a special profession for doing it called rhetors. In a sense poetry and jazz as such began about mid-nineteenth century with a friend of Baudelaire and Verlaine, Charles Cros, who recited his poems to the jivy music of the three piece bands of the *bals musettes* and *cafés chan-*

tants. He was a very great and very wise poet as well. This should set to rest the cooked-up dispute as to who invented it. I am sure I didn't and, as I say, I started in the early Twenties.

Why to jazz specifically? Well, I, for one, don't make any distinction between jazz and "serious music." Jazz is serious music; some people think it is the only American music worth taking seriously. Not in lush or brutal clip joints, but in the best jazz rooms and concerts, poetry gains from jazz an audience of widely diversified character, people who are seriously concerned with music, but who do not ordinarily read verse and who care nothing for the conflicts and rituals of the literary scene. The audience poetry has today, its official audience, is what is killing it. And, of course, the poet himself gains by the test of popular presentation. Naturally all poetry is not, nor should it be, able to meet this test. But we could do with more. Jazz gains by a new vocal content which can match its own seriousness, depth and complexity. Some jazz is "abstract" like Bach, but most of it is a kind of "program music" like Stravinsky, and obviously the better the program—all other things considered—the better the results. I might mention that Stravinsky's *Persephone* does not differ formally from what we are trying to do. Poetry and jazz is not a gimmick, a freak gig, something for the sockless cats and the unwashed chicks of the marijuana circuit. It is not new, but as old as music and poetry, and to be treated with the dignity and respect, by performers and audience respectively, which those ancient expressions of mankind should always merit.

POETRY AND YOUTH

I think that, by and large, poetry is a dying art in modern civilization, dying for lack of a significant audience. Kids who can't make the team or build a hot rod or toss chicks around in the air jitterbugging tend to gravitate to "The Lit." and thence to the reputedly adult literary quarterly. Poetry won't get the chicks that even the poorest hot rod will, but in extremity it will serve. And like poet, like audience. It is not just the Babbitts who think there's something odd about people who read poetry. I think so, and I know. Odd, and very, very few. And so poetry itself has become insufferably odd and cranky. I think this is due to the lack of living contact with the audience, as well, of course, as to general social and economic factors. There isn't much to be done about the big factors by any one individual anyway, but it is possible to keep plugging away at putting the poet back into actual physical touch with a live audience. In San Francisco we have led the world in that effort. Today, more than anywhere in the world except possibly Japan, poetry is a real factor in the life of the community and poets enjoy widespread influence—not on literature, but on life.

Jazz poetry reading puts poetry back in the entertainment business, where it was with Homer and the troubadours. Even Victorian epics like *Idylls of the King* and *Evangeline* were written to be read to the whole family around the fire in the evening by papa—not, certainly, to be studied for their ambiguities by a seminar of five Ph.D. candidates, conducted by another poet.

The musicians get a chance to work with words that mean something, something approximating the really profound levels attained by much modern jazz which certainly does not belong in the banal world of the Tin Pan Alley lyric. Also, the rhythms of modern poetry are extremely complex and the problems they set the musicians are comparable to those he sets himself when he "takes off" from the hackneyed rhythm structure of the popular tune. Actually, much modern poetry is too complex for jazz, which, *aficionados* to the contrary, is not as complicated as much quite ordinary classical music.

There is a widespread belief that real jazz is just blown, spontaneously, out of nowhere, and that if it isn't improvised it isn't jazz. Nothing could be less true. The most spontaneous improvisation works with an immense repertory of stereotyped patterns, melodic, harmonic, rhythmic, which every musician knows, and into which he pours the new life of the immediate performance as he goes along. At any given moment everybody in the band has a pretty clear idea of what is going to happen next. By very definition the great swing bands were elaborately arranged and exhaustively rehearsed. So the idea that you can just get up in front of a band and everybody blow poetry and sounds out of dreams is just plain silly.

PRECISION EFFORT

We have found that the effects we want are obtained by making sure that each musician knows exactly what the poet is doing—what he means, and what technical effects he employs, for instance the rhythms of his speech, to put his meaning across. Each musician has a sheet with the text in front of him, which he also uses as a cue sheet and for all sorts of other marginal musical notation. Then comes plenty of careful rehearsal, each one taped and played back and carefully analyzed. Rehearsals are pretty elaborate, far more finicky than the average band rehearsal, but the constant effort is to increase spontaneity, not to limit it. We find, like all artists, that you have to work hard to earn freedom of expression. One thing, there is very little room for the intensely competitive self-expression of the bop era. We don't try to blow each other down. We find that jazz poetry is an exacting, co-operative, precision effort, like mountaineering. Everybody has to be perfectly co-ordinated; there is no place for the bitter musical dogfights immortalized on some bop records; everybody has to be as socialized as six men on a rope working across the face of a cliff.

I, for one, have tried to treat the voice as another instrument in the band. Whenever the voice takes on the character of a solo singer or the band sinks to background music, we feel we have failed, and we scrap that effort and start over. You can readily see that, contrary to popular belief, this poetry and jazz combination is harder work than either of the arts taken separately. So, as a warning to other poets and musicians, if you don't work, but hard, you are going to fall on your face. It's time and trouble, but the final product is worth it; what they call the creative satisfactions are terrific, a real joy, and Lord, Lord, Lord, look how it packs them in!

Kenneth Rexroth at New York
University, April 22, 1960.
Della Brief of the Village Voice
eating ice cream.

Bass player Charles Mingus
and West Coast poet Kenneth
Patchen do a performance of
poetry and jazz at the Living
Theatre, March 14, 1959.

Brigid Murnaghan at the West Village
International Café, corner of Perry and
Greenwich Avenue, reading with Danny
McCabe and John Sweenhart,
November 15, 1959.

Michael McClure at City College, November 9, 1959, where he read from Hymns to St. Geryon and Other Poems. *Philip Whalen read from* Three Satires, *one of his earliest works.*

A poetry reading in the Artist's Studio. Left to right: Jud Yalkut, Ray Bremser (reading), William Morris, Marc Schleifer, Bonnie Bremser (on floor), Clint Nichols, artist-poet George Preston, October 25, 1959. Nichols's poem "bordentown" in "Beat Coast East," was dedicated to the warden.

Paul Blackburn and Big Table *editor Paul Carroll, March 7, 1960, who read selections from the banned magazine.*

KEROUAC AT THE VILLAGE VANGUARD

by Dan Wakefield

The Nation, January 4, 1958

Jack Kerouac opened at the Village Vanguard in New York on the Thursday night before Christmas, as part of a holiday bill which included the J. J. Johnson quartet and Beverly Kenny. J. J. Johnson is an old pro, a trombone man of dignity and distinction. Beverly Kenny is a red-head who sings a deep-throated, swinging style, and Jack Kerouac is the "spokesman" of the Beat Generation by merit of his recent novel, *On the Road*. Kerouac, the uncompromising hipster, was billed as reading from his own "works," to the background accompaniment of a jazz pianist. A beer at the Village Vanguard bar goes for $1.25, and the minimum for sitting at a table is $4 per person, so it was understandable that not too many "beat" characters were able to enjoy Kerouac's debut on the nightclub circuit. There were, however, one seaman, one poet and one blonde in Kerouac's corner (the dimly lit corner at the back) for Friday night's performance.

An agent of *The Nation* showed up late, ordered a beer at the bar and turned to face the stage, where Kerouac stood beneath several smoky beams with a large sheaf of manuscript in his hands and recited to a cold (as distinguished from cool) audience from a piece about life in the famous "Cellar" bar in San Francisco. Kerouac wore his hair in need of a cut; brown slacks, brown shoes, cotton argyles and a gold-thread open-neck sport-shirt that glistened in the dark and hung out over his belt.

Kerouac was reading a passage about his friendship with the bartenders at the "Cellar." A gentleman known as Lou, tending bar at the Vanguard, turned to his clients and remarked quietly, "He won't make many bartender friends if he keeps on usin' *that* stuff." Lou was a man in his late forties, and no doubt unfamiliar with the Beat Generation.

There were, however, signs of genuine liberal tendencies among the audience. A table of what looked to be the leftovers of an office party from around Times Square was shuffling restlessly when one of the gentlemen "ssshdd" them and explained, "Some people like this stuff." Back in Kerouac's corner, the blonde explained to the newly seated *Nation* agent that Jack didn't like the idea of this nightclub business but thought it might help *On the Road*. "If it gets back on the bestseller list, they may take it as a movie. If he sells it as a movie, he won't have to do *this* sort of thing any more."

Kerouac finally finished with "this sort of thing," and retired to the back room where J. J. Johnson and his pros were taking their break. Johnson and his sidemen were supremely sober and Kerouac came back drunk to sit at the edge of their table. He was at first politely ignored and was finally recognized after asking Mr. Johnson, "What did you think of what I read?" Johnson looked at him, the lion-tamer in the circus looking at the kid who had just won the amateur hog-calling contest, and asked him if he had written it. Kerouac admitted he had written it and Johnson, after a pause, judged that "it sounded very deep." Kerouac said how much he enjoyed Johnson's trombone, and said that he personally had always wanted to be a tenor sax man.

"Man, I could really work with a tenor sax," said Kerouac.

Johnson looked up without expression and said, "You look more like a trumpet man to me."

Kerouac's next "set" opened with a reading called "The Life of a Sixty Year Old Mexican Junkie." It seemed this junkie had been picked up while a young man by an American female junkie and finally got the monkey on his back. The story was sad indeed. It met with applause from the audience of the Village Vanguard. After that episode, Kerouac looked out blinking from beneath the spotlights and asked, "Has anyone here ever heard of Allen Ginsberg?"

Kerouac's corner clapped, and a few scattered claps came from across the floor. Kerouac then announced that he had Ginsberg's latest poem right there with him and that he would read it. He raised the sheaf of manuscripts before him, pointed his finger to the smoky ceiling, and began to proclaim. In the dark, it was impossible to note down all the verses, but the key refrain seemed to be, "Mother, with your six vaginas."

Kerouac did not state where Ginsberg is at present, and for all we know he is still in San Francisco. It seems only reasonable, though, that he soon will be opening at El Morocco. If Kerouac has made the nightclub circuit, Ginsberg should not be far behind.

It seems only yesterday that Ginsberg was sitting on a deserted railroad tie in California with Jack Kerouac, writing poetry about his beat friends who challenged the status quo and bewailed the rape of American letters by Philistine forces. Was it only yesterday that Ginsberg dedicated his almost-banned book of poems, *Howl,* to Jack Kerouac, "the new Buddha of American prose" whose eleven books were "published in heaven"? And now one is published by the Viking Press and the others are being read at the Village Vanguard by the Buddha himself. The glow-in-the-dark, gold-thread shirt worn by the Buddha in his Vanguard readings seems to be the principal symbol of his "protest" still remaining. One recalls the lines of Kenneth Rexroth's poem dealing with the death of Dylan Thomas: "You killed him, in your goddam Brooks Brothers suit." We can only shudder at the genocide that should be wreaked by Kerouac's haberdashery.

But all is not beat. It so happened, by one of those wonderful plots of the Muse, that on the same night Kerouac was reading from his testament at the Vanguard, a young poet named Richard Wilbur was about four blocks across the Village reading from his work at New York University.

Richard Wilbur was born in 1921, and is thereby entitled to inclusion as a member of the Beat Generation. He wears, however, a Brooks Brothers suit, has never recited from his work in the Village Vanguard, quotes heavily from Greek and medieval philosophers, and is currently teaching a Shakespeare course at Wesleyan University. Richard Wilbur is 36 years old and Jack Kerouac is 35. The painful difference is that Wilbur is a man and Kerouac a kid.

To go from the university lecture hall to the Village Vanguard the Friday night before Christmas was to realize that there is no such thing as a "generation"; that there are born each year a certain number of men and a certain number of boys; that out of each era in our national history there come a few poets and a few poor boys who wander with words, and that no grand generalization can tie them together. Jack Kerouac sweats beneath the spotlights of a nightclub to bring his novel back to the bestseller list. He is now "On the Town." Lo and behold—it is Richard Wilbur who is on the road; who has been, all along.

A reading, February 15, 1959, at the Artist's Studio, an informal poetry center run by George Preston, 48 East 3rd Street. Kerouac on ladder reading a passage from On the Road. *Left to right: poets Ted Joans, Jose Garcia Villa, Allen Ginsberg, Edward Marshall, Gregory Corso, LeRoi Jones (now Amiri Baraka).*

Kerouac relaxing with fans during recess in poetry reading at Artist's Studio, February 15, 1959.

Corso lights up during poetry reading break at Artist's Studio, February 15, 1959. Filipino poet Jose Garcia Villa sits on his right.

Artist's Studio audience at poetry reading, 48 East 3rd Street, February 22, 1959.

Artist's Studio, 48 East 3rd Street, Robert La Soda, Steve Levine, Albert Xoc, February 22, 1959. Levine read from his collection, A Resonance of Hope.

OFF THE ROAD, INTO THE VANGUARD, AND OUT

by Howard Smith

Village Voice, December 25, 1957

Out front the J. J. Johnson Quartet heats up the buzzing, jammed-in, packed house to a supercharged, pregnant pitch. In a back alcove, near the men's room, sits Jack Kerouac, who has come off his road into the spotlight of the literary world and his sometime home, Greenwich Village, for a stay at the Village Vanguard that was supposed to be indefinite—and it was. It lasted seven nights.

His receding hair tousled, sweating enough to fill a wine cask, Kerouac looks like a member in good standing of the generation he called "beat." Anxious drags on cigarette after cigarette, walking around in tight little circles, fast quick talk to anyone nearby, swigs from an always handy drink, gulps of an always handy coffee, tighten Paisley tie, loosen tie, tighten tie.

"What am I going to read?" . . . and he leafs through a suitcaseful and suddenly realizes no one remembered to bring a copy of his *On the Road.* His combination manager–literary agent talks slowly and carefully in the assuring way they get paid to talk in, but the girl jazz singer is lilting a flip version of "Look to the Rainbow," and Jack knows he's on next.

He leafs through lots of little pads filled with the tiniest hand-lettered notes. "When I write I print everything in pencil. My father was a printer. He lost his shop on the horses. If he didn't, I'd be a printer today. I'd probably be publishing the fresh, young poets. . . ."

He's getting more nervous, but his speech comes easy in answer to certain questions. "You don't know what a square is? Well, old Rexroth says I'm a square. If he means because I was born a French Canadian Catholic . . . sometimes devout . . .

then I guess that makes me a square. But a square is someone who ain't hip. Hipness? Him" (pointing to me) "and I, we're hip."

Trying to keep up with the questions, he goes on at an even faster rate. "I was sitting with Steve Allen out front for a while; he said he wished he had his old *Tonight* show, so he could put me on. I told him he should wire Jack Paar. . . . Jazz-men and poets are both like babies. . . . No, I decided not to read to music because I feel they don't mix. . . . Well, maybe Allen will sit in on the piano for a while, though. . . . Yair, whatever I write about is all true. . . . I think Emily Dickinson is better than Whitman, as a wordman, that is."

The drink, the sweat, the smoke, the nerves are taking effect. It's time for him to go on. He grabs some of those pads and begins making his way through the maze of tiny night-club tables. They all came to see him, and a few tieless buddies from the old days, a little proud and a little jealous, the fourth estate, the agents, the hand-shakers, the Steve Allens, the Madison Avenue bunch trying to keep ultra-current; all treating him like a Carmine DeSapio or Floyd Patterson.

He's shorter than they expected, this writer who has been likened to Sandburg but looks like a frightened MC on his first job. They applaud wildly for this 35-year-old who was drunk for the first three weeks that his book made the best-seller list, and now stands before them wearing an outfit of fair middle-class taste, but with a thick, hand-tooled, large-buckled leather belt.

"I'm going to read like I read to my friends." A too-easy murmur of laughter, the crowd is with him. He reads fast, with his eyes untheatrically glued to the little pad, rapidly, on and on as if he wants to get it over with. "I'll read a junky poem." He slurs over the beautiful passages as if not expecting the crowd to dig them, even if he went slower. "It's like kissing my kitten's belly. . . ." He begins to loosen up and ad lib, and the audience is with him. A fast 15 minutes and he's done.

The applause is like a thunderstorm on a hot July night. He smiles and goes to sit among the wheels and the agents, and pulls a relaxed drag on his cigarette.

He is prince of the hips, being accepted in the court of the rich kings who, six months ago, would have nudged him closer to the bar, if he wandered in to watch the show. He must have hated himself in the morning—not for the drinks he had, but because he ate it all up the way he really never wanted to.

As I was leaving I heard some guy in an old Army shirt, standing close to the bar, remark: "Well, Kerouac came off the road in high gear . . . I hope he has a good set of snow tires."

Jack Kerouac, Gloria McDarrah, Lew Welch, and Albert Saijo writing a poem at Fred and Gloria's apartment, 304 West 14th Street, December 10, 1959.

Kerouac at 304 West 14th Street, December 10, 1959, with Gloria McDarrah at typewriter.

Kerouac at 304 West 14th Street, December 10, 1959.

Albert Saijo and Lew Welch at 304 West 14th Street, December 10, 1959.

KING OF THE BEATS

by Seymour Krim

Commonweal, January 2, 1959

With each passing book Jack Kerouac begins to come down to earth a little more, to reveal what he's made of and allow for some practical judgments. There has been such a gossip campaign about our so-called wild man, the King of the Beats, that ordinarily serious literary people have come to assume a fighting stance (either for or against) that has little to do with Kerouac's actual performance.

Let us take a look at his newest book, *The Dharma Bums* (Viking, $3.95), before trying to generalize. Once again Kerouac is writing in the first person—a transparent autobiographical device, calling himself Ray Smith where before he wore the dream-names of Sal Paradise and Leo Percipied—and the scene of the book is the San Francisco–Berkeley area where the young beats live a kind of Ashcan School type of life, sparked up with wine and the bed. It is essentially the same Kerouac environment that was pictured in the first two books of his current spurt; the only truly new arrival on the scene is Zen, and a good deal of the dialogue and the references play around with Buddhist notions.

Ray Smith, the hero of the present chapter in Kerouac's nonstop gush (and each of the three novels that have recently been published are mere episodes in the unwinding scroll of his experience), adds mountain-climbing and meditation to the typical Kerouacian staple of batting madly around the country. In a sense, this book is gentler and less pretentious than both *On the Road* and *The Subterraneans;* Kerouac-Smith is in a more thoughtful and introspective mood than previously, and spends much time by himself digging the beauties and possibilities of nature. A genuine pastoral charm can be found in the *Bums,* and it is quite refereshing until it becomes overdone.

But although this new facet of Kerouac's sensitivity has been seized upon by some conventional critics who couldn't see what all the fuss was about before, Kerouac's sensuous response to nature should not be hoisted high as proof that he is a good boy after all, wholesome and bracketable.

That's too easy: witness the fact that it enabled Mr. J. Donald Adams to hop on the Kerouac Lambretta with some fulsome verbiage about Kerouac's being the finest nature writer since Hemingway (which is untrue) and altogether dodging the other implications in the work (which formerly caused Adams to consign Kerouac to the noisome pit). Kerouac's back-to-nature theme in the present book is obviously part of his total drive for a direct, vitalistic marriage with reality in all its senses. Literary teetotalers and nice old ladies who now pat Kerouac's head kindly because he celebrates the birds and bees forget that he loves (but loves, man!) his booze and sex as much as ever; his next book may very well revive the original horror and condemnation.

The most widely quoted reviews of *On the Road* compared Kerouac to Thomas Wolfe as a rolling, roaring, all-American type of prose bard. As his writing now tumbles out into book form (rumor has it that Kerouac has at least six already-written books waiting for publishers), we can see that this original comparison was misleading. Kerouac does not have the classic verbal equipment or majesty of Wolfe at his best, and anyone who goes to his books looking for the same thrilling bombast won't find it. As a handler of words, Kerouac is often careless and slangy, the language often dripping colorlessly into an undifferentiated puddle. And in this latest book we see that the writing is thin as well, with none of the rotundity or resonance that the Wolfe-Whitman comparisons implied.

I think it is illuminating to poke into his actual prose itself because so much hazy misinformation has found its way into the press concerning it. The most interesting writing of Kerouac's three recent books can be found in *The Subterraneans*, where the sentences are thick, clotted, almost unreadable in their fidelity to what the "I" experiences, down to the most hair-fine detail. I have been told that this is the only one of Kerouac's books that has not been edited; and it shows in the final tediousness of the writing and, more importantly, in the attempt on Kerouac's part to tell *all* about his painful affair with a young colored girl. It is a strong and vivid piece of writing, one that stays in the mind like a burr, but it also points up the recklessness of his method of composition and, probably, his entire philosophy. This is important, I think, because Kerouac's virtues and excesses are yoked very tightly, almost inseparably, together.

After publishing the semi-conventional *The Town and the City* in his late twenties, Kerouac (now thirty-six) felt a dissatisfaction with the academic notion of the novel-form; he turned his back on every falsity that he felt in the made-up, "fictional" conception of the novel, carried over from the nineteenth century and embalmed in the universities, and tried to find a form that was more on a level with his actual experience. With much fumbling, he at last hit upon what his buddy Allen Ginsberg, the young howling poet, has described a little pretentiously as "spontaneous bop prosody." Broken down, this means completely spontaneous composition with none of the super-ego restraints formerly enjoined upon the writer; and also, very important to the method, *no rewriting* once the original words and the shape of sentences are first cast by the mind.

Kerouac's "bop prosody" represented a breakthrough for him as a writer which should be appreciated even if one has doubts about the method: it enabled him to express his experience with much greater accuracy and reality than if he still wore around his neck what he felt as heavy stones of "responsibility" and "literature." The bulk of highbrow young writers Kerouac's own age were strangling themselves, he believed, with grueling and ultra-sober notions of "wit," "tension," "density" and "complexity" in writing—a set of catchwords coming out of the New Criticism and the high-powered little magazines. All this seemed falsely over-intellectual and forced to Kerouac and his band of guerrillas. Writing, they thought, loses all of its value to the individual if it has to be put through such a grotesquely convoluted process. Kerouac felt he had to return to the primary reality of his experience and forget the consequences; otherwise he could never have gotten under way and reached a pitch in his faith and certainty where he could really "let go" with some of the actuality that he had undergone. Thus Kerouac's "rhythm writing"—no censoring, no rationalizing, no tampering with the flow—was a most dramatic counterpart to the kind of statically intellectual work he felt was slowing down the literary scene. He wanted to tear open all the vents of being and let the actual thought at the moment it was conceived drop upon the page without apology.

In this Kerouac wasn't without precedent, of course. It is an ancient artistic notion, and in our time Jackson Pollock of the so-called "action painters" of the abstract expressionist group had reached comparable conclusions and John Cage done similar things in music. But in Kerouac's case, especially after the publication of *On the Road* (which was edited and cleaned up by Viking before being offered to the public) a barrage of moral criticism was leveled at him which artists like Pollock and Cage never had to cope with. Because the work of these two men is abstract, critics could wrangle about the method but the ambiguity of the content presented a challenge which had to be brooded upon. But in Kerouac's case people hardly noticed the method because the life he seemed to glorify—promiscuity, pot-smoking, the hot pursuit of speed, kicks, excitement—was so much more tangible than "art." What was particularly refreshing or shocking about Kerouac's content (depending on the readers) was that he brought out into the open—could not help doing so, once committed to his method—some facts about contemporary American life which don't find their way into the Sunday *Times,* for instance, because they aren't the kind of news thought fit enough to print.

The life Kerouac writes about may be judged to be "good" or "bad" or "destructive"; unquestionably it foams over with confusion and waste, but then so does our national scene. And there is the objective fact that many young people—often quite gifted ones, in the sense of creativity, response to experience, trying to think for themselves—are living a life similar to the kind that Kerouac writes about. What once was the inner circle of bohemia has expanded its values through modern jazz and the dissemination of avant garde art of all kinds to the very gates of the middle-class, and if you leaf through the men's magazines today you will see that the so-called bohemian values have now become a part of American life; the dividing-line separating the bearded, horn-rimmed types from our former images of bourgeois respectability seems not so sharp anymore. Many Americans seem to be living, or as Kerouac would perhaps more honestly say, trying to make it, on this same screwy scene.

Thus I believe that Kerouac, by throwing over the literary restraints, has succeeded in letting some of the real experience of our decade escape into his pages in crude, free-swinging, even shapeless form. Unlike most of his contemporaries, who haven't been spared a similar life, Kerouac doesn't apologize for his pursuit of pleasure; he refuses to look down on his experience or to measure it against any ideal. He is determined simply to find joy in his life, even at extravagant cost and risk.

What sets Kerouac apart from the "writer writers," and makes his voice carry despite its comparative frailty and childishness, is that he has the courage to put down the unaccustomed rhythm and details of the frantic modern scene exactly the way he's lived it. This may not be a literary achievement which will survive beyond the present. But can we be sure what will?

Kerouac at 304 West 14th Street, December 10, 1959.

THE BEAT DEBATED—IS IT OR IS IT NOT?

by Marc D. Schleifer

Village Voice, November 19, 1958

"Let the cats in," someone shouted, while an overflow crowd of hundreds pushed against doors barred by anxious college girls. The place was Hunter College Playhouse on November 6, [1958,] where there was a debate scheduled on the theme, "Is There a Beat Generation?"

Sponsor of the affair was Brandeis University, whose dean, Joseph Kauffman, peered at the audience and looked uncomfortable, glanced at guests Kingsley Amis, Ashley Montagu, James Wechsler, and then looked more uncomfortable. When the evening's festivities of hoots, cheers, insults, and poetry were over, Dean Kauffman's discomfort was so great that I feared for his supper. *But he was still smiling.* And after all, isn't discomfort a small price for enlightened academicians to pay when they carry the creative process into lecture-hall operating rooms on a stretcher and then dissect it as they would a bloodless corpse?

Thoughts, somewhat excerpted, in order of their appearance:

KEROUAC (dashing offstage a dozen times, clowning with a hat to the final stumble and wild dragging of poet Allen Ginsberg onstage toward the end of the "debate"): "Live your lives out, they say; nah, love your lives out, so when they come around and stone you, you won't be living in any glass house— only a glassy flesh. What is called the 'beat generation' is really a revolution in manners . . . being a swinging group of new American boys intent on life. James Dean was not the first to express this. Before him there was Bogart and the private

79

eyes. Now college kids have started to use the words 'hung up.' . . . I'm hung up, you know—words I first heard on Times Square in the '40s. Being beat goes back to my ancestors, to the rebellious, the hungry, the weird, and the mad. To Laurel and Hardy, to Popeye, to Wimpy looking wild-eyed over hamburgers, the size of which they make no more; to Lamont Cranston, the Shadow, with his mad heh-heh-heh knowing laugh. And now there are two types of beat hipsters—the Cool: bearded, sitting without moving in cafes, with their unfriendly girls dressed in black, who say nothing; and the Hot: Crazy, talkative, mad shining eyes, running from bar to bar only to be ignored by the cool subterraneans. I guess I'm still with the hot ones. When I walk into a club playing jazz, I still want to shout: 'Blow, Man, Blow.'"

KINGSLEY AMIS (author of *Lucky Jim,* wearing a conservative light brown suit, perplexed by the mad audience, but in a friendly way trying to understand the madness): "There is a general impression that the beat generation has opened a branch in England, or at least made an alliance with a group called 'the Angry Young Men.' Thus a Detroit critic says: 'America's angry young men are called the beat generation.' Is there a group of young English writers united and unique in protesting about creative stagnation in contemporary life? No, emphatically, no. 'The Angry Young Men' is an invention of literary middlemen, desperate journalists who thrive on classifications and clichés, who put writers in pigeonholes and save people the trouble of reading. This nonsense can also be traced to the Anglo-American cult of youth. In England, anybody who writes and is under pensionable age is put under the title of AYM. Any day I expect to see Boris Pasternak so labeled. Yes, Osborne *is* angry, that's his privilege. But all the English writers who have been so categorized are doing what writers have always done—they are going about the job of writing. There is no Angry Young Men movement. There may be a beat generation, but I doubt it."

JAMES WECHSLER (editor of the *New York Post* and author of *Revolt on the Campus,* looking angry if not young, vigorously chewing his gum with openmouthed liberal sincerity, staring at Kerouac with incomprehension whenever Jack mentioned God, Poetry, or the Cross): "I am one of the few unreconstructed radicals of my generation. Much of what has happened in the past 20 or so years has challenged my basic beliefs, but I still adhere to them. *[Turning to Kerouac]* Life is complicated enough without having to make it into a poem. I am convinced that ethical values will reemerge. What gives meaning to life is the survival of these values. It is a sad thing for America that this beat generation is supposed to represent rebellion and un-orthodoxy. After listening to Kerouac I understand less about what they stand for than before. I see no virtue in organized confusion. The beat generation as a symbol is sort of a joke. The issue is not whether there is a beat generation, but whether civilization will survive. There is no valor in their [the beats'] kind of flight and irresponsibility."

ASHLEY MONTAGU (Princeton anthropologist, author of *Immortality and Man: The First Million Years,* white-haired, calm, slightly amused, and slightly sleepy-looking just the way the Ladies League thinks a professor should look): "James Dean symbolized the beat generation. His death was consistent with the BG philosophy—life is like Russian Roulette. Their only conformity is nonconformity. The beats give personal testimony to the breakdown of Western values. These are the children who were failed by their parents. Compassion, not con-demnation, is called for. The BG is the ultimate expression of a civilization whose moral values have broken down. While not everybody born in the past 30 years is beat, and while there were beat people born more than 30 years ago, the beat writers are describing this generation."

In May 1959, traffic went in both directions on Fifth Avenue and buses drove through Washington Square Park. Folk singing in the park drew people from all over.

In the mid-1950s there was actually quaint folk dancing in Washington Square Park.

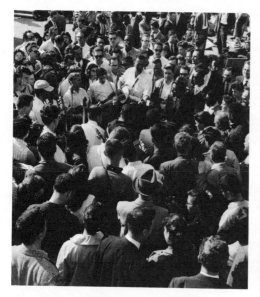

The Shanty Boys in the mid-1950s provided regular Sunday-afternoon entertainment in Washington Square Park. The players are Mike Cohen on guitar, Roger Sprung on banjo, and Lionel Kilberg on wash tub.

William Morris reading poetry, July 26, 1959, in Washington Square Park while friend Malcolm Soule looks on. Police had arrested Morris the week before on a disorderly conduct charge for attracting a crowd.

Writer-critic Nat Hentoff, left, and journalist Gilbert Millstein minding their children in Washington Square Park, April 8, 1960.

Fred McDarrah, Norman Mailer, Marvin Frank, and Harold (Doc) Humes, in Washington Square Park, May 15, 1960.

John Filler with daughter Erika in Washington Square Park, March 27, 1960.

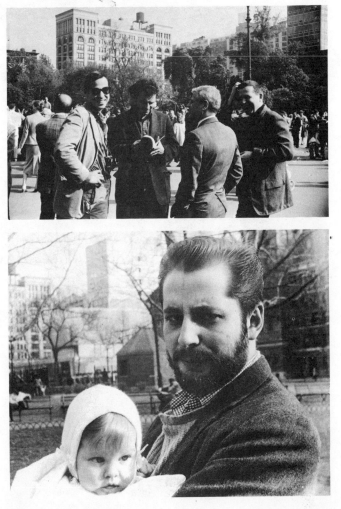

Joyce and Ted Joans in Washington Square Park, June 7, 1959, with their children. All four are now married and the youngest one has made Ted Joans a grandfather.

Dick Bellamy and Alfred Leslie in Washington Square Park, September 12, 1959. Both worked on Pull My Daisy.

Village Voice *auto columnist Daniel List, left, with cartoonist Shel Silverstein in Washington Square Park, June 7, 1959.*

Howard Hart and friend Cindy Lee (Cindia Laracuen) on Fifth Avenue and 21st Street, September 4, 1959.

Provincetown Review *editors William V. Ward and Harriet Sohmers in Washington Square Park, April 24, 1960.*

SCORE HERE FOR
JAZZ AND JUNK
THE
CONNECTION
THE LIVING THEATRE
6TH AVE AT 14 ST
THE FREDDIE REDD
QUARTET
WITH
JACKIE MC LEAN

Harry Proach of the Living Theatre takes the message into Washington Square Park, July 19, 1959.

THE ROAMING BEATNIKS

by Jack Kerouac

Holiday, October 1959

The beat night life of New York strangely has nothing to do with night clubs or spending money and yet it is a complete night life in the truest sense. Take, for example, this typical evening among the characters:

Emerging from the Seventh Avenue subway on 42nd Street, you pass the john, which is the beatest john in New York: you can never tell if it's open or not, usually there's a big chain in front of it saying it's out of order, or else it's got some white-haired decaying monster slinking outside; a john which all seven million people in New York City have at one time passed and taken strange notice of—past the new charcoal-fried-hamburger stand, Bible booths, operatic jukeboxes, and a seedy underground used-magazine store smelling of subway arcades—here and there a used copy of that old bard Plotinus sneaked in with the remainders of collections of German high-school text-books—where they sell long, ratty-looking hotdogs (no, actually they're quite beautiful, particularly if you haven't got 15 cents and are looking for someone in Bickford's Cafeteria who can lay some smash on you (lend you some change).

Coming up that stairway, people stand there for hours and hours drooling in the rain, with soaking-wet umbrellas; lots of boys in dungarees scared to go into the Army standing halfway up the stairway on the iron steps waiting for God Who knows what; certainly among them some romantic heroes just in from Oklahoma, with ambitions to end up yearning in the arms of some unpredictable sexy young blonde in a penthouse on the Empire State Building—some of them probably stand there dreaming of owning the Empire State Building by virtue of a magic spell which they've dreamed up by a creek in the back-woods of a ratty old house on the outskirts of Texarkana.

Ashamed of being seen going into the dirty movie (what's its name?) across the street from the New York *Times*—The lion and the tiger passing, as Tom Wolfe used to say about certain types passing that corner.

Leaning against that cigar store with a lot of telephone booths on the corner of 42nd and Seventh, where you make beautiful telephone calls looking out into the street and it gets real cozy in there when it's raining outside and you like to prolong the conversation, who do you find? Basketball teams? Basketball coaches? All those guys from the rollerskating rink go there? Cats from the Bronx again, looking for some action, really looking for romance? Strange duos of girls coming out of dirty movies? Did you ever see them? Or bemused drunken businessmen with their hats tipped awry on their graying heads staring catatonically upward at the signs floating by on the Times Building, huge sentences about Khrushchev reeling by, the populations of Asia enumerated in flashing lightbulbs, always five hundred periods after each sentence. Suddenly a psychopathically worried policeman appears on the corner and tells everybody to go away. This is the center of the greatest city the world has ever known and this is what beatniks do here. "Standing on the street corner waiting for no one is Power," sayeth poet Gregory Corso.

Instead of going to night clubs—if you're in a position to make the nightclub scene (most beatniks rattle empty pockets passing Birdland)—how strange to stand on the sidewalk and just watch that weird eccentric from Second Avenue looking like Napoleon going by feeling cooky crumbs in his pocket, or a young 15-year-old kid with a bratty face, or suddenly somebody swishing by in a baseball hat (because that's what you see), and finally an old lady dressed in seven hats and a long, ratty fur coat in the middle of the July night carrying a huge Russian woolen purse filled with scribbled bits of paper which say "Festival Foundation Inc., 70,000 Germs" and moths flying out of her sleeve—she rushes up and importunes Shriners. And duffelbag soldiers without a war—harmonica players off freight trains. Of course there are the normal New Yorkers, looking ridiculously out of place and as odd as their own neat oddity, carrying pizzas and *Daily Newses* and headed for brown basements or Pennsylvania trains—W. H. Auden himself may

be seen fumbling by in the rain—Paul Bowles, natty in a
Dacron suit, passing through on a trip from Morocco, the ghost
of Herman Melville himself followed by Bartleby the Wall
Street Scrivener and Pierre the ambiguous hipster of 1848
out on a walk—to see what's up in the news flashes of the
Times—— Let's go back to the corner newsstand. SPACE BLAST.
. . . POPE WASHES FEET OF POOR.

Let's go across the street to Grant's, our favored dining place.
For 65 cents you get a huge plate of fried clams, a lot of French
fried potatoes, a little portion of cole slaw, some tartar sauce, a
little cup of red sauce for fish, a slice of lemon, two slices of fresh
rye bread, a pat of butter, another ten cents brings a glass of rare
birch beer. . . . What a ball it is to eat here! Migrations of Span-
iards chewing on hotdogs, standing up, leaning over big pots of
mustard. Ten different counters with different specialties. Ten-
cent cheese sandwiches, two liquor bars for the Apocalypse, oh
yeah and great indifferent bartenders—and cops that stand in
the back getting free meals—drunken saxophone players on the
nod—lonely, dignified ragpickers from Hudson Street supping
soup without a word to anybody, with black fingers, woe. Twenty
thousand customers a day—fifty thousand on rainy days—one
hundred thousand on snowy days. Operation twenty-four hours
a night. Privacy: Supreme under a glary red light full of conversation. Toulouse-Lautrec, with his deformity and cane, sketch-
ing in the corner. You can stay there for five minutes and gobble
up your food, or else stay there for hours having insane philosophical conversation with your buddy and wondering about the
people. "Let's have a hotdog before we go to the movie!" and you
get so high in there you never get to the movies, because it's
better than a show about Doris Day on a holiday in the Carib-
bean.

"But what are we gonna do tonight? Marty would go to a
movie but we're going to connect for some junk. Let's go down
to the Automat."

"Just a minute, I've got to shine my shoes on top of a fire
hydrant."

"You wanta see yourself in the fun mirror?"

"Wanta take four pictures for a quarter? Because we're on
the eternal scene. We can look at the picture and remember it
when we're wise old white-haired Thoreaus in cabins."

"Ah, the fun mirrors are gone, they used to have fun mirrors here."

"How about the Laff Movie?"

"That's gone too."

"They got the flea circus."

"They still got donzinggerls?"

"The burlesque is gone, millions and millions of years ago."

"Shall we go down by the Automat and watch the old ladies eating beans, or the deaf-mutes that stand in front of the window there and you watch 'em and try to figure the invisible language as it flees across the window from face to face and finger to finger . . . ? Why does Times Square feel like a big room?"

Across the street is Bickford's, right in the middle of the block under the Apollo Theater marquee and right next door to a little bookshop that specializes in Havelock Ellis and Rabelais, with thousands of sex fiends leafing at the bins. Bickford's is the greatest stage on Times Square: many people have hung around there for years, man and boy, searching, God alone knows for what, maybe some angel of Times Square who would make the whole big room home, the old homestead . . . civilization needs it. What's Times Square doing there anyway? Might as well enjoy it. Greatest city the world has ever seen. Have they got a Times Square on Mars? What would the Blob do on Times Square? Or St. Francis?

A girl gets off a bus in the Port Authority Terminal and goes into Bickford's. Chinese girl, red shoes, sits down with coffee, looking for daddy.

There's a whole floating population around Times Square that has always made Bickford's their headquarters day and night. In the old days of the beat generation some poets used to go in there to meet the famous character "Hunkey" who used to come in and out in an oversized black raincoat and a cigarette holder, looking for somebody to lay a pawnticket on—Remington typewriter, portable radio, black raincoat—to score for some toast (get some money) so he can go uptown and get in trouble with the cops or any of his boys. Also a lot of stupid gangsters from 8th Avenue used to cut in—maybe they still do—the ones from the early days are all in jail or dead. Now the poets just go there, and smoke a peace pipe, looking for the ghost of Hunkey or his boys, and dream over the fading cups of tea.

The beatniks make the point that if you went there every night and stayed there you could start a whole Dostoevski season on Times Square by yourself and meet all the midnight newspaper peddlers and their involvements and families and woes; religious fanatics who would take you home and give you long sermons over the kitchen table about the "new apocalypse" and similar ideas: "My Baptist minister back in Winston-Salem told me the reason that God invented television was that when Christ comes back to earth again, they shall crucify Him right on the streets of this here Babylon and they gonna have television cameras pointin' down on that spot and the streets shall run with blood and every eye shall see."

Still hungry, go out, down to the Oriental Cafeteria— "favored dining spot" also—some night life—cheap—down in the basement across the street from the Port Authority monolith bus terminal on 40th Street and eat big oily lambs' shanks with Greek rice for 90¢. Oriental zig-zag tunes on the jukebox.

Depends how high you are by now—assuming you've picked up someone on one of the corners—say 42nd Street and Eighth Avenue, near the great Whelan's drug store, another lonely haunt spot where you can meet people—Negro whores, ladies limping in a Benzedrine psychosis. Across the street you can see the ruins of New York already started—the Globe Hotel being torn down there, an empty tooth hole right on 44th Street—and the green McGraw-Hill building gaping up in the sky, higher than you'd believe—lonely all by itself down towards the Hudson River where freighters wait in the rain with their Montevideo limestone.

Might as well go on home. It's getting old. Or: "Let's make the Village or go to the Lower East Side and play Symphony Sid on the radio—or play our Indian records—and eat big dead Puerto Rican steaks—or lung stew—see if Bruno has slashed any more car roofs in Brooklyn—though Bruno's gentled now, maybe he's written a new poem."

Or look at Television. Night life—Oscar Levant talking about his melancholia.

The Five Spot, on 5th Street and Bowery, sometimes features Thelonious Monk on the piano and you go on there. If you know the proprietor you sit down at the table free with a beer, but if you don't know him you can sneak in and stand by the ventilator and listen. Always crowded weekends. Monk cogitates with deadly abstraction, clonk, and makes a statement, huge foot beating delicately on the floor, head turned to one side listening, entering the piano.

Lester Young played there just before he died and used to sit in the back kitchen between sets. Poet Allen Ginsberg went back and got on his knees and asked him what he would do if an atom bomb fell on New York. Lester said he would break the window in Tiffany's and get some jewels anyway. He also said, "What you doin' on your knees?" not realizing he is a great hero of the beat generation, and now enshrined. The Five Spot is darkly lit, has weird waiters, good music always; sometimes John "Train" Coltrane showers his rough notes from his big tenor horn all over the place. On weekends, parties of well-dressed uptowners jam-pack the place, talking continuously—nobody minds.

O for a couple of hours, though, in the Egyptian Gardens in the lower West Side Chelsea district of Greek restaurants. Glasses of ouzo, Greek liqueur, and beautiful girls dancing the belly dance in spangles and beaded bras, the incomparable Zara on the floor and weaving like mystery to the flutes and tingtang beats of Greece—when she's not dancing she sits in the orchestra with the men, plopping a drum against her belly, dreams in her eyes. Huge crowds of what appear to be Suburbia couples sit at the tables clapping to the swaying Oriental idea. If you're late you have to stand along the wall.

Wanta dance? The Garden Bar on Third Avenue where you can do fantastic sprawling dances in the dim back room to a jukebox, cheap, the waiter doesn't care.

Wanta just talk? The Cedar Bar on University Place where all the painters hang out and a 16-year-old kid who was there one afternoon squirting red wine out of a Spanish wine skin into his friends' mouths and kept missing. . . .

The night clubs of Greenwich Village known as the Half Note, the Village Vanguard, the Café Bohemia, the Village Gate also feature jazz (Lee Konitz, J.J. Johnson, Miles Davis), but you've got to have mucho money and it's not so much that you've got to have mucho money, but the sad commercial atmosphere is killing jazz, and jazz is killing itself there, because jazz belongs to open, joyful ten-cent beer joints, as in the beginning.

There's a big party at some painter's loft, wild loud flamenco on the phonograph, the girls suddenly become all hips and heels, and people try to dance between their flying hair. Men go mad and start tackling people, flying wedges hurtle across the room, men grab men around the knees and lift them nine feet from the floor and lose their balance and nobody gets hurt, blonk. Girls are balanced hands on men's knees, their skirts falling and revealing frills on their thighs. Finally everybody dresses to go home and the host says dazedly, "You all look so *respectable*."

Or somebody just had an opening, or there's a poetry reading at the Living Theater, or at the Gaslight Café, or at the Seven Arts Coffee Gallery, up around Times Square (Ninth Avenue and 43rd Street, amazing spot) (begins at midnight Fridays), where afterward everybody rushes out to the old wild bar. Or else a huge party at LeRoi Jones's—he's got a new issue of *Yugen* magazine which he printed himself on a little cranky machine and everybody's poems are in it, from San Francisco to Gloucester, Mass., and costs only 50 cents. Historic publisher, secret hipster of the trade. LeRoi's getting sick of parties, everyone's always taking off his shirt and dancing, three sentimental girls are crooning over poet Raymond Bremser, Gregory Corso is arguing with the New York *Post* reporter saying, "But you don't understand Kangaroonian weep! Forsake thy trade! Flee to the Enchenedian Islands!"

Let's get out of here, it's too literary. Let's go get drunk on the Bowery or eat those long noodles and tea in glasses at Hong Pat's in Chinatown. What are we always eating for? Let's walk over the Brooklyn Bridge and build up another appetite. How about some okra on Sands Street?

Shades of Hart Crane!

Ah, let's go back to the Village and stand on the corner of 8th Street and Sixth Avenue and watch the intellectuals go by. AP reporters lurching home to their basement apartments on Washington Square, lady editorialists with huge German police dogs breaking their chains, lonely dikes melting by, unknown experts on Sherlock Holmes with blue fingernails going up to their rooms to take scopolamine, a musclebound young man in a cheap, gray German suit explaining something weird to his fat girl friend, great editors leaning politely at the newsstand buying the early edition of the *Times,* great, fat furniture movers out of 1910 Charlie Chaplin films coming home with great bags full of chop suey (feeding everybody), Picasso's melancholy harlequin now owner of a print and frame shop musing on his wife and newborn child lifting up his finger for a taxi, rolypoly recording engineers rush in fur hats, girl artists down from Columbia with D. H. Lawrence problems picking up 50-year-old men, old men in the Kettle of Fish, and the melancholy specter of New York Women's Prison that looms high and is folded in silence as the night itself—at sunset their windows look like oranges—poet e. e. cummings buying a package of cough drops in the shade of that monstrosity. If it's raining you can stand under the awning in front of Howard Johnson's and watch the street from the other side.

Beatnik Angel Peter Orlovsky in the supermarket five doors away buying Uneeda Biscuits (late Friday night), ice cream, caviar, bacon, pretzels, soda-pop, *TV Guide,* Vaseline, three toothbrushes, chocolate milk (dreaming of roast suckling pig), buying whole Idaho potatoes, raisin bread, wormy cabbage by mistake, and fresh-felt tomatoes and collecting purple stamps. Then he goes home broke and dumps it all on the table, takes out a big book of Mayakovsky poems, turns on the 1949 television set to the horror movie, and goes to sleep.

And this is the beat night life of New York.

Albert Saijo, Gloria McDarrah, Jack Kerouac, Lew Welch, and Fred McDarrah in Egyptian Gardens, December 10, 1959, after completin an original poem in two hours.

Belly dancing at the Egyptian Gardens, December 10, 1959.

Alfred Leslie and Harold (Doc) Humes at the Jazz Gallery, 80 St. Mark's Place, December 1 1959. Horace Silver Quintet, A Farmer, and Benny Golsson played that night.

Art Blakey & His Jazz Messengers at the Jazz Gallery, 80 St. Mark's Place, February 6, 1960. The club was popular with the beat poets and writers.

Mimi Margeaux recites an ode to autumn, George Preston scatters leaves, Jack Micheline climbs the picket fence. After a McClure-Whelan poetry reading on City College campus.

Micheline, birdlike, jumps!

Outside the Cedar Street Tavern, 24 University Place, August 18, 1959. The tavern relocated six blocks away some years later, when the building was torn down.

The White Horse Tavern, 567 Hudson Street, was the most important literary bar in the West Village in the mid-1950s, made famous by Dylan Thomas, who drank there while in New York. The beats later went to the Cedar Street Tavern.

LeRoi Jones and Diane DiPrima relaxing in the Cedar Street Tavern, April 5, 1960.

Meg Randall, painter Edward Avedisian, sculptor Ronald Bladen, and model Ann Schwertley at 4:00 a.m., Riker's Café, East 8th Street, March 19, 1960. Bladen did drawings for Randall's Giant of Tears, *a book of poems.*

LeRoi Jones (now Amiri Baraka) with editor Irving Rosenthal and John Fles in Cedar Street Tavern, October 21, 1959. Picture was originally taken for a Kulchur *magazine advertisement.*

Poets Bill Godden, Bruce Fearing, and Jack Micheline in Cedar Street Tavern, October 9, 1959. Godden's poems appeared in Exodus *and* Birth *and were published under the title* Famous People Thoughts and Poems, *by Birth Press.*

Poet Frank O'Hara, left, with New York School abstract expressionist Franz Kline in Cedar Street Tavern, 24 University Place, the artists' and poets' hangout. March 6, 1959.

Bartender John Bodnar, Julian Beck, and Allen Ginsberg in Cedar Street Tavern, August 19, 1959.

The night the Cedar Street Tavern closed, March 30, 1963. View looking to front of tavern.

*The night the Cedar Street Tavern closed, March 30, 1963.
View looking to rear of tavern.*

*Sylvia Topp and Tuli
Kupferberg in front of
the Cedar Street
Tavern.*

THE UPBEAT BEATNIK

by Art Buchwald

New York Herald Tribune, January 4, 1960

PARIS. The last time we saw our good friend the beat poet Gregory Corso, he was struggling to be heard in a world filled with squares. But in less than a year and a half the picture, according to him, has changed and beatniks are here to stay.

Mr. Corso, who recently returned from a successful tour of American universities where they let him read his poetry, told us: "Beatniks in America are now a majority, even though they're still being treated like a minority. Every face you see is a beatnik face. It won't be long before everyone will sit in bed and eat big fat pies."

The philosophy of the beatniks, Mr. Corso explained to us, was that no man should work. "They got machines now to do the work," he said. "People got to start thinking. That's what's going to save us. Everyone staying in bed eating big fat pies and thinking. As soon as the bankers become beatniks they'll open the vaults and then everyone will have money."

We asked Mr. Corso how he explained the success of the beatniks in such a short time.

"We owe it all to Henry Luce."

"How's that?"

"Well, when we first started, the literary magazines tried to put us down. But they had no luck, so they asked Henry Luce to help them. They said: 'Henry, we ain't got the circulation to stop them. It's up to you.' So Mr. Luce put *Time, Life, Fortune,* and *Sports Illustrated* at their disposal.

"Well, the elevators in the Time and Life Building went on a twenty-four-hour shift and everyone went to work. Pretty soon they were writing all about us. But instead of it becoming a drag, they were spreading the gospel faster than Western

Union. People that never heard of beatniks suddenly became aware of us, and the little Frankenstein zoomed.

"Pretty soon it got just too much for Luce. One of his boys was sent out to interview us and he never went back. He gave up his worldly goods and he's now sitting underneath the Acropolis muttering about centaurs and Minotaurs.

"When Luce saw there was nothing he could do, he called in J. Edgar Hoover and the cops and said: 'This thing is bigger than me and Mrs. Luce.'

"So J. Edgar Hoover called the cops out and they started raiding coffee houses. They were even thinking of having a Sullivan law for poets. They wanted to make it a criminal offense to carry a poem on your person. I had an arsenal at home— maybe 150 poems.

"But the cops got nowhere because instead of making arrests they started writing poetry to each other. Where can a thing like this end? The beatniks are a plague and the plague is on."

Mr. Corso said that during his travels in the United States he found a great interest in poetry. "People are getting hooked on poetry," he said. "It's like dope. Whether the beatniks did it with notoriety or silliness, America is getting conscious of poetry. When they start locking poets up, man, you know we've arrived.

"I even have college kids now who write to me and ask me how to become beatniks."

"What do you reply?"

"I say: 'I'm no Norman Vincent Peale. You got to find it in your own way.' A lot of them are laying their arsenal of poems on me and they want me to comment on them. But I can't comment on poetry. When a man sings out something, it's marvelous just to have the song.

"This is going to be a great age," he said. "I can feel it. If we can only get some beatniks in the armies of the world, we can burn down war."

"How?" we wanted to know.

"All you have to do is get beatniks into an army and they'll do away with the uniforms. Now an army can't fight without uniforms. It's no fun. So instead, everybody will stay in their barracks and write poetry. Of course, the colonels will write better poetry than the captains, the captains will write better poetry than the sergeants, and the privates will get all the rejection slips."

So far, though, Mr. Corso said, beatniks haven't become rich. "The concept of an artist starving to death to paint good is going out. Maybe next it will be the poets. There would be nothing more perfect or beautiful than an elegant beatnik. We would bring back red-lined capes, velvet suits, and big bow ties."

"What about baths?"

"We're not against baths. Henry Luce thinks we're against baths. In order for him to distinguish, he has to say there are people who smell nice and there are people who don't."

"Have you ever met Mr. Luce?" we asked him.

"You don't have to meet him," Mr. Corso said. "He's everywhere."

Barbara Moraff, Ray Bremser (with bottle), and Gregory Corso in trench coat at Living Theatre, 530 Sixth Avenue, January 26, 1959.

Gregory Corso, center, borrowing phone money from friend (possibly Kerouac); Allen Ginsberg, right. At the Living Theatre, 530 Sixth Avenue, for performance of Many Loves (William Carlos Williams), January 13, 1959.

Corso and Ginsberg at artist Dody Mueller's exhibit at the Hansa Gallery, Central Park South, March 16, 1959.

PORTRAIT OF A BEAT

by *Alfred G. Aronowitz*

Nugget, October 1960

In Chicago once, a woman asked Allen Ginsberg: "Why is it that you have so much homosexuality in your poetry?"

"I sleep," he has since said, "with men and with women. I am neither queer, nor am I bisexual. My name is Allen Ginsberg and I sleep with whoever I want."

Obviously, Mr. Ginsberg also says what he wants. But then it is as the most outspoken of the Beat Generation poets that he has become the most spoken about. In the salons of literary respectability the name Ginsberg today is on more lips than care to pronounce it, even with a sneer. Nevertheless, Ginsberg, although he may believe, as do so many of his Beat colleagues, that life is an illusion, has no illusions about life, and especially about sex life. He lives it, as he presumes to do everything else, in the best of poetic traditions, if not the best of social ones.

"I don't know whether it's a great sociological problem or not," he says, "but I think that it's pretty shameful that in this culture people have to be so frightened of their own normal sex lives and frightened of other people knowing about it to the point where they have to go slinking around making ridiculous tragedies of their lives. So it seems, for one thing, at this point, that it's necessary for the poets to speak out directly about intimate matters, if they come into the poetry, which they do in mine, and not attempt to hide them or evade the issues. Life is full of strange experiences."

Certainly Ginsberg's has been.

He has handled luggage in the baggage room at Greyhound, carrying suitcases as heavy as his thoughts. He has written speeches for a candidate for Congress. He has taken off his clothes at somewhat genteel parties, proclaiming that those who objected to his body were really ashamed of their own. He has run copy for the Associated Press. He has shipped out as a seaman on tramp steamers, sailing to places as remote as some people find his verse. He has been a Young Liberal, running a mimeograph machine in a labor union organizing office but now he considers labor unions cut from the same stencil as managements. He has washed dishes in greasy spoon restaurants, which, by the way, are his usual eating places. He has harbored thieves and helped them store their loot, justifying himself with the thought that Dostoevsky would have smiled upon him. He has hitchhiked over most of the country. He has undergone eight months of treatment in an insane asylum, suspecting all the while that it was everyone else who was insane. He has taken heroin, cocaine, and what has been called "the true morphine," and he says he's never had a Habit. And, between New York and San Francisco, among young American poets who once didn't know that one another existed, he has organized what the literary crust seems to think is a literary underground.

If Jack Kerouac is, as he has been called, the St. Jack of the Beat Generation, then Allen Ginsberg is its Prophet.

His first published contribution to the growing library of Beat books was a poem which he calls *Howl* and which others with what may be less foresight call blasphemous.

"*Howl* is written," says Ginsberg, peering as he does through his glasses with a friendly intermingling of smile and solemnity, "in some of the rhythm of Hebraic liturgy—chants as they were set down by the Old Testament prophets. That's what it's supposed to represent—prophets howling in the Wilderness. That, in fact, is what the whole Beat Generation is, if it's anything—prophets howling in the Wilderness against a crazy civilization. It was Jack Kerouac, you know, who gave the poem its name. I mailed him a copy just after I wrote it—it was still untitled—and he wrote back, 'I got your howl. . . .'"

The critics got *Howl*, too, or at least they received it. "Nothing goes to show how square the squares are so much as the *favorable* reviews they've given it," groaned poetic colleague Kenneth Rexroth, who himself called *Howl* "much more than the most sensational book of poetry of 1957." Almost overnight,

Howl became the Manifesto of the Beat Generation. And if that wasn't enough to insure Ginsberg's rise, or plummet, to fame, depending upon whether one looks up toward him or down, the San Francisco Department of Police gave him the final shove. It tried to ban the book.

"Allen seems to think he is a latter-day Ezra Pound," says Norman Podhoretz, who has been the most critical of the critics, although he wasn't quite square enough to give *Howl* a favorable review. "In Ginsberg's letters I see the epistolary style of Pound, who, you know, was always writing letters to editors, letters full of profanity, encouraging them to publish his boys. Pound was the great literary talent scout of his day—he discovered T.S. Eliot and helped Yeats become a great poet. He acted not only as leading poet and leading brain but also pushed all the other poets. . . . Now Allen is doing the same thing. . . ."

Ginsberg, of course, takes Pound with a grain of salt and Podhoretz with a pound. Although Ginsberg considers the Beat movement to be heir poetic to the movement which Pound once led, Ginsberg rejects Pound much the same as Pound eventually rejected his former colleagues. And as for Podhoretz, Ginsberg has commented: "He is totally and technically incompetent." For his part, Podhoretz is not so sweeping in his opinion of Ginsberg. A freshman at Columbia College when Ginsberg was an upperclassman there, Podhoretz, writing in a constant complaint that his is a generation without a literary voice, refuses to accept the Beat Generation even as a falsetto. Insisting that there isn't enough vitality in other American writing and that there is too much violence in the Beat, he has, consequently, become as much a villain to the Beats as he considers them to literature. There have, however, been attempts at reconciliation.

"I was working at home one Saturday night," Podhoretz recalls, "when I got a telephone call from some kid—it must have been Ginsberg's friend, Peter Orlovsky. He said, 'Allen and Jack are here having a ball. Why don't you come down and have some kicks.' I told him no, I was busy, and he said, 'Wait, Allen'll talk to you.' So Ginsberg came to the phone—I knew him at Columbia but I hadn't talked to him in years—and he started talking in bop language. So I told him to come off it and he said, 'Come on down, we're having a party. We'll teach you the Dharma.' Well, I guess I was crazy. I went. But it turned out not to be a party at all. There was just Ginsberg, Orlovsky and Kerouac at the apartment of one of Kerouac's girl friends. Kerouac asked me, 'Why is it that all the biggest young critics . . . Why are you against us? Why aren't you for the best talent in your generation?' I said I didn't think he was the best talent in my generation. . . . Kerouac was indignant and said that I said he wasn't intelligent. He really didn't argue, he kept making cracks and being charming, and he *is* charming. But I think much more highly of Ginsberg's literary abilities than Kerouac's. I've always thought highly of Ginsberg as a poet, you know. This Beat stuff is a fairly recent kick of his. He may still become a great poet. He may write important poetry some day. Ginsberg has a superb ear—he can do most anything he wants to do with verse. As an undergraduate in college he was writing fantastic things."

Although the meeting was not quite a meeting of minds, there is evidence that some of their opinions have since mellowed. In any event, the parallel Podhoretz has drawn between Ginsberg and Pound is almost letter-perfect. From his soapbox-furnished tenement flat in the cheap-rent district of New York's Lower East Side, Ginsberg's outgoing mail is exceeded only by his incoming mail, which, daily, brings him new correspondents to answer. Among the regular correspondents, there is, for example, William Seward Burroughs, author of *The Naked Lunch,* writing from a flea hotel in Paris or from Tangiers, telling about the shortcomings of French mysticism, reporting on incidents and sights that could be seen only by an eye as naked as his own, letters that will make another novel, "endless," as Ginsberg says of *The Naked Lunch,* and "that will drive everybody mad." Another is Gregory Corso, sending letters from France or Italy or Crete or Greece, where "I shall surely sleep a night in the Parthenon," telling of a vision of skinless air, questioning death and denouncing its fear, writing a poem about it and enclosing the manuscript. Another is Robert Creeley, a modern jazz poet, editor of *The Black Mountain Review,* not Beat himself, perhaps, but with a beat, writing from Majorca or the Grand Canyon, enclosing poems, too, that fascinate and delight Ginsberg and he sends his own in answer. Another is poet Gary Snyder, his missives inked with a calligraphy that once marked other illuminated manuscripts, a penmanship borrowed from the monks of Middle Aged monasteries, writing now from San Francisco, now from Japan, with an ancient alphabet that speaks a whole new hip language. And there is Lawrence Ferlinghetti, owner of the San Francisco book store called City Lights, a beacon for the Beats and other poets, publisher of *Howl,* a poet like the rest, exchanging manuscripts and compliments, sometimes urgently, by telegram: ALLEN: I READ "APOLLINAIRE'S TOMB" STRUCK DUMB & POOR. YOU ARE HUGEST DARK GENIUS VOICE STILL UNRECOGNIZED.

"Allen is always sending me copies of poems written by his friends, and he's always scrawling notes on the margins," says Ferlinghetti. "He always writes, 'You must publish this—this is mad, this is wild!'"

In addition to his vast correspondence with the various agents of his Underground at their various outposts on The Road, Ginsberg receives a daily deluge of unsolicited letters, some from publications asking for articles or looking for arguments, some from publishers seeking publication rights for an aroused and enthusiastic overseas audience, and many from colleges and universities asking Ginsberg to give poetry readings, a task Ginsberg has been happy to perform for nothing, even happier to perform for money, but lately is just as happy not to perform at all—he doesn't do it any more.

Ginsberg, of course, had become a literary figure even before he wrote *Howl.* Certainly his name, or at least suitable aliases thereof, had already been imprinted in a large, although largely unpublished, body of literature. By 1957, when *Howl* came off the presses, he was a major, if not heroic, character in most of Kerouac's books and also had put in an appearance as David Stofsky, the so-called mad poet, in John Clellon Holmes' *Go.* But all this, naturally, was of little satisfaction to Ginsberg, who had insisted on following his own angel and whose ambitions were written in his own manuscripts.

"I can be pretty persuasive," Ginsberg has said on occasion, and the fact of the matter is that he can. A deft and positive logician, even though he believes in intuition over rationality, Ginsberg is at his best in conversation, and he has changed many minds by the sheer power of his own, so much so that critics who started out doubting Ginsberg's idea of his destiny are now beginning to doubt their own ideas of it.

Culturally, he has charmed Chicago, captured San Francisco and corrupted Los Angeles. "In California," he recalls with a gentle glee, "in L.A., we went down for a poetry reading among what was a bunch of, basically, social Philistines. We came down, offered ourselves, free, to read poetry for them—we were going to Mexico to meet Jack. They were a rather unruly audience, but they were all right, there were some interesting people there. But there was one creepy red-haired guy who kept on saying, 'What are you guys trying to prove?' And I said, 'Nakedness'—he was interrupting the poetry. So he said, 'Nakedness? What do you mean by nakedness?' So I suddenly understood that I had to show him what I meant in some way that would really get across and a way that would move him. So I pulled my clothes off, which shut him up."

Ginsberg concedes that his poetry readings in Chicago were a bit more dignified. Certainly they were accepted with more dignity. Sponsoring one reading was the Chicago Shaw Society, to whom Ginsberg announced, "*. . . this poetry is droppings of the mind . . .*" and whose members, according to the Shaw Society bulletin, responded by dropping the preconceptions from *their* minds. In fact, the only real heckler at the Chicago readings apparently was *Time* magazine (February 9, 1959): ". . . In the richly appointed Lake Shore Drive apartment of Chicago Financier Albert Newman, the guests chatted animatedly, gazed at the original Picasso on the wall, and the Monet, the Jackson Pollock. . . . At length Poet Ginsberg arrived, wearing blue jeans and a checked black-and-red lumberjack shirt with black patches at the elbows. With him were two other shabbily dressed Beatniks. One was Ginsberg's intimate friend, a mental-hospital attendant named Peter Orlovsky, twenty-five, who writes poetry *(I talk to the fire hydrant, asking: 'Do you have bigger tears than I do?');* the other was Gregory Corso, twenty-eight, a shabby, dark little man who boasts that he has never combed his hair—and never gets an argument."

According to Ginsberg, there is much that *Time* hasn't said, either about the Chicago readings or about all the other occasions when *Time* has turned on the Beats. "Knowing what I do about the way they've exaggerated and distorted actual events which concern me," he says, "I shudder to think of what they've done to international events, news that's really important. Think of how many people read *Time* every week and get their picture of the world from it." The result has been something of a feud. *"Are you going to let your emotional life be run by Time Magazine?"* Ginsberg asks in a poem. *"I'm obsessed by Time Magazine. I read it every week. Its cover stares at me every time I slink past the corner candystore."* Once a *Life* magazine reporter assaulted Ginsberg's flat seeking an interview, and Ginsberg threw him out, although not bodily.

"He tried to tell me why I should talk to him even though the article was going to be unfriendly," Ginsberg says. "Why should I talk to him?"

The flat in which Ginsberg is not at home to *Life* reporters is of the type that might be expected to house a poet who has taken a vow of poverty the better to be untrammeled by modern society, a vow which modern society—the economics of poetry publishing being what they are—has helped him keep. Two stories above a Puerto Rican storefront church, it lies behind a large, enchanted door that most of the time is locked and unresponding but sometimes answers with a "Who is it?" A few steps past the bathroom, with its eternal light, because someone has to climb on the rim of the tub to turn it off, and there is the kitchen, light green or light blue behind the wall soot on which someone has finger painted, with convincing expertness, a mystical Chinese or Japanese legend that has no explanation. Over the refrigerator, sketched on brown wrapping paper, is Kerouac's drawing of Dr. Sax just as it appears on the title page of his book, *Dr. Sax*. On a ledge over the brown metal table, usually cluttered with slightly used dishes, glasses, cups, sugar, salt and an extensively used typewriter, a tiny souvenir bust of Napoleon faces the wall, his back toward everyone. A few inches away on the same ledge, another souvenir, a post card with a picture of the house in Rome where Shelley once lived. And on the wall in the corner is the photograph of another hero, William Carlos Williams, silhouetted atop Garrett Mountain overlooking his city, once Ginsberg's, Paterson.

Ginsberg and Orlovsky share the apartment with Corso, when he is in New York, and with a continuum of visitors, many uninvited or unannounced. There is no telephone to announce their coming. At the kitchen table there may be novelist Paul Bowles for dinner, a friend from Tangiers, or Jack

Kerouac, arrived for the weekend, or Philip Whalen and Michael McClure, San Francisco poets, houseguests, or Fernando Arrabal, French novelist, paying a social call, or friends and literati.

In the largest of the three bedrooms, with its balcony, a fire escape, there is television, a second-hand set worth its weight in mahogany, offering treasures such as Popeye, The Three Stooges, and occasional Marx Brothers films, comedies of a life that is frightening to live, scripts whose writers of old Hollywood probably never even realized were copied from Kafka. In Ginsberg's flat on quiet evenings at home sometimes all the occupants are on separate typewriters in separate rooms listening to separate voices, working late into the night, sleeping late into the day, with Ginsberg, his digestive tract as sensitive as all of him, awakening sometimes ill, the after-effect of hostile audiences, perhaps, or of cough-syrup euphoria or perhaps of simple poetic brooding. Once a bum from the nearby Bowery knocked on the door, came in and told of hearing that Ginsberg was really a secret philanthropist, a benefactor of mankind. Ginsberg gave him his total assets, a dollar and change.

"People used to ask me if Allen wrote poetry, too," recalls Ginsberg's father, Louis Ginsberg, an English teacher in Paterson, and a poet as well. "And I would tell them, 'No—he's the only one in the family who's normal.' Then I found out he had all these poems hidden in his room at Columbia.

"As a father, I'm happy that Allen has made his success in poetry, and I certainly like some of his poems very much," the elder Ginsberg says. "My poetry is a little different but I guess each one has his inner nature that he has to satisfy."

Allen Ginsberg was born June 3, 1926. While he was a boy growing up in Paterson, his mother was in and out of mental hospitals. She died in Pilgrim State Hospital in 1955. Ginsberg has written several poems for his mother, including, curiously enough, *Howl*—curiously, because its full title is *Howl for Carl Solomon*.

"I realized after I wrote it that it was addressed to her," he says, sitting on the bed with two cats playing at his feet and a parakeet in a cage intruding an occasional raucous reminder of its existence. "I realized that *Howl* is actually to her rather than to Carl in a sense. Because the emotion that comes from it is built on my mother, not on anything as superficial as a later acquaintance, such as Carl."

Ginsberg was with Solomon at the New York State Psychiatric Institute. Born in 1928, Solomon, according to other bits of biography, was proclaimed a child prodigy at the age of seven, when several New York newspapers commemorated, with headlined awe, his ability to memorize the batting averages of all the players in the National and American leagues. Educated in New York and at the Sorbonne, and later an editor with a New York publishing house, he, like Ginsberg, spent time in the Merchant Marine as well as in the asylum.

"Carl?" says Ginsberg, stroking a cat purring on his lap, as the clock ticks loudly on the makeshift night table. "I met him in the bug house. The New York State Psychiatric Institute. Our first meeting was funny. I mean, my mother had been in that hospital, and here *I* was in the hospital now. I walked down to the ward with my bags and sat down at the table at the end of the corridor in the afternoon sunlight and Carl was just coming up in a big bathrobe, just out of shock. And he walked up to me, you know, new meat in the ward, and said, 'Who are you?' So I said, 'I'm Alyosha'—you know, the saintly character in Dostoevsky's *Brothers Karamazov*. So Carl said, 'Well, I'm Kirilov—Wait'll you meet the other saints here.'"— and Ginsberg laughs. "We immediately had a rapport. Carl had a great project. He was going to publish my work, Kerouac's work, William S. Burroughs' work, John Holmes' work, Jean Genet's work, if he could, Louis Ferdinand Céline's work, if he could—all the new literature that's coming out now. He would have made a million dollars, I guess. But they thought he was crazy. Now he's back in Pilgrim State. But he's not crazy at all."

At Columbia, from which he received a degree, Ginsberg is remembered not with reverent silence, perhaps, but usually with silence, and mention of him brings a great shushing of lips from former professors and classmates alike. Part of the shushing, of course, covers his commitment to the New York State Psychiatric Institute, even though the doctors there finally conceded he was not a schizophrenic but merely a neurotic. Also covered by the shushing, however, is the year Ginsberg was suspended for tracing obscene odes on a dusty window in Columbia's Hartley Hall.

Professor Lionel Trilling played a major role in Ginsberg's undergraduate life and has continued to play bit parts in Ginsberg's life ever since. In retrospect, Trilling seems to look upon Ginsberg with a professorial and growing affection. Certainly Ginsberg courted this affection, although during his studenthood it wasn't apples which Ginsberg brought to his teacher but revelations of Kerouac and Burroughs and what Ginsberg had learned of the reality outside the Nineteenth Century coffin he considers his classes to have been. "In the early years, I tried to be open with him," Ginsberg says, "and laid on him my understanding of Burroughs and Jack—stories about them, hoping he would be interested or see some freshness or light, but all he or the others at Columbia could see was me searching for a father or pushing myself or bucking for an instructorship or whatever they have been conditioned to think in terms of." Ginsberg invaded Trilling's after-school privacy with samples of his own poetry, which at first pleased Trilling much as Ginsberg's present poetry displeases him. Because he *is* displeased. Unwilling, even as a literary critic, to be drawn into any public discussion of his former student's literature—or even of Beat literature—Trilling has, in more private company, said that he is bored both with Ginsberg's manner and Ginsberg's doctrine and is not much interested in his poetry, either, but has, on occasion, defended it.

By his travels through the seamier side of life, Ginsberg has come to believe that civilization is coming apart at the seams. Ginsberg's guide, of course, was Jack Kerouac, whose friendship is at least one debt that Ginsberg owes Columbia. It was with Kerouac that Ginsberg found his way to the neon connections of Times Square, the switchblade dives of Eighth Avenue and the society that William S. Burroughs introduced them to, a society which can be found in the writings of all of them. Together, Ginsberg and Kerouac launched an investigation of the Underworld that might have pleased Dostoevsky but probably would have irked that other expert on crime, also a boyhood hero of Kerouac, The Shadow. But then it was souls they said they were seeking, not criminals.

Sometimes it was difficult to tell the guide from the guided. "Allen . . ." says Kerouac, "Allen's a great influence on me." But Neal Cassady, another great influence on Kerouac, adds, "Jack's always putting Allen down. We'll be riding along and we'll pass a beach and it'll be a big Jewish resort, see, and Jack'll say to Allen, 'How come there's no beach for French-Canadians, huh?'" In any event, the relationship between Kerouac and Ginsberg has had its effect not only on the writing of each other but apparently on that of a whole new generation of poets, building on a writing style which Ginsberg and Kerouac call *spontaneous bop prosody,* based on rhythms of hipster speech and drawn from jazz and everyday talk, words meant to be music and set down on paper in the same mystical pattern in which they appear in the mind.

Ginsberg's poetry has been translated into Japanese, German, Spanish and Bengali and he has read it to audiences in at least a dozen countries. The Chilean government has had him as its guest for an international literary conference, at which, by the way, other guests were Arnold Toynbee and Pierre Mendès-France. And if he has read in coffee houses and bars all over the United States he also has read, by invitation, at the Library of Congress, where, for the benefit of a tape recorder and the archives, he chose a special poem denouncing America: *". . . Millions of tons of human wheat were burned in the halls of Congress while India starved and screamed and ate mad dogs full of rain . . ."*

"If I were living in Russia," he said later, "I probably would have written a poem denouncing Russia."

In other more recent experiences, he has undergone electric shock treatment just to see what it would do to his mind, he has attended, with full beard, a Brooklyn convention of Hassidic rabbis, and he has taken lysergic acid, a new wonder drug that he thinks might undermine the price of heroin.

"It seems to have approximated and reaffirmed my memory of the Harlem 'sensation,'" he says.

Traveling in Europe, he has sought out Samuel Beckett in Paris, talked with Dame Edith Sitwell in London, and walked with W. H. Auden on Oxford campus.

He has visited the graves of Shelley, Apollinaire and Blake.

"They didn't say a word," Ginsberg reports. "Not a word."

Today, Ginsberg, dressed in eternal blue jeans and living on scattered royalties and honorariums which sometimes total as much as eighty dollars a month, continues seeking new experience, new gnostic insight and new poetry along with Corso, Orlovsky and weekend friend Kerouac, who, when asked why he has never used Ginsberg as the prototype for a central figure in any of his novels, answered:

"Oh, because he's not an interesting character, to me. He doesn't do anything but talk."

But he adds: "Let the world know that I love Allen Ginsberg."

"Kerouac," commented poet Ray Bremser, "is a genius. But Allen . . . Allen's more important!"

Sometimes saddened by the jeers of a daily press that knows little more than the word "Beatnik," Ginsberg says quietly and with sureness: "Well, I guess it doesn't matter in the long run . . . I write for God's ear."

Ginsberg typing a poem, 170 East 2nd Street, January 9, 1960.

Ginsberg with his Siamese cat at 170 East 2nd Street, January 9, 1960.

Ginsberg and Herbert Hunke at 170 East 2nd Street, January 9, 1960.

*Herbert Hunke and
Peter Orlovsky in
Ginsberg's flat, 170
East 2nd Street,
January 9, 1960.*

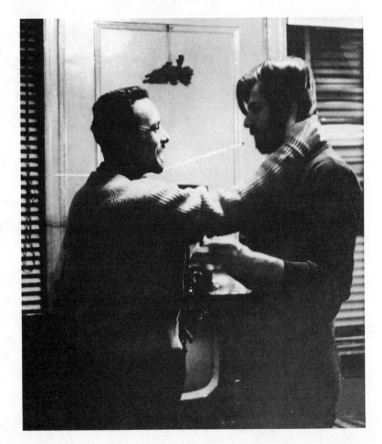

Ginsberg's fridge with Poe on the left, Baudelaire on right, 170 East 2nd Street January 9, 1960.

Ginsberg's sink in his tenement flat, 170 East 2nd Street, January 9, 1960.

Ginsberg and Kerouac at artist Dody Müller's exhibition at the Hansa Gallery, Central Park South, March 16, 1959.

Norman Mailer and Allen Ginsberg at a book party given by Grove Press.

William Burroughs
with Allen Ginsberg
at a Grove Press
party.

Allen Ginsberg howling
at the Artist's Club New Year's
Eve party, 1958. The club,
at 73 Fourth Avenue, was the
meeting place of the 1950s
abstract expressionists.

Buddhists Find a Beatnik 'Spy'

Special to The New York Times

SAIGON, Vietnam, June 5 —The Buddhists, who are in conflict with the Vietnamese Government, asserted today that they believed the Americans had sent a "spy to look at us."

A Buddhist spokesman told this to newsmen. The newsmen, incredulous, asked if the spokesman would be good enough to describe the "spy."

"Well, he was tall and had a very long beard and his hair was very long in back and curly," the Buddhist said. "He said he was a poet and a littlec razy and that he liked Buddhists. We didn't know what else he was so we decided he was a spy."

At this point the newsmen burst out laughing. The alleged spy was the American poet, Allen Ginsberg, a well-known beatnik. Mr. Ginsberg was here briefly for several days on his way to British Columbia after a long stay in India.

The Budhist controversy with the Government involves their resentment over Govern-ment curbs on their activities, including a ban on raising the Budhist flag.

Allen Ginsburg

HORN ON *HOWL*

by Lawrence Ferlinghetti

Evergreen Review No. 4, 1957

Fahrenheit 451, the temperature at which books burn, has finally been determined not to be the prevailing temperature at San Francisco, though the police still would be all too happy to make it hot for you. On October 3 last, Judge Clayton Horn of Municipal Court brought in a 39-page opinion finding Shigeyoshi Murao and myself not guilty of publishing or selling obscene writings, to wit Allen Ginsberg's *HOWL and Other Poems* and issue 11&12 of *The Miscellaneous Man*.

Thus ended one of the most irresponsible and callous police actions to be perpetrated west of the Rockies, not counting the treatment accorded Indians and Japanese.

When William Carlos Williams, in his Introduction to *HOWL*, said that Ginsberg had come up with "an arresting poem" he hardly knew what he was saying. The first edition of *HOWL*, Number Four in the Pocket Poet Series, was printed in England by Villiers, passed thru Customs without incident, and was published at the City Lights bookstore here in the fall of 1956. Part of a second printing was stopped by Customs on March 25, 1957, not long after an earlier issue of *The Miscellaneous Man* (published in Berkeley by William Margolis) had been seized coming from the same printer. Section 305 of the Tariff Act of 1930 was cited. The San Francisco *Chronicle* (which alone among the local press put up a real howl about censorship) reported, in part:

> Collector of Customs Chester MacPhee continued his campaign yesterday to keep what he considers obscene literature away from the children of the Bay Area. He confiscated 520 copies of a paperbound volume of poetry entitled *HOWL and*

Horn on HOWL

> *Other Poems.* . . . "The words and the sense of the
> writing is obscene," MacPhee declared. "You
> wouldn't want your children to come across it."

On April 3 the American Civil Liberties Union (to which I
had submitted the manuscript of *HOWL* before it went to the
printer) informed Mr. MacPhee that it would contest the legal-
ity of the seizure, since it did not consider the book obscene. We
announced in the meantime that an entirely new edition of
HOWL was being printed within the United States, thereby re-
moving it from Customs jurisdiction. No changes were made in
the original text, and a photo-offset edition was placed on sale
at City Lights bookstore and distributed nationally while the
Customs continued to sit on the copies from Britain.

On May 19, book editor William Hogan of the San Francisco
Chronicle gave his Sunday column to an article by myself, defending *HOWL* (I recommended a medal be made for Collector
MacPhee, since his action was already rendering the book famous. But the police were soon to take over this advertising
account and do a much better job—10,000 copies of *HOWL*
were in print by the time they finished with it.) In defense of
HOWL I said I thought it to be "the most significant single long
poem to be published in this country since World War II, perhaps since T. S. Eliot's *Four Quartets.*" To which many added
"Alas." Fair enough, considering the barren, polished poetry
and well-mannered verse which had dominated many of the
major poetry publications during the past decade or so, not to
mention some of the "fashionable incoherence" which has
passed for poetry in many of the smaller, avant-garde magazines and little presses. *HOWL* commits many poetic sins; but
it was time. And it would be very interesting to hear from critics who can name another single long poem published in this
country since the War which is as significant of its time and
place and generation. (A reviewer in the *Atlantic Monthly* recently wrote that *HOWL* may well turn out to be *The Wasteland* of the younger generation.) The central part of my article
said:

> . . . It is not the poet but what he observes which
> is revealed as obscene. The great obscene wastes

of *HOWL* are the sad wastes of the mechanized
world, lost among atom bombs and insane na-
tionalisms. . . . Ginsberg chooses to walk on the
wild side of this world, along with Nelson Algren, Henry Miller, Kenneth Rexroth, Kenneth
Patchen, not to mention some great American
dead, mostly in the tradition of philosophical
anarchism. . . . Ginsberg wrote his own best defense of *HOWL* in another poem called "America." Here he asks:

> "What sphinx of cement and aluminum bashed
>   open their
>   skulls and ate up their brains and imagination?
> Moloch! Solitude! Filth! Ugliness! Ashcans and
>   unobtainable dollars! Children screaming under
>   the stairways! Boys sobbing in armies! Old men
>   weeping in the parks!"

A world, in short, you wouldn't want your children to come across. . . . Thus was Goya
obscene in depicting the Disasters of War, thus
Whitman an exhibitionist, exhibiting man in
his own strange skin.

On May 29 Customs released the books it had been holding,
since the United States Attorney at San Francisco refused to
institute condemnation proceedings against *HOWL*.

Then the police took over and arrested us, Captain William
Hanrahan of the juvenile department (well named, in this case)
reporting that the books were not fit for children to read. Thus
during the first week of June I found myself being booked and
fingerprinted in San Francisco's Hall of Justice. The city jail
occupies the upper floors of it, and a charming sight it is, a
picturesque return to the early Middle Ages. And my enforced
tour of it was a dandy way for the city officially to recognize the
flowering of poetry in San Francisco. As one paper reported,
"The Cops Don't Allow No Renaissance Here."

The ACLU posted bail. Our trials went on all summer, with
a couple of weeks between each day in court. The prosecution
soon admitted it had no case against either Shig Murao or myself as far as the *Miscellaneous Man* was concerned, since we

were not the publisher of it, in which case there was no proof we knew what was inside the magazine when it was sold at our store. And, under the California Penal Code, the willful and lewd *intent* of the accused had to be established. Thus the trial was narrowed down to *HOWL*.

The so-called People's Case (I say so-called, since the People seemed mostly on our side) was presented by Deputy District Attorney Ralph McIntosh whose heart seemed not in it nor his mind on it. He was opposed by some of the most formidable legal talent to be found, in the persons of Mr. Jake ("Never Plead Guilty") Ehrlich, Lawrence Speiser (former counsel for the ACLU), and Albert Bendich (present counsel for the ACLU)—all of whom defended us without expense to us.

The critical support for *HOWL* (or the protest against censorship on principle) was enormous. Here is some of what some said:

Henry Rago, editor of *Poetry* (Chicago)—

> ... I wish only to say that the book is a thoroughly serious work of literary art. ... There is absolutely no question in my mind or in that of any poet or critic with whom I have discussed the book that it is a work of the legitimacy and validity contemplated by existing American law, as we know it in the statement of Justice Woolsey in the classic *Ulysses* case, and as we have seen it reaffirmed just recently by the Supreme Court in the Butler case. ... I would be unworthy of the tradition of this magazine or simply of my place as a poet in the republic of letters ... if I did not speak for the right of this book to free circulation, and against this affront not only to Allen Ginsberg and his publishers, but to the possibilities of the art of poetry in America. ...

William Hogan of the San Francisco *Chronicle*:

> ... *HOWL and Other Poems,* according to accepted, serious contemporary American literary

standards, is a dignified, sincere and admirable work of art. . . .

Robert Duncan and Director Ruth Witt-Diamant of the San Francisco (State College) Poetry Center:

> . . . *HOWL* is a significant work in American poetry, deriving both a spirit and form from Walt Whitman's *Leaves of Grass*, from Jewish religious writings. . . . It is rhapsodic, highly idealistic and inspired in cause and purpose. Like other inspired poets, Ginsberg strives to include all of life, especially the elements of suffering and dismay from which the voice of desire rises. Only by misunderstanding might these tortured outcryings for sexual and spiritual understanding be taken as salacious. The poet gives us the most painful details; he moves us toward a statement of experience that is challenging and finally noble.

Thomas Parkinson (University of California):

> . . . *HOWL* is one of the most important books of poetry published in the last ten years. Its power and eloquence are obvious, and the talent of Mr. Ginsberg is of the highest order. Even people who do not like the book are compelled to testify to its force and brilliance. . . .

James Laughlin (*New Directions*):

> I have read the book carefully and do not myself consider it offensive to good taste, likely to lead youth astray, or be injurious to public morals. I feel, furthermore, that the book has considerable distinction as literature, being a powerful and artistic expression of a meaningful philosophical attitude. . . .

Kenneth Patchen:

> The issue here—as in every like case—is not the merit or lack of it of a book but of a Society which traditionally holds the human being to be by its very functional nature a creature of shameful, outrageous, and obscene habits. . . .

Eugene Burdick (novelist and critic):

> The poem *HOWL* strikes me as an impressionistic, broadly gauged, almost surrealistic attempt to catch the movement, color, drama, and inevitable disappointments of life in a complex, modern society. *HOWL* is a pessimistic, and indeed, almost a tragic view of life. . . . It is my impression that the total impact of the poem is far from lascivious or obscene. It is depressing, but not licentious or extravagant in its use of harsh words. . . . .

Northern California Booksellers Association:

> It may or may not be literature but it does have literary merit. . . . The proposition that adult literature must meet the standards of suitability for children is manifestly absurd. . . . To quote Supreme Court Justice Frankfurter in a similar case—". . . the effect of this is to reduce the adult population to reading only what is fit for children . . . surely this is to burn the house down to roast the pig."

Barney Rosset and Donald Allen, editors of the *Evergreen Review* (in which *HOWL* was reprinted during the trial):

> The second issue of *Evergreen Review*, which was devoted to the work of writers in the San Francisco Bay Area, attempted in large part to show the kinds of serious writing being done by the

postwar generation. We published Allen Ginsberg's poem *HOWL* in that issue because we believe that it is a significant modern poem, and that Allen Ginsberg's intention was to sincerely and honestly present a portion of his own experience of the life of his generation. . . . Our final considered opinion was that Allen Ginsberg's *HOWL* is an achieved poem and that it deserves to be considered as such. . . .

At the trial itself, nine expert witnesses testified in behalf of *HOWL*. They were eloquent witnesses, together furnishing as good a one-sided critical survey of *HOWL* as could possibly be got up in any literary magazine. These witnesses were: Mark Schorer and Leo Lowenthal (of the University of California faculty), Walter Van Tilburg Clark, Herbert Blau, Arthur Foff, and Mark Linenthal (all of the San Francisco State College faculty), Kenneth Rexroth, Vincent McHugh (poet and novelist), and Luther Nichols (book editor of the San Francisco *Examiner*). A few excerpts from the trial transcript—

Dr. Mark Schorer: The theme of the poem is announced very clearly in the opening line, "I saw the best minds of my generation destroyed by madness, starving hysterical naked." Then the following lines that make up the first part attempt to create the impression of a kind of nightmare world in which people representing "the best minds of my generation," in the author's view, are wandering like damned souls in hell. That is done through a kind of series of what one might call surrealistic images, a kind of state of hallucinations. Then in the second section the mood of the poem changes and it becomes an indictment of those elements in modern society that, in the author's view, are destructive of the best qualities in human nature and of the best minds. Those elements are, I would say, predominantly materialism, conformity and mechanization leading toward war. And then the third part is a personal address to a friend, real or fictional, of the poet or of the person who is speaking in the poet's voice—those are not always the same thing—who is mad and in a madhouse, and is the specific representative of what the author regards as a general condition, and with that final statement the poem ends. . . .

Mr. McIntosh (*later in cross-examination*): I didn't quite follow your explanation to page 21, "Footnote to *HOWL*." Do you call that the second phase?

Mark Schorer: I didn't speak about "Footnote to *HOWL*." I regard that as a separate poem.

Mr. McIntosh: Oh, I'm—

Mark Schorer: It is not one of the three parts that make up the first poem. It's a comment on, I take it, the attitude expressed in *HOWL* proper, and I think what it says—if you would like my understanding of it—is that in spite of all of the depravity that *HOWL* has shown, all of the despair, all of the defeat, life is essentially holy and should be so lived. In other words, the footnote gives us this state in contradistinction to the state that the poem proper has tried to present.

Mr. McIntosh (*later*): Did you read the one in the back called "America"? . . . What's the essence of that piece of poetry?

Mark Schorer: I think that what the poem says is that the "I," the speaker, feels that he has given a piece of himself to America and has been given nothing in return, and the poem laments certain people who have suffered at the hands of—well, specifically, the United States Government, men like Tom Mooney, the Spanish Loyalists, Sacco & Vanzetti, the Scottsboro boys and so on.

Mr. McIntosh: Is that in there?

Mark Schorer: That's on page 33. In other words, that is the speaker associating himself with those figures in American history whom he regards as having been martyred. He feels that way about himself.

Mr. McIntosh: Well, "America" is a little bit easier to understand than *HOWL*, isn't it? . . . Now [*referring to shorter poems in the back of the book*]—you read those two? You think they are similar, in a similar vein?

Mark Schorer: They are very different. Those are what one would call lyric poems and the earlier ones are hortatory poems.

Mr. McIntosh: What?

Mark Schorer: Poems of diatribe and indictment, the mood is very different, hortatory.

Mr. McIntosh: That's all.

Dr. Leo Lowenthal: In my opinion this is a genuine work of literature, which is very characteristic for a period of unrest and tension such as the one we have been living through the last decade. I was reminded by reading *HOWL* of many other literary works as they have been written after times of great upheavals, particularly after World War One, and I found this work very much in line with similar literary works. With regard to the specific merits of the poem *HOWL*, I would say that it is structured very well. As I see it, it consists of three parts, the first of which is the craving of the poet for self-identification, where he roams all over the field and tries to find allies in similar search for self-identification. He then indicts, in the second part, the villain, so to say, which does not permit him to find it, the Moloch of society, of the world as it is today. And in the third part he indicates the potentiality of fulfillment by friendship and love, although it ends on a sad and melancholic note actually indicating that he is in search for fulfillment he cannot find.

Kenneth Rexroth: . . . The simplest term for such writing is prophetic, it is easier to call it that than anything else because we have a large body of prophetic writing to refer to. There are the prophets of the Bible, which it greatly resembles in purpose and in language and in subject matter. . . . The theme is the denunciation of evil and a pointing out of the way out, so to speak. That is prophetic literature. "Woe! Woe! Woe! The City of Jerusalem! The Syrian is about to come down or has already and you are to do such and such a thing and you must repent and do thus and so." And *HOWL*, the four parts of the poem—that is including the "Footnote to *HOWL*" as one additional part—do this very specifically. They take up these various specifics seriatim, one after the other. . . . And "Footnote to *HOWL*," of course, again, is Biblical in reference. The reference is to the Benedicite, which says over and over again, "Blessed is the fire, Blessed is the light, Blessed are the trees, and Blessed is this and Blessed is that," and he is saying, "Everything that is human is Holy to me," and that the possibility of salvation in this terrible situation which he reveals is through love and through the love of everything Holy in man. So that, I would say, that this just about covers the field of typically prophetic poetry. . . .

Herbert Blau: The thing that strikes me most forcefully about *HOWL* is that it is worded in what appears to be a contemporary tradition, one that did not cause me any particular consternation in reading, a tradition most evident in the modern period following the First World War, a tradition that resembles European literary tradition and is defined as "Dada," a kind of art of furious negation. By the intensity of its negation it seems to be both resurrective in quality and ultimately a sort of paean of possible hope. I wouldn't say that the chances for redemption or chances for salvation in a work of this kind are deemed to be very extensively possible but, nonetheless, the vision is not a total vision of despair. It is a vision that by the salvation of despair, by the salvation of what would appear to be perversity, by the salvation of what would appear to be obscene, by the salvation of what would appear to be illicit, is ultimately a kind of redemption of the illicit, the obscene, the disillusioned and the despairing. . . .

Vincent McHugh: In this case . . . we have a vision of a modern hell. Now, we have certain precedents for that, for example, the book that it makes me think of, or the work of literature that it makes me think of offhand, the work of literature which is ferociously sincere in the same way, is Mr. Pound's—some of Mr. Pound's *Cantos*, especially Canto XIV and Canto XV. These, for example, in turn derive certainly from Dante and from the famous so-called cantos in Dante, and Dante, in turn, derives from the *Odyssey*, and so on into all the mythologies of the world. . . .

The prosecution put only two "expert witnesses" on the stand—both very lame samples of academia—one from the Catholic University of San Francisco and one a private elocution teacher, a beautiful woman, who said, "You feel like you are going through the gutter when you have to read that stuff. I didn't linger on it too long, I assure you." The University of San Francisco instructor said: "The literary value of this poem is negligible. . . . This poem is apparently dedicated to a long-dead movement, Dadaism, and some late followers of Dadaism. And, therefore, the opportunity is long past for any significant literary contribution of this poem." The critically devastating things the prosecution's witnesses could have said, but didn't, remain one of the great Catholic silences of the day.

So much for the literary criticism inspired by the trial. Cross-examination by the Prosecutor was generally brilliant, as in the following bit:

Mr. McIntosh: Does Mr. Ferlinghetti attend your poetry writing workshop?

Dr. Mark Linenthal: He does not.
Mr. McIntosh: Do you attend his?
Dr. Linenthal: I do not.
Mr. McIntosh: You haven't been over there hearing him read poetry?
Dr. Linenthal: No, I haven't.
(etc.)

Legally, a layman could see that an important principle was certainly in the line drawn between "hard core pornography" and writing judged to be "social speech." But more important still was the court's acceptance of the principle that if a work is determined to be "social speech" the question of obscenity may not even be raised. Or, in the words of Counsel Bendich's argument:

"The first amendment to the Constitution of the United States protecting the fundamental freedoms of speech and press prohibits the suppression of literature by the application of obscenity formulae unless the trial court first determines that the literature in question is utterly without social importance." (*Roth* v. *U.S.*)
. . . What is being urged here is that the majority opinion in *Roth* requires a trial court to make the constitutional determination; to decide in the first instance whether a work is utterly without redeeming social importance, *before* it permits the test of obscenity to be applied. . . .
. . . The record is clear that all of the experts for the defense identified the main theme of *HOWL* as social criticism. And the prosecution concedes that it does not understand the work, much less what its dominant theme is.

Judge Horn agreed, in his opinion:

I do not believe that *HOWL* is without even "the slightest redeeming social importance." The first part of *HOWL* presents a picture of a nightmare world; the second part is an indictment of those elements in modern society destructive of the best qualities of human nature; such elements are predominantly identified as materialism, conformity, and mechanization leading toward war. The third part presents a picture of an individual who is a specific representation of what the author conceives as a general condition. . . . "Footnote to *HOWL*" seems to be a declamation that everything in the world is holy, including parts of the body by name. It ends in a plea for holy living. . . .

And the judge went on to set forth certain rules for the guidance of authorities in the future:

1. If the material has the slightest redeeming social importance it is not obscene because it is protected by the First and Fourteenth Amendments of the United States Constitution, and the California Constitution.
2. If it does not have the slightest redeeming social importance it *may* be obscene.
3. The test of obscenity in California is that the material must have a tendency to deprave or corrupt readers by exciting lascivious thoughts or arousing lustful desire to the point that it presents a clear and present danger of inciting to anti-social or immoral action.
4. The book or material must be judged as a whole by its effect on the *average adult* in the community.
5. If the material is objectionable only because of coarse and vulgar language which is not erotic or aphrodisiac in character it is not obscene.
6. Scienter must be proved.
7. Book reviews may be received in evidence if properly authenticated.
8. Evidence of expert witnesses in the literary field is proper.

9. Comparison of the material with other similar material previously adjudicated is proper.

10. The people owe a duty to themselves and to each other to preserve and protect their constitutional freedoms from any encroachment by government unless it appears that the allowable limits of such protection have been breached, and then to take only such action as will heal the breach.

11. Quoting Justice Douglas: "I have the same confidence in the ability of our people to reject noxious literature as I have in their capacity to sort out the true from the false in theology, economics, politics, or any other field."

12. In considering material claimed to be obscene it is well to remember the motto: *Honi soit qui mal y pense* (Evil to him who thinks evil).

At which the Prosecution was reliably reported to have blushed.

Under banner headlines, the *Chronicle* reported that "the Judge's decision was hailed with applause and cheers from a packed audience that offered the most fantastic collection of beards, turtle-necked shirts and Italian hair-dos ever to grace the grimy precincts of the Hall of Justice." The decision was hailed editorially as a "landmark of law." Judge Horn has since been re-elected to office, which I like to think means that the People agree it was the police who here committed an obscene action.

Allen Ginsberg reading HOWL and Other Poems *at the Living Theatre, November 23, 1959.*

Ginsberg at the Living Theatre, November 23, 1959.

Ginsberg at the Living Theatre, November 23, 1959.

Prof. Fred Dupee of the Columbia University English Department introduces Peter Orlovsky, Gregory Corso, and Allen Ginsberg for a historic poetry reading, February 5, 1959. Kerouac was also scheduled to read but never showed up.

Gregory Corso at Columbia University, February 5, 1959, reading from his poem "Marriage," described as a compulsive poem about a compulsive subject. Ginsberg read his poems "The Ignu" and "Lion in the Room," which he dedicated to Lionel Trilling.

Peter Orlovsky reading his poem "Lines of Feelings" at Columbia, February 5, 1959: "The mountain bear has a hole in his pants— trouble . . ."

Gregory Corso, Allen Ginsberg, William Burroughs, and Maretta Greer at opening of Timothy Leary's Meditation Center on Hudson Street, February 15, 1967.

On April 17, 1975, Gregory Corso, William Burroughs, Allen Ginsberg, and Peter Orlovsky gave a poetry reading at Columbia University. All except Burroughs had read there 16 years before, on February 15, 1959.

Composer and French horn artist David Amram with Ginsberg and Kerouac at Dody Müller Art Show, March 16, 1959. All three participated in Robert Frank film Pull My Daisy.

Kerouac with photographer-filmmaker Robert Frank (who did Pull My Daisy) *at the Hansa Gallery, March 16, 1959.*

THE OTHER NIGHT AT COLUMBIA: A REPORT FROM THE ACADEMY

by Diana Trilling

Claremont Essays, 1964

The "beats" were to read their poetry at Columbia on Thursday evening and on the spur of the moment three wives from the English department had decided to go hear them. But for me, one of the three, the spur of the moment was not where the story had begun. It had begun much farther back, some twelve or fourteen years ago, when Allen Ginsberg had been a student of my husband's and I had heard about him much more than I usually hear of students for the simple reason that he got into a great deal of trouble which involved his instructors, and had to be rescued and revived and restored; eventually he had even to be kept out of jail. Of course there was always the question, should this young man be rescued, should he be restored? There was even the question, shouldn't he go to jail? We argued about it some at home but the discussion, I'm afraid, was academic, despite my old resistance to the idea that people like Ginsberg had the right to ask and receive preferential treatment just because they read Rimbaud and Gide and undertook to be writers themselves. Nor was my principle, if one may call it that, of equal responsibility for poets and shoe clerks so firm that I didn't need to protect it by refusing to confront Ginsberg as an individual or potential acquaintance. I don't mean that I was aware, at the time, of my motive for disappearing on the two or three occasions when he came to the house to deliver a new batch of poems and report on his latest adventures in sensation-seeking. If I'd been asked to explain, then my wish not to meet and talk with this disturbing young man who had managed to break through the barrier of student anonymity, I suppose I'd have rested with the proposition that he made life too messy, although then I'd have had to defend myself against the charge, made in the name of art, of a strictness of judgment which was too little tolerant of deviation from more usual and respectable standards of behavior. But ten, twelve, fourteen years ago, there was still something of a challenge in the "conventional" position; I still enjoyed defending the properties and proprieties of the middle class against friends who persisted in scorning them. Of course, once upon a time—that was in the thirties—one had had to defend even having a comfortable chair to sit in, or a rug on the floor. But by the forties things had changed; one's most intransigent literary friends had capitulated by then, everybody had a well-upholstered sofa and I was reduced to such marginal causes as the Metropolitan Museum and the expectation that visitors would put their ashes in the ashtray and go home by 2:00 A.M. Then why should I not also defend the expectation that a student at Columbia, even a poet, would do his work, submit it to his teachers through the normal channels of classroom communication, stay out of jail, and, if things went right, graduate, start publishing, be reviewed, and see what developed, whether he was a success or failure?

Well, for Ginsberg, things didn't go right for quite a while. The time came when he was graduated from Columbia and published his poems, but first he got into considerable difficulty, beginning with his suspension from college and the requirement that he submit to psychiatric treatment, and terminating—but this was quite a few years later—in an encounter with the police from which he was extricated by some of his old teachers who knew he needed a hospital more than a prison. The suspension had been for a year, when Ginsberg had been a senior; the situation was not without its grim humor. It seems that Ginsberg had traced an obscenity in the dust of a dormitory window; the words were too shocking for the Dean of Students to speak, so he had written them on a piece of paper which he pushed across the desk to my husband: "Fuck the Jews." Even the part of Lionel that wanted to laugh couldn't; it was too hard for the Dean to have to transmit this message to a Jewish professor—this was still in the forties when being a Jew in the university was not yet what it is today. "But he's a Jew himself," said the Dean. "Can you understand his writing a thing like that?" Yes, Lionel could understand; but he couldn't explain it to the Dean. And anyway, he knew that to appreciate why Ginsberg had traced this particular legend on the window required more than an understanding of Jewish self-hatred, and also that it was not the sole cause for administrative uneasiness about Ginsberg and his cronies. It was ordinary good sense for the college to take protective measures with Ginsberg and for him.

I now realize that even at this early point in his career I had already accumulated a fund of information about young Ginsberg which accurately forecast his later talent for self-promotion although it was surely disproportionate to the place he commanded in his teacher's mind and quite failed to jibe with the physical impression I had caught in opening the door to him when he came to the apartment. He was middling tall, slight, dark, sallow; his dress suggested shabby gentility, poor brown tweed gone threadbare and yellow. The description would have fitted any number of undergraduates of his or any Columbia generation; it was only the personal story that set him acutely apart. He came from New Jersey, where his father was a schoolteacher, or perhaps a principal, who wrote poetry too—I think for the *Saturday Review*, which would be as good a way as any of defining the separation between father and son. His mother was in a mental institution, and she had been there, off and on, for a long time. This was the central and utterly persuasive fact of the young man's life; I knew this before I was told it in poetry at Columbia the other night, and doubtless it was this knowledge that at least in some part accounted for the edginess with which I responded to so much as the mention of Ginsberg's name. Here was a boy on whom an outrageous unfairness had been perpetrated: his mother had fled from him into madness and now whoever crossed his path became somehow responsible, caught in the impossibility of rectifying what she had done. It was an unjust burden for Ginsberg to put, as he so subtly did, on those who were only the later accidents of his history and it made me defensive instead of charitable with him. No boy, after all, could ask anyone to help him build a career on the terrible but gratuitous circumstance of a mad mother; it was a justification for neither poetry nor prose nor yet for "philosophy" of the kind young Ginsberg liked to expound to his teacher. In the question period which followed the poetry-reading the other night at Columbia, this matter of a rationale for the behavior of Ginsberg and his friends came up: someone asked Ginsberg to state his philosophy. It was a moment I had been awaiting and I thought: "Here we go; he'll tell us how he's crazy like a daisy and how his friend Orlovsky is crazy like a butterfly." I had been reading *Time*; who hadn't? But, instead of repeating the formulations of earlier interviews, Ginsberg answered that he had no philosophy; he spoke of inspiration, or perhaps it was illumination, ecstatic illumination, as the source of his poetry, and I was more than surprised; I was curiously pleased for him because I took it as a considerable advance in self-control that he could operate with this much shrewdness and leave it, if only for this occasion, to his audience to abstract a "position" from his and his friends' antics while he himself moved wild, mild, and innocent through the jungle of speculation. Back in the older days, it had always been my feeling that so far as his relationship with his teacher was concerned, this trying to formulate a philosophy must reveal its falseness even to himself; his recourse to it was somehow beneath his intelligence. Apart from the need to force a recognition of his personal suffering upon certain figures who, in his mind, stood for society, two motives, it seemed to me, impelled him then: the wish to shock his teacher, and the wish to meet the teacher on equal ground. The first of these motives was complicated enough, involving as it did the gratifications of self-incrimination and disapproval, and then forgiveness; but the second was more tangled still. To talk with one's English professor who was also a writer, a critic, and one who made no bones about his solid connection with literary tradition, about one's descent from Rimbaud, Baudelaire or Dostoevsky was clearly to demonstrate a good-sized rationality and order in what was apparently an otherwise undisciplined life. Even more, or so I fancied, it was to propose an alliance between the views of the academic and the poet-rebel, the unity of a deep discriminating commitment to literature which must certainly one day wipe out the fortuitous distance between boy and man, pupil and teacher. Thus, Ginsberg standing on the platform at Columbia and refusing the philosophy gambit might well be announcing a new and sounder impulse toward self-definition for which one could be grateful.

The Other Night at Columbia: A Report from the Academy

But I remind myself: Ginsberg at Columbia on Thursday night was not Ginsberg at Chicago—according to *Time*, at any rate—or Ginsberg at Hunter either, where Kerouac ran the show, and a dismal show it must have been, with Kerouac drinking on the platform and clapping James Wechsler's hat on his head in a grand parade of contempt—they were two of four panelists gathered to discuss "Is there such a thing as a beat generation?"—and leading Ginsberg out from the wings like a circus donkey. For whatever reason—rumor had it he was in a personal crisis—Kerouac didn't appear on Thursday night, and Ginsberg at Columbia was Ginsberg his own man, dealing with his own history, and intent, it seemed to me, on showing up the past for the poor inaccurate thing it so often is: it's a chance we all dream of but mostly it works the other way around, like the long-ago perhaps-apocryphal story of the successful theater director coming back to Yale and sitting on the fence weeping for a youth he could never rewrite no matter how many plays of Chekhov he brought to Broadway, no matter how much money he made. I suppose I have no right to say now, and on such early and little evidence, that Ginsberg had always desperately wanted to be respectable, or respected, like his instructors at Columbia, it is so likely that this is a hindsight that suits my needs. It struck me, though, that this was the most unmistakable and touching message from platform to audience the other night, and as I received it, I felt I had known something like it all along. Not that Ginsberg had ever shown himself as a potential future colleague in the university; anything but that. Even the implied literary comradeship had had reference, not to any possibility of Ginsberg's assimilation into the community of professors, but to the professor's capacity for association in the community of rebellious young poets. Still, it was not just anyone on the campus to whom Ginsberg had come with his lurid boasts which were also his confession; it was Lionel, it was Mark Van Doren; if there was anyone else it would very likely be of the same respectable species, and I remember saying, "He wants you to forbid him to behave like that. He wants you to take him out of it, or why does he choose people like you and Mark Van Doren to tell these stories to?" To which I received always the same answer: "I'm not his father," a response that of course allowed of no argument.

And yet, even granting the accuracy of this reconstruction

of the past, it would be wrong to conclude that any consideration of motive on Ginsberg's part was sufficiently strong to alter one's first and most forceful image of Ginsberg as a "case"—a gifted and sad case, a guilt-provoking and nuisance case, but, above all, a case. Nor was it a help that my husband had recently published a story about a crazy student and a supposedly normal student in which the author's affection was so plainly directed to the former; we never became used to the calls, often in the middle of the night, asking whether it wasn't the crazy character who was really sane. Allen Ginsberg, with his poems in which there was never quite enough talent or hard work, and with his ambiguous need to tell his teacher exactly what new flagrancy had opened to his imagination as he talked about Gide with his friends at the West End Café, had at any rate the distinction of being more crudely justified in his emotional disturbance than most. He also had the distinction of carrying mental unbalance in the direction of criminality, a territory one preferred to leave unclaimed by student or friend.

Gide and the West End Café in all its upper-Broadway dreariness: what could the two conceivably have in common except those lost boys of the forties? How different it might have been for Ginsberg and his friends if they had come of age ten or fifteen years sooner was one of the particular sadnesses of the other evening; it virtually stood on the platform with them as the poets read their poems, whose chief virtue, it seemed to me, was their "racial-minority" funniness, their "depressed-classes" funniness of a kind which has never had so sure and live a place as it did in the thirties, the embittered fond funniness which has to do with one's own impossible origins, funniness plain and poetical, always aware of itself, of a kind which would seem now to have all but disappeared among intellectuals except as an eclecticism or a device of self-pity. It's a real loss; I hadn't quite realized how much I missed it until Thursday night when Ginsberg read his poem "The Ignu," and Corso read his poem "Marriage" (a compulsive poem, he called it, about a compulsive subject), and they were still funny in that old racial-depressed way but not nearly as funny and authentic as they would have been had they been written before the Jews and the Italians and the Negroes, but especially the Jews, had been awarded a place as Americans-like-everyone-else instead of remaining outsiders raised in the Bronx or on Ninth Avenue or even in Georgia. The Jew in particular is a loss to literature and life—I mean the Jew out of which was bred the Jewish intellectual of the thirties. For a few short years in the thirties, as not before or since, the Jew was at his funniest, shrewdest best; he perfectly well knew the advantage he could count on in the Gentile world, and that there was no ascendancy or pride the Gentile comrades could muster against a roomful of Jewish sympathizers singing at the tops of their voices, "A SOCialist union is a NO good union, is a COM-pan-y union of the bosses," or against Michael Gold's mother, who wanted to know did her boy have to write books the whole world should know she had bedbugs. If Ginsberg had been born in an earlier generation it would surely have been the Stewart Cafeteria in the Village that he and his friends would have frequented instead of the West End, that dim waystation of undergraduate debauchery on Morningside Heights—and the Stewart Cafeteria was a well-lighted place and one of the funniest places in New York; at least, at every other table it was funny, and where it was decadent or even conspiratorial, that had its humor too, or at least its robustness. As for Gide—the Gide of the thirties was the "betrayer of the Revolution," not the Gide of the *acte gratuite* and homosexuality in North Africa. One didn't use pathology in those days to explain or excuse or exhibit oneself and one never had to be lonely; there was never a less lonely time for intellectuals than the Depression, or a less depressed time—unless, of course, one was recalcitrant, like Fitzgerald, and simply refused to be radicalized, in which stubborn case it couldn't have been lonelier. Intellectuals talk now about how, in the thirties, there was an "idea" in life, not the emptiness we live in. Actually, it was a time of generally weak intellection— or so it seems to me now—but of very strong feeling. Everyone judged everyone else; it was a time of incessant cruel moral judgment; today's friend was tomorrow's enemy; whoever disagreed with oneself had sold out, God knows to or for what; there was little of the generosity among intellectuals which nowadays dictates the automatic "Gee, that's great" at any news of someone else's good fortune. But it was surely a time of quicker, truer feeling than is now conjured up with marijuana or the infantile camaraderie of Kerouac's *On the Road*. And there was paradox but no contradiction in this double truth, just as there was no contradiction in the fact that it was a time in which the neurotic determination of the intellectual was being so universally acted out and yet a time in which, whatever his dedication to historical or economic determinism, personally he had a unique sense of free will. In the thirties one's clinical vocabulary was limited to two words, escapism and subjectivism, and both of them applied only to other people's wrong political choices.

Well, the "beats" weren't lucky enough to be born except when they were born. Ginsberg says he lives in Harlem, but it's not the Harlem of the Scottsboro boys and W. C. Handy and the benign insanity of trying to proletarianize Striver's Row; their comrades are not the comrades of the Stewart Cafeteria nor yet of the road, as Kerouac would disingenuously have it, but pickups on dark morning streets. But they have their connection with us who were young in the thirties, their intimate political connection, which we deny at risk of missing what it is that makes the "beat" phenomenon something to think about. As they used to say on Fourteenth Street, it is no accident, comrades, it is decidedly no accident that today in the fifties our single overt manifestation of protest takes the wholly non-political form of a group of panic-stricken kids in blue jeans, many of them publicly homosexual, talking about or taking drugs, assuring us that they are out of their minds, not responsible, while the liberal intellectual is convinced that he has no power to control the political future, the future of the free world, and that therefore he must submit to what he defines as political necessity. Though of course the various aspects of a culture must be granted their own autonomous source and character, the connection between "beat" and respectable liberal intellectual exists and is not hard to locate: the common need to deny free will, divest oneself of responsibility and yet stay alive. The typical liberal intellectual of the fifties, whether he is a writer or a sociologist or a law-school professor, explains his evolution over the last two decades—specifically, his current attitudes in foreign affairs—by telling us that he has been forced to accept the unhappy reality of Soviet strength in an atomic world, and that there is no alternative to capitulation—

not that he calls it that—except the extinction of nuclear war. Even the diplomacy he invokes is not so much flexible, which he would like to think it is, as disarmed, an instrument of his impulse to surrender rather than of any wish to win or even hold the line. Similarly docile to culture, the "beat" also contrives a fate by predicating a fate. Like the respectable established intellectual—or the organization man, or the suburban matron—against whom he makes his play or protest, he conceives of himself as incapable of exerting any substantive influence against the forces that condition him. He is made by society, he cannot make society. He can only stay alive as best he can for as long as is permitted him. Is it any wonder, then, that *Time* and *Life* write as they do about the "beats"—with such a conspicuous show of superiority, and no hint of fear? These periodicals know what genuine, dangerous protest looks like, and it doesn't look like Ginsberg and Kerouac. Clearly, there is no more menace in "Howl" or *On the Road* than there is in the Scarsdale PTA. In the common assumption of effectlessness, in the apparent will to rest with a social determination over which the individual spirit and intelligence cannot and perhaps even should not try to triumph, there merge any number of the disparate elements of our present culture—from the liberal intellectual journals to Luce to the Harvard Law School, from Ginsberg to the suburban matron.

But then why, one ponders, do one's most relaxed and nonsquare friends, alongside of whom one can oneself be made to look like the original object with four sides of equal length, why do one's most politically "flexible" friends, alongside of whom one's own divergence from dominant liberal opinion is regularly made to look so ungraceful, so like a latter-day sectarianism, feel constrained to dispute Columbia's judgment in giving the "beats" a hearing on the campus and my own wish to attend their poetry reading? Why, for instance, the dissent of Dwight MacDonald, whom I happened to see that afternoon; or of W. H. Auden, who, when I afterward said I had been moved by the performance, gently chided me, "I'm ashamed of you"; or of the editor of *Partisan Review*, who, while he consents to my going ahead with this article for his magazine, can't hide his editorial puzzlement, even worry, because I want to give the "beats" so much attention? In strict logic, it would seem to me that things should go in quite the other direction and that I, who insist upon at least the asumption of free will in our political choices, who insist upon what I call political responsibility, should be the one to protest a university forum for the irresponsibles whereas my friends whose politics are what I think of as finally a politics of passivity and fatedness, should be able to shrug off the "beats" as merely another inevitable, if tasteless, expression of a *Zeitgeist* with which I believe them to be far more in tune than I am. I do not mean, of course, to rule out taste, or style, as a valid criterion of moral judgment. A sense of social overwhelmment which announces itself in terms of disreputableness or even criminality no doubt asks for a different kind of moral assessment than the same emotion kept within the bounds of a generally recognized propriety. But I would simply point to the similarities which are masked by the real differences between the "beats" and those intellectuals who most overtly scorn them. Taste or style dictates that most intellectuals behave decorously, earn a regular living, disguise instead of flaunt any private digressions from the conduct society considers desirable; when they seek support for the poetical impulse or ask for light on their self-doubt and fears, they don't make the naked boast that they are crazy like daisies but they elaborate a new belief in the indispensability of neurosis to art, or beat the bushes for some new deviant psychoanalysis which will generalize their despair though of course without curing it. And these differences of style are undeniably important, at least for the moment. It is from the long-range view of our present-day cultural situation, which bears so closely upon our continuing national crisis, that the moral difference between a respectable and a disreputable acceptance of defeat seems to me to constitute little more than a cultural footnote to history.

But perhaps I wander too far from the other night at Columbia. There was enough in the evening that was humanly immediate to divert one from this kind of ultimate concern. . . .

It was not an official university occasion. The "beats" appeared at Columbia on the invitation of a student club—interestingly enough, the John Dewey Society. Whether the club first approached Ginsberg or Ginsberg initiated the proceedings, I don't know, but what had happened was that Ginsberg in his undergraduate days had taken a loan from the university—$200? $250?—and recently the Bursar's office had caught up with him in his new incarnation of successful literary itinerant, to demand repayment. Nothing if not ingenious, Ginsberg now proposed to pay off his debt by reading his poetry at Columbia without fee. It was at this point that various members of the English department, solicited as sponsors for the operation, had announced their rejection of the whole deal, literary as well as financial, and the performance was arranged without financial benefit to Ginsberg and without official cover; we three wives, however, decided to attend on our own. We would meet at 7:45 at the door of the theater; no, we would meet at 7:40 at the door of the theater; no, we would meet no later than 7:30 across the street from the theater: the telephoning back and forth among the three women was stupendous as word spread of vast barbarian hordes converging on Columbia's poor dull McMillin Theater from all the dark recesses of the city, howling for their leader. The advance warnings turned out to be exaggerated. It was nevertheless disconcerting that Fred Dupee of the English Department had consented, at the request of the John Dewey Society, to be moderator, chairman, introducer of Ginsberg and his fellow-poets, for while it provided the wives of his colleagues with the assurance of seats in a section of the hall reserved for faculty, it was not without its uncomfortable reminder that Ginsberg had, in a sense, got his way; he was appearing on the same Columbia platform from which T. S. Eliot had last year read his poetry; he was being presented by, and was thus bound to be thought under the sponsorship of, a distinguished member of the academic and literary community who was also one's long-time friend. And indeed it was as Dupee's friend that one took a first canvass of the scene: the line of policemen before the entrance to the theater; the air of suppressed excitement in the lobbies and one's own rather contemptible self-consciousness about being a participant in the much-publicized occasion; the shoddiness of an audience in which it was virtually impossible to distinguish between student and camp-follower; the always-new shock of so many young girls, so few of them pretty, and so many blackest black stockings; so many young men, so few of them—despite the many black beards—with any promise of masculinity. It was distressing to think that Dupee was going to be "faculty" to such an incoherent assembly, that at this moment he was backstage with Ginsberg's group, formulating a deportment which would check the excess of which one knew it to be capable, even or especially in public, without doing violence to his own large tolerance.

For me, it was of some note that the auditorium smelled fresh. The place was already full when we arrived; I took one look at the crowd and was certain that it would smell bad. But I was mistaken. These people may think they're dirty inside and dress up to it. But the audience was clean and Ginsberg was clean and Corso was clean and Orlovsky was clean. Maybe Ginsberg says he doesn't bathe or shave; Corso, I know, declares that he has never combed his hair; Orlovsky has a line in one of the two poems he read—he's not yet written his third, the chairman explained—"If I should shave, I know the bugs would go away." But for this occasion, at any rate, Ginsberg, Corso and Orlovsky were all beautifully clean and shaven; Kerouac, in crisis, didn't appear, but if he had come he would have been clean and shaven too—he was entirely clean the night at Hunter; I've inquired about that. Certainly there's nothing dirty about a checked shirt or a lumberjacket and blue jeans; they're standard uniform in the best nursery schools. Ginsberg has his price, as do his friends, however much they may dissemble.

And how do I look to the "beats," I ask myself after that experience with the seats, and not only I but the other wives I was with? We had pulled aside the tattered old velvet rope which marked off the section held for faculty, actually it was trailing on the floor, and moved into the seats Dupee's wife had saved for us by strewing coats on them; there was a big gray overcoat she couldn't identify: she stood holding it up in the air murmuring wistfully, "Whose is this?"—until the young people in the row in back of us took account of us and answered sternly, "*Those* seats are reserved for faculty." If I have trouble unraveling undergraduates from "beats," neither do the wives of the Columbia English department wear their proper manners with any certainty.

But Dupee's proper manners, that's something else again: what could I have been worrying about, when had Dupee ever failed to meet an occasion, or missed the right style? I don't suppose one could witness a better performance than his on Thursday evening: its rightness was apparent the moment he walked onto the stage, his troupe in tow and himself just close enough and yet enough removed to indicate the balance in which he held the situation. Had there been a hint of betrayal in his deportment, of either himself or his guests—naturally, he had made them his guests—the whole evening might have been different: for instance, a few minutes later when the overflow audience outside the door began to bang and shout for admission, might not the audience have caught the contagion and become unruly too? Or would Ginsberg have stayed with his picture of himself as poet serious and triumphant instead of succumbing to what must have been the greatest temptation to spoil his opportunity? "The last time I was in this theater," Dupee began quietly, "it was also to hear a poet read his orks. That was T. S. Eliot." A slight alteration of inflection, from irony to mockery, from wit to condescension, and it might well have been a signal for near-riot, boos and catcalls and whistlings; the evening would have been lost to the "beats," Dupee and Columbia would have been defeated. Dupee tranformed a circus into a classroom. He himself, he said, welcomed the chance to hear these poets read their works—he never once in his remarks gave them their name of "beats" nor alluded even to San Francisco—because in all poetry it was important to study the spoken accent; he himself didn't happen especially to admire those of their works that he knew; still, he would draw our attention to their skillful use of a certain kind of American imagery which, deriving from Whitman, yet passed Whitman's use of it or even Hart Crane's. . . . It was Dupee speaking for the Academy, claiming for it its place in life, and the performers were inevitably captive to his dignity and self-assurance. Rather than Ginsberg and his friends, it was a photographer from *Life*, exploding his flashbulbs in everybody's face, mounting a ladder at the back of the stage the more effectively to shoot his angles, who came to represent vulgarity and disruption and disrespect; when a student in the audience disconnected a wire which had something to do with the picture-taking, one might guess that Ginsberg was none too happy that his mass-circulation "story" was being spoilt but it was the photographer's face that became ugly, the only real ugliness of the evening. One could feel nothing but pity for Ginsberg and his friends that their front of disreputableness and rebellion should be this vulnerable to the seductions of a clever host. With Dupee's introduction, the whole of their armor had been penetrated at the very outset.

Pity is not the easiest of our emotions today; now it's "understanding" that is easy, and more and more—or so I find for myself—real pity moves hand in hand with real terror; it's an emotion one avoids because it's so hard; one "understands" the crippled, the delinquent, the unhappy so as not to have to pity them. But Thursday night was an occasion of pity so direct and inescapable that it left little to the understanding that wasn't mere afterthought—and pity not only for the observed, the performers, but for us who had come to observe them and reassure ourselves that we were not implicated. One might as readily persuade oneself one was not implicated in one's children! For this was it: these *were* children, miserable children trying desperately to manage, asking desperately to be taken out of it all, so that I kept asking myself, where had I had just such an experience before, and later it came to me: I had gone to see O'Neill's *Long Day's Journey into Night,* and the play had echoed with just such a child's cry for help; at intermission time all the mothers in the audience were so tormented and anxious that they rushed in a body to phone home: was the baby really all right, was he really well and warm in his bed; one couldn't get near the telephone booths. A dozen years ago, when Ginsberg had been a student and I had taxed Lionel with the duty to forbid him to misbehave, he had answered me that he wasn't the boy's father, and of course he was right. Neither was Mark Van Doren the boy's father; a teacher is not a father to his students and he must never try to be. Besides, Ginsberg had a father of his own who couldn't be replaced at will: he was in the audience the other night. One of the things Ginsberg read was part of a long poem to his mother, who, he told us, had died three years ago, and as he read it, he choked and cried; but no one in the auditorium tittered or showed embarrassment at this public display of emotion, and I doubt whether there was a young Existentialist in the audience who thought, "See he has existence: he can cry, he can feel." Nor did anyone seem very curious when he went on to explain, later in the evening, that the reason he had cried was because his father was in the theater. I have no way of knowing what Ginsberg's father felt the other night about his son being up there on the stage at Columbia (it rather obsesses me), but I should guess he was proud; it's what I'd conclude from his expression at the end of the performance when Ginsberg pressed through the admirers who surrounded him to get to his father as quickly as he could: surely that's nice for a father. And I should suppose a father was bound to be pleased that his son was reading his poems in a university auditorium: it would mean the boy's success, and this would be better than a vulgarity; it would necessarily include the chairman's critical gravity and the fact, however bizarre, that T. S. Eliot had been the last poet in this place before him. In a sense, Orlovsky and Corso were more orphans than Ginsberg the other night, but this was not necessarily because they were without fathers of their own in the audience; I should think it would go back much farther than this, to whatever it was that made them look so much more masked, less openly eager for approval; although they were essentially as innocent and childlike as Ginsberg, they couldn't begin to match his appeal; it was on Ginsberg that one's eye rested, it was to the sweetness in his face and to his sweet smile that one responded; it was to him that one gave one's pity and for him one felt one's terror. Clearly, I am no judge of his poem "Lion in the Room," which he announced was dedicated to Lionel Trilling; I heard it through too much sympathy, and also self-consciousness. The poem was addressed as well as dedicated to Lionel; it was about a lion in the room with the poet, a lion who was hungry but refused to eat him; I heard it as a passionate love-poem; I really can't say whether it was a good or a bad poem, but I was much moved by it, in some part unaccountably. It was also a decent poem, and I am willing to admit this surprised me; there were no obscenities in it as there had been in much of the poetry the "beats" read. Here was something else one noted about the other evening: most of the audience was very young, and Ginsberg must have realized this because when he read the poem about his mother and came to the place where he referred to the YPSLs of her girlhood, he interposed his only textual exegesis of the evening; in an aside he explained, "Young People's Socialist League"—he was very earnest about wanting his poetry to be understood. And it wasn't only his gentility that distinguished Ginsberg's father from the rest of the audience; as far as I could see, he was the only man in the hall who looked old enough to be the father of a grown son; the audience was crazily young, there were virtually no faculty present: I suppose they didn't want to give this much sanction to the "beats." For this young audience the obscenities read from the stage seemed to have no force whatsoever; there was not even the shock of silence, and when Ginsberg forgot himself in the question period and said that something or other was bull-shit, I think he was more upset than his listeners; I can't imagine anything more detached and scientific outside a psychoanalyst's office, or perhaps a nursery school, than this young audience at Columbia. And even of Corso himself one had the sense that he mouthed the bad word only with considerable personal difficulty: this hurts me more than it hurts you.

Obviously, the whole performance had been carefully planned as to who would read first and what, then who next, and just how much an audience could take without becoming bored and overcritical: it would be my opinion we could have taken a bit more before the question period, which must have been an anti-climax for anyone who had come to the reading as a fellow-traveler. I've already reported how Ginsberg dealt with the philosophy question. There remains, of the question period, only to report his views on verse forms.

I don't remember how the question was put to Ginsberg— but I'm sure it was put neutrally: no one was inclined to embarrass the guests—which led him into a discussion of prosody; perhaps it was the question about what Ginsberg as a poet had learned at Columbia; but anyway, here, at last, Ginsberg had a real classroom subject: he could be a teacher who wed outrageousness to authority in the time-honored way of the young and lively, no-pedant-he performer of the classroom, and suddenly Ginsberg announced firmly that no one at Columbia knew anything about prosody; the English department was stuck in the nineteenth century, sensible of no meter other than the old iambic pentameter, whereas the thing about him and his friends was their concern with a poetic line which

moved in the rhythm of ordinary speech; they were poetic inno-
vators, carrying things forward the logical next step from William Carlos Williams. And now all at once the thing about
Ginsberg and his friends was not their social protest and existentialism, their whackiness and beat-upness: suddenly it had
become their energy of poetic impulse that earned them their
right to be heard in the university, their studious devotion to
their art: Ginsberg was seeing to that. Orlovsky had made his
contribution to the evening; he had read his two whacky up-
roarious poems, the entire canon of his work, and had won his
acclaim. Corso had similarly given his best, and been approved.
The question period, the period of instruction, belonged to
Ginsberg alone, and his friends might be slightly puzzled by
the turn the evening had taken, the decorousness of which they
suddenly found themselves a part—Corso, for instance, began
to look like a chastened small boy who was still determined,
though his heart was no longer in it, to bull his way through
against all these damned grown-ups—but they had no choice
except to permit their companion his deviation into high-mind-
edness. And thus did one measure, finally, the full tug of something close to respectability in Ginsberg's life, by this division
in the ranks; and thus, too, was the soundness of Dupee's
reminder, that there is always something to learn from hearing a poet read his poems aloud, borne in on one. For the fact
was that Ginsberg, reading his verse, had naturally given it
the iambic beat: after all, it is the traditional beat of English
poetry where it deals with serious subjects, as Ginsberg's
poems so often do. A poet, one thought—and it was a poignant
thought because it came so immediately and humanly rather
than as an abstraction—may choose to walk whatever zany
path in his life as a man; but when it comes to mourning and
mothers and such, he will be drawn into the line of tradition; at
least in this far he is always drawn toward "respectability."

The evening was over, we were dismissed to return to our
homes. A crowd formed around Ginsberg; he extricated himself
and came to his father a few rows ahead of us. I resisted the
temptation to overhear their greeting. In some part of me I
wanted to speak to Ginsberg, tell him I had liked the poem he
had written to my husband, but I didn't dare: I couldn't be sure
that Ginsberg wouldn't take my meaning wrong. Outside, it

had blown up a bit—or was it just the chill of unreality against which we hurried to find shelter?

There was a meeting going on at home of the pleasant professional sort which, like the comfortable living room in which it usually takes place, at a certain point in a successful modern literary career confirms the writer in his sense of disciplined achievement and well-earned reward. It is of course a sense that all writers long for quite as much as they fear it; certainly it is not to be made too conscious, nor ever to be spoken of except without elaborate irony, lest it propose a life without risk and therefore without virtue. I had found myself hurrying as if I were needed, but there was really no reason for my haste; my entrance was an interruption, even a disturbance of the orderly scene, not the smallest part of whose point for me lay, now, in the troubling contrast it made with the world I had just come from. Auden, alone of the eight men in the room not dressed in a proper suit but wearing a battered old brown leather jacket, was first to inquire about my experience. I told him I had been moved; he answered gently that he was ashamed of me. In a dim suffocated effort of necessary correction, I said, "It's different when it's human beings and not just a sociological phenomenon," and I can only guess, and hope, he took what I meant. Yet as I prepared to get out of the room so that the men could sit down again with their drinks, I felt there was something more I had to add—it was so far from enough to leave the "beats" as no more than human beings— and so I said, "Allen Ginsberg read a love-poem to you, Lionel. I liked it very much." It was an awkward thing to say in the circumstances, perhaps even a little foolish as an attempt to bridge the unfathomable gap that was all so quickly and meaningfully opening up between the evening that had been and the evening that was now so surely reclaiming me. But I'm certain that Ginsberg's old teacher knew what I was saying, and why I was impelled to say it.

BELIEF AND TECHNIQUE FOR MODERN PROSE

by Jack Kerouac

Evergreen Review, Vol. 2, No. 8, 1959

List of Essentials

1. Scribbled secret notebooks, and wild typewritten pages, for yr own joy
2. Submissive to everything, open, listening
3. Try never get drunk outside yr own house
4. Be in love with yr life
5. Something that you feel will find its own form
6. Be crazy dumbsaint of the mind
7. Blow as deep as you want to blow
8. Write what you want bottomless from bottom of the mind
9. The unspeakable visions of the individual
10. No time for poetry, but exactly what is
11. Visionary tics shivering in the chest
12. In tranced fixation dreaming upon object before you
13. Remove literary, grammatical and syntactical inhibition
14. Like Proust be an old teahead of time
15. Telling the true story of the world in interior monolog
16. The jewel center of interest is the eye within the eye
17. Write in recollection and amazement for yourself
18. Work from pithy middle eye out, swimming in language sea
19. Accept loss forever
20. Believe in the holy contour of life
21. Struggle to sketch the flow that already exists intact in mind

22. Dont think of words when you stop but to see picture better
23. Keep track of every day the date emblazoned in yr morning
24. No fear or shame in the dignity of yr experience, language & knowledge
25. Write for the world to read and see yr exact pictures of it
26. Bookmovie is the movie in words, the visual American form
27. In Praise of Character in the Bleak inhuman Loneliness
28. Composing wild, undisciplined, pure, coming in from under, crazier the better
29. You're a Genius all the time
30. Writer-Director of Earthly movies Sponsored & Angeled in Heaven

Kerouac at the Underwood, typing corrections to "This is a poem By Albert Saijo, Lew Welch and Jack Kerouac," created on the spot at McDarrah's apartment, 304 West 14th Street on December 10, 1959.

Jerrold Heiserman (rear), Mimi Margeaux, Stella Pittelli, Philip Lamantia, and Kirby Doyle at 24 Cornelia Street apartment of Dave Lambert.

Edwin Fancher, publisher, and Daniel Wolf, editor, of the Village Voice, *in front of its first office, 22 Greenwich Avenue, March 16, 1959. They published more articles, poetry, criticism, book reviews on the beat generation than any other newspaper or magazine in America.*

Richard Seaver and Irving Rosenthal, editors of Evergreen Review, *editing a manuscript by French poet and playwright Fernando Arrabal, right, in office of Grove Press, February 1, 1960.*

Norman Mailer, novelist and co-owner of the Village Voice, *with editor Daniel Wolf at newspaper office, 22 Greenwich Avenue, March 16, 1960. Wolf also edited* Exodus.

HOW TO TELL THE BEATNIKS FROM THE HIPSTERS

by Herbert Gold

The Noble Savage, March 1960

When you take dehydrated hipster and add watery words to make Instant Beatnik, the flavor is gone but the lack of taste lingers on.

Once again Time, Inc., has done the work of creation. Unlike the Lord, who made something from nothing, creating the universe out of void, the anonymous scribes at *Time* and *Life* have labored to create nothing from a something which was merely *almost* nothing. They have invented the Beatnik, an all-purpose subject for satire and shuddering in lectures on the real, true-hearted America.

Exactly what is a beatnik, who is it? The beatnik is the hipster squeezed into shape by the popular media, seen as through a gloss darkly by radio, television, films, and magazines. But he is not mere fantasy, either. He exists in too, too solid flesh in the persons of those lads who wander about Greenwich Village, North Beach in San Francisco, the Near North Side in Chicago, and other selected drill fields, wearing turtleneck sweaters beneath the free-form silver crucifixes pendant from ribbons around their necks, dark glasses, and a world-historical pout on the face; or the girls in jeans and waxy eye makeup; or the crowds at bongo and poetry conferences. As their spokesmen put it, they are Waiting for Something; but they are not waiting for some rough beast slouching toward Venice, Calif., to be born. They need the message. They are waiting with their 19¢ for the next issue of *Life.* They need to find out what they are up to next.

In other words, they have taken their cue from the pictures in *Life* as another obedient generation took its cue from the dialogue in Hemingway. Hemingway's followers imitated fictional characters imitating the Lost Generation. Rockefeller Center's fictional people are imitating fictional characters imitating fictional people. The significant difference is one of increasing abstraction from any vital internal compulsion. There is a decline of energy. There is a policy of massive retractionof reality.

Question: Is this a definition? "The beatnik is like a hipster, like."

Answer: Not in the conventional definition of a definition, which asks us to locate a thing or a concept by putting it in its general class and then describing how it differs from all other members of the class. let us try to arrive at some understanding of the beatnik by chronological pointing (ostensive definition) and value orientation (viewing with alarm); since we shall argue that the shadowy beatnik's detached body is a hipster, we shall loyally define him, too.

1946. We are back there. Zoot suits and the Black Market; the calendars with daring Rita Hayworth and glibly amorous Betty Grable still decorate country garages where proud purchasers try to get their new hollow bullet-shaped Hudsons to run properly. A flood of veterans with G.I. clothes and clogged psyches has returned to the campus. Boyd Raeburn, bop, Existentialism, strange quarrels with the Russians, and the quonset hut for raising children. It is already hard to keep apart, keep up. Both the gifted and the stupefied need to find ways of setting themselves apart from a massified society. A secret cowboy group of them has beenlet in on a discovery: marijuana doesn't cause any hangover; a still smaller few has learned that heroin, injected straight into the vein, will not cause death from an air bubble; and marijuana teases, but heroin causes *real* trouble, something to do.

A line of speech from this season: "Are you enlightened?"

This means, Do you dig?

A year or two later. Rebop is dead, Long Live Bop. Also progressive jazz, cool jazz, bop glasses, and a quiet music while dreamy young writers remember the day they liberated Paris (their wives wish they could liberate a G.I. loan). A child raised according to the principles of permissiveness really smells up the place. Henry Wallace just won't do. A phrase: "Are you hep?"

This means, Do you dig?

Still later. Less politics, less memory of the war, less insistence on the real true comfort of the G.I. shoe; Milton Berle and Fulton Sheen ("Uncle Miltie and Uncle Fultie") were hilarious and profound; more music, more talk, and a few jazz chapparoonies trickling out of Juilliard. A phrase: "Are you hip?"

This means, Do you dig?

In 1949 Anatole Broyard wrote an essay in the *Partisan Review,* entitled "Portrait of the Hipster." But the world was not yet ready. Attention, attention was not paid this modern man. Jack Kerouac had just left college. Clellon Holmes was writing his novel *Go,* and "hipster" was a mere word to dscribe a mere little thing. This little thing: a child who does not care. Perhaps the best projection of the hipster fantasy is that of a recent movie, *Teen-Agers from Outer Space.* This quickie, made on a small budget of dollars and a large one of greed, invents hotrodders from some other planet who wish to destroy Earth and all its appurtenances, such as Friendly Dogs, Kindly Gramps, and Adults. Why? Well, they don't really have anything against us. It's not personal. Wearing their black space uniforms, with untied Keds on their feet and Vaseline in their hair, they are careening about the universe in their souped-up spaceships, lookin' for somethin' to do, pops. (For plot purposes there are also outerspace monsters who grow too damn fast and eat people.) Occasionally the teenager whips out his molecular disintegrator and molecularly disintegrates some boring square.

The hipster doesn't want to feel; he keeps cool. He has checked up on experience and found it wanting; he is enlightened, hep, hip, and doesn't dig overmuch. He carries books without reading them, drives cars without going anyplace, goes places without arriving anywhere. He is beat. In other words, he's in trouble about feeling.

Now, how does this frigid soul get to be a hero? Well, Jack Kerouac transforms his frigidity ito the nymphomaniacal jitters. He looks like the opposite of what he is; he is less a lover than a call boy; he is beat down and beat up, but under the auspices of a lucky pun, he is also beatific, by the same logic that makes Harry James identical with Henry James. They sound alike. The English language glitters with such treasure-troves of truth for the lucky, free-associating searcher, i.e., pants can be both heavy breathing and blue jeans. Truth comes of enthusiastic delving into these cosmic juxtapositions. In Allen Ginsberg, an alert, intelligent, fantastical young juxtapositioner, the passion for poetry and a passion for display create the greatest publicist for a literary fashion since Ezra Pound made it big with imagism. Then a few established literary runners picked up the torch. Kenneth Rexroth turned his temper on the new idea; Norman Mailer discovered that the hipster is really a White Negro, that is, a nonpolitical rebel outcast, and in fact, Raskolnikov had something like this in mind. (A colored hipster, by this definition, is a Negro Negro.) The industry of writing about mass culture swung into production. *(Mea Culpa.)*

In other places *(mea culpa, mea culpa),* I have defined the hipster as follows: He is the criminal with no motivation in hunger, the delinquent with no zest, the gang follower with no love of the gang; i.e., the worker without ambition or pleasure in work, the youngster with undescended passions, the organization man with sloanwilsonian gregorypeckerism in his cold, cold heart. He has entered a deep cavern where desire and art are unknown; swimming blind, scarred, and silent, he eats whatever is alive—a symptom of trouble, but hardly feeling it any more.

The hipster writer admires this slouching male impersonator. He performs a modern miracle of the fishes, transforming the skim milk of poverty into the nonfat milk of middle-class reducing diets. In this difficult hour of the midcentury, he drinks at the fount of uncreative frigidity, of conformity without a cause and rebellion with claws—in other words, everything that a writer must not endure. He admires those who labor in silence on street corners in order to produce a tautology and a vacuum. He has found a new Symbol of Our Age.

All right, like it or not, the hipster writer really existed, some of them talented, and the hipster creature really existed, some of them genuinely pathetic and suffering in their hope of finding a reason for being alive through acts of sabotage. But who received the fruit of their sacrifice? (They sacrificed mainly others.) How do we make room for the beatnik amid the ruins?

Enter *Time* and *Life* with fanfare of donkeys. Let us speed up the record here and pass beyond that shrill quarrel about who whomped together that phrase, The Beat Generation. Someone thought to tack the Russian suffix "nik" on the tail of the word "beat" in order to name the vaguest quantity since you last held the smell of an opinion in your hand.* For the popular media, this is an ideal situation. The vaguer the thing discussed, the more freedom to the curt, concise, complete newsinventor. The hipster is a straw horse trying to be a dead horse; the beatnik is a horse that never was, and it can be whipped in the empty air with loud satisfying cracks and no danger of being tuckered out; it draws its burden as well as it ever did. Writing about the hipster is dangerous; one might be tempted by loyalty to the facts. But since the beatnik was invented solely as an item for journalistic use, it is the property of journalists.

In principle, therefore, it can mean anything, but in order to be interesting, it has to have qualities. Therefore it drinks espresso coffee, splashes paint on huge canvases, chants poetry to jazz, and sits without dancing the whole night through. If a girl, it is available; if a boy, it is also available. It is above all photogenic.

The beatnik, then, is the hipster parodied and packaged as a commercial product. It is a commodity. It bears the same relation to the hipster as the cornflake does to a field of corn. The cornfield has a certain corny splendor, waving its tassels under the gaudy skies of authentic Americana. The cornflake has broken the vegetable barrier, being pounded, chipped, flavored with sugar and malt, preserved, wrapped, and sold with no flavor at all of the original kernel; the legend on the box, read at breakfast by millions of ardent kids, is far more important than that ancient organic starch which now lies gluey in the bowl.

It is perhaps a tribute to the vitality of the hipster's image that he needed to undergo this change in order to attain the proper degree of unreality for use by the unreality mongers. His identity, faint at best, had to be annihilated by destroying

*My best information is that Herb Caen, a columnist for the *San Francisco Chronicle,* invented the word. If my research budget were larger, I would try to find out if Li'l Abner is carried by the *Chronicle.* Can the word "beat" be an etymological borrowing from the Lower Slobbovian? Correspondence from linguists invited.

his name; a real hipster might criticize a public foolishness about him, or at least stand in silent reproach near that Atlas of Rockefeller Center which carries an empty, airy globe on its straining back. But since there are no real beatniks, who can either quarrel or libel? Who can defend a fantasy against slander? It was a stroke of exemplary cunning. At about the same time that the Soviet scientists gave the world the sputnik, some American media specialists launched the beatnik.

And Jack Kerouac and buddies went swiftly into orbit. Their own sense of reality was rather tremulous to begin with, and it leaned heavily on the breast of publicity. If publicity needed the word "beatnik," then they would adopt its soul for their very own. Lifelessness imitated artlessness. Kerouac has celebrated "the beatnik angel," asleep before his television horror movie, in *Escapade, Holiday, Encounter, Playboy, Evergreen Review,* and elsewhere, usually along the lines of his *Encounter* essay, which was originally a lecture given at a New York university: "Woe unto those who spit on the Beat Generation. Woe unto those who don't realize that America must, will, is, changing now, for the better I say. . . . This necessarily'll have to be about myself. I'm going all out." Or in *Holiday:* "Standing on a street corner waiting for no one is Power."

The no one who comes along and takes his hand is the beatnik.

At present writing, in September 1959, *Life* has come up with the latest idea for utilizing the product. In a picture story they have contrasted the life of a small town—happy folks a-watchin' of the tellyvision machine—with them Beatneck critters a-recitin' of the poetry to the jazz. The paragraphs describing the beatniks are headlined with that jagged, half-legible, arty type invented to advertise offbeat but commercial films like *The Man with the Golden Armnik* and *Anatomy of a Murdernik,* a typeface which can be called Preminger Bold, or No-Point Hipsville. The smalltown togetherness heroes are a little blurred in the pictures. They are not such skilled models. The beatniks from Venice, Calif., know how to hold the pose—jazz in mouth, aghast dreaming in eyes.

Americans are a convinceable people, and lo, snap your fingers twice and the beatnik really exists, sprung into full flake while the corn is still green. On Eighth Street in Greenwich Village, on the North Beach hills of San Francisco, and on the

Near North Side of Chicago, the hipster has folded his hypodermic and silently stolen away. Perhaps he still digs jazz, heists caviar, borrows cars, makes love without pleasure, but he takes these traditional thrills without the fresh joy of the avantgarde innovator. He is passé. He is as dead as yoyos and miniature golf and the American Veterans Committee. He may as well get into line, heading for the suburbs of silence, in deathly procession behind the lost generation, the zoot suiters, and those who believe that large heavy automobiles bring prestige. (*Musica morbida.* Can Gian-Carlo Menotti write a dirge for a fad?)

The hipster has not been rubbed out by the beatnik; he has been rubbed in. While old Kronos was devoured by his own sons, the hipster has been defrocked by those attendant angels who only come to swell a progress, increase an editorial penetration. As the anonymous tunesmiths of *Time* refer to Jacques Barzun as an elitenik (will Santa Claus turn into a Saint Nicknik?), the once mighty hipster stands humbly in the wings, ready to speak his few lines as a puny beatnik:

> His life is gentle, and the elements
> So mix'd in him that Nature might stand up
> And say to all the world, "This is a man?"

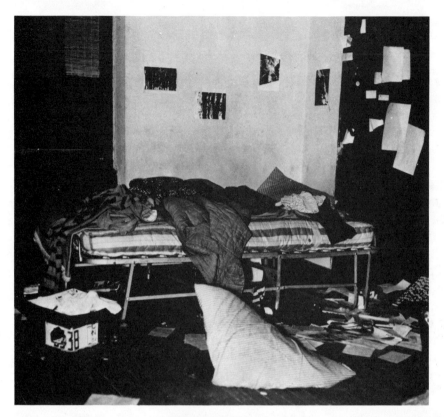

Artist-poet William Morris's beatnik pad, 212 Sullivan Street, May 24, 1959.

Poet Hugh Romney (later called Wavy-Gravy, the Hog Farm Guru) posing with art work by action painter William Morris in his beatnik cellar pad at 212 Sullivan Street, May 24, 1959.

Dan Propper in William Morris's beatnik pad, 212 Sullivan Street, May 24, 1959.

William Smith, a beatnik candidate for President, in Ninth Circle Bar, 139 West 10th Street, August 15, 1960.

William Morris reading poetry at the Caravan Café, 102 West 3rd Street, May 24, 1959. His love-oriented poem "Return to New York" began: "I want to score for love my sweet; I want to hear once more the bedspring music of your kiss. . . ."

Hugh Romney reading poetry in the Caravan Café, 102 West 3rd Street, May 24, 1959. His poem "Let the Last Be First," an ode to love, began: "Wings beat noisily! Golden harps rejoice! Angels copulate . . ."

Ray Bremser reading
Poems of Holy
Madness _in the_
Epitome Café, 165
Bleecker Street, June
_6, 1959._

Diane DiPrima in Gaslight Café, June 28,
1959, reading from her book of poetry This
Kind of Bird Flies Backwards.

Manager Frank Lo Piccolo of the
Caravan Café, 102 West 3rd
Street, is issued a summons by
6th Precinct Officer George Parker
for conducting poetry readings
without a cabaret license, May 24,
_1959._

Listening to beat poetry in the Café Bizarre, 106 West 3rd Street, June 7, 1959.

Taylor Mead reading Excerpts from the Anonymous Diary of a New York Youth *in the Gaslight Café, 116 MacDougal Street, June 7, 1959.*

Richard Davidson reading his poem "Moon over MacDougal Street" in the Epitome Café, July 19, 1959.

Poets from Frank Dalia's Intermezzo Café, MacDougal Street. Tony Jordan (top left), Frank Dalia, second from left, Bruce Paige (second from right), Marcia Lord (trench coat), Penny Carol (scarf), John Hicken (seated), September 12, 1959. Some were beat poets in training.

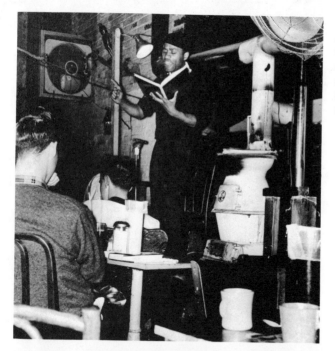

Ted Joans at the Café Bizarre, 106 West 3rd Street, May 24, 1959, made a big hit with his beat and dada poems, surrealist prose and jazz shouts.

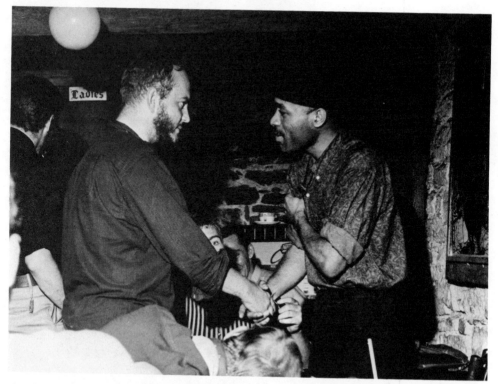

Washington poet Dick Dabney and Ted Joans in the Gaslight Café, July 18, 1959. Dabney gave up the beat life and was a columnist for the Washington Post; Joans went to Africa.

Poet Ambrose Hollingsworth in Manny Roth's Cock 'n' Bull Café, 147 Bleecker Street, May 24, 1959.

Thomas McGrath reading his poetry from A Double World in the Gaslight Café, September 4, 1959.

Jazz poet Jim Lyons with Malcolm Soule in the Gaslight Café, September 21, 1959. Lyons's "Hotel Blues" was published in the Gaslight Poetry Review.

A view in the Gaslight Café, 116 MacDougal Street, September 21, 1959. Ed Freeman (with sunglasses) had his work in the Gaslight Poetry Review.

Village Voice *"Saloon Society" columnist Bill Manville, right, with novelist Rosemary Santini and Jack Malick in the San Remo Café, 93 MacDougal Street, a postwar literary tavern that closed down in the 1970s.*

THEY DIG BOOZE, JAZZ AND SEX

by Edward Klein

New York Daily News, February 19, 1958

The cool hipsters of the "Beat Generation," driven to the walls of cold water tenements on the Lower East Side by soaring prices and soaring apartment houses, are likely to be the last of the bohemians of Greenwich Village.

"The real-crazy-man avant-garde of our real-crazy-man times," as they were described in an article in the *Village Voice,* the Beat people live a frantic life of alcohol, jazz music, sex and, for some, dope, in search of thrills, kicks and a new approach to life.

Born in the throes of the Great Depression, maturing in the years of World War II and living now in a cold war era of H-bombs and ballistic missiles, the Beat Generation considers itself disillusioned, bored and—above all—"beat."

Unlike the bohemians of the '20s and '30s who denounced society from corner soap boxes, crusaded in parades and wrote bitter novels, the hipsters have no ambition to make over the world and ask only to be left alone so they can "dig" the most from what they call "their" generation.

As F. Scott Fitzgerald represented the "Lost Generation" of the '20s, a new, young novelist, Jack Kerouac, has come to be the unofficial spokesman of the "Beat." Tall, gaunt and cool, Kerouac, author of *On the Road,* and the soon-to-be-released *The Subterraneans,* personifies this new movement.

For six years, Kerouac says, he was "hopping freights, hitchhiking, and working as railroad brakeman, deck hand and scullion on merchant ships and government fire lookout and at hundreds of jobs." He slept in mountains and deserts in a sleeping bag and roamed all over America.

Since then, he has spent his time "in skid row or in jazz joints or with personal poet madmen. I'm only a jolly story teller and have nothing to do with politics or schemes and my

179

only plan is the old Chinese way of the Tao: 'Avoid the authorities!'"

THEIR EDGY NERVES DEMAND STIMULATION

Now he lives part of the year in Orlando, Fla., and part in New York and is working on a novel "about American Zen Lunatics (poets and rucksack wanderers)."

As Kerouac says, some of the Beat Generation smoke weed (marijuana) for the kicks. On the Lower East Side, between Houston and 14th Sts. and as far east as Avenue A—"America's Left Bank"—the pusher plies his trade among eager characters whose nerves demand constant stimulation.

Unfortunately, there is a hitch to the Beat's never-ending search for thrills. Each new kick dulls the nerves, so that the hipster becomes harder to satisfy.

"Man," said one sallow-faced, emaciated Beat character in the San Remo on MacDougal St., "there just ain't no word in hip-talk for 'enough.' Either you're way out, pops, or you're hung up. That's IT! Yes. Yes."

The same goes for jazz and sex. Jazz is the music of the Beat Generation and the late jazzman Charlie Parker is their god. Before the wailing saxophones of Stan Getz and Phil Woods, the driving rhythm of bassmen Oscar Pettiford and Charlie Mingus or the intricate piano playing of Thelonious Monk and Oscar Peterson, the Beat people go into trances of ecstasy and oblivion.

The Five-Spot, Half-Note, Café Bohemia and Village Vanguard swing the kind of jazz the hipsters "dig."

THEY EAT IT UP; YES, MAN, THAT'S IT

"This place gets like a sweaty smoker on a long train ride," says Iggie Termini, co-owner of the Five-Spot. "By around 2:30, everybody feels like they've known each other for a long time. Some take off their jackets and sit as close as they can to the jazz—swaying and mumbling—and they don't miss a note or a phrase. Sometimes, between sets, one of these guys asks me or my brother, Joe, if he can take a turn at the drums or bass. If we know he's good, we let him. They like it and their friends eat it up and yell, 'Yes, man. Yes. That's it.'"

One of the Half-Note's regulars, a youngish-looking cat in blue jeans and T shirt, tried to explain why he goes for jazz in such an all-out way.

"Now don't think that we don't dig Beethoven-oorini," he said, talking in the manner of a Marlon Brando or James Dean. "We dig everything, man. It's just that jazz is it—It has it, it means it, it says it."

IT HAS THE BEAT THAT MAKES 'EM MOVE

His short, attractive girl friend, in a heavy black sweater, added: "Jazz is cool and it has a beat and it makes us move. That's what we've got to do—move and go."

In recent months, Greenwich Village has experienced the most important contribution of the Beat Generation, as poetry and jazz got together, with poets reading their free verse to jazz accompaniment. Max Gordon, the enterprising owner of the Village Vanguard, stepped up the trend by hiring Kerouac himself to give poetry-jazz readings on Sunday afternoons.

Word went out all over the country to the Beat people in Chicago, Denver or San Francisco or rushing aimlessly somewhere on the road. They descended from cold-water flats and uptown penthouses on the Vanguard, eager to hear their "voice." Most of them were penniless and Max says he made no money on the deal.

TEAMED UP, BROUGHT THE HOUSE DOWN

After only a week, Kerouac began to get restless.

"I didn't want it. I didn't want anything behind me," Kerouac complained, pointing to the jazz pianist on the stage. "Max Gordon said he wanted me to try it out for a few weeks. I won't do it ever again, not for a million dollars. I'm no Jackie Gleason. I'm a poet."

Others have had more success. Poet Jim Grady teamed up with bassist Charlie Mingus at the Half-Note and brought the house down. At Goody's Bar, Robert Claremont and Anca Vrbovska read their poetry to jazz and the experiment proved successful. The Half-Note is now the center of the movement.

The Beat Generation divides life into halves: work life and love life. Work life usually means an occasional job as a dishwasher or longshoreman for enough money to buy whisky and a little food—for a few weeks.

Love life, however, ranks in order with dope and jazz, demanding much of the hipster's time and devotion. The cats play everything cool and sex is no exception. It is not unusual for one Beat character to be having simultaneous affairs with two or three girls—and each of the girls must feel completely free to see other men. Things tend to get complicated but no one seems to care as long as they are satisfied they are "digging" life.

A pert blonde at the Kettle of Fish put it this way: "Daddy-o, if someone wants to make it with me, and I have eyes for him, he don't need no vaccination certificate—only a pad (room). But, man, who's got a pad these days?"

IT WON'T BE LONG UNTIL THEY'RE GONE

She was referring to the trouble Beat people have finding a place in which they can afford to live. Since the war the Village has been going chichi and at least a dozen middle and upper-class apartment buildings have already replaced the colorful old dwellings that gave the Village its famous flavor.

"In 10 years, there won't be a Village—even though it'll be called the Village," says Jimmy Garofolo, a lifelong Villager and owner of the Café Bohemia. "The bohemians are being pushed out over east and, after a while, there'll be only the East River for them. A lot of my artist friends who 10 years ago wouldn't have thought of leaving are moving uptown. It won't be long until everybody's gone."

The lofts on the "Left Bank" have absorbed some of the displaced bohemians and a new artistic colony has sprung up where once Polish, Romanian and German families lived as their fathers did in Europe. But most people feel it is only a matter of time before high rents and slum clearance projects destroy this last stronghold of bohemianism.

THE WRECKERS CLOSE IN ON THE LAST BOHEMIANS

by *Edward Klein*

New York Daily News, February 20, 1958

The Beat Generation is composing an obituary for Greenwich Village. The only proclaimed big bohemian group left in the Village, its adherents seek blindly for thrills among the sounds of a building boom that will eventually drive them out.

When the $75 million Washington Square Village housing project (just south of the square) is opened this fall, another 12 acres of Bohemia will be lost to respectability. At $60 a room, these three glass and glazed-brick buildings replace six square blocks of picturesque studios, crooked houses and dilapidated business lofts.

The Village is probably the only place in the U.S. where a shout of protest goes up when the government plans a slum clearance project. But efforts to save it as a combination of family community and artistic utopia are proving futile. There are now under construction, or soon will be, at least a dozen modern apartment buildings and a mammoth expansion program by New York University.

George F. Baughman, vice president in charge of business affairs for NYU, estimates that the school is going to spend $20 million in development. In fact, NYU owns or controls three-quarters of Washington Square, which some people claim will soon become its private campus.

THEY'RE UP IN ARMS OVER THE HIGHWAY

In addition, a bitter fight has developed between the Greenwich Village Association and Parks Commissioner Robert Moses over the proposed 48-foot, four-lane highway extending Fifth Ave. through Washington Square to Canal St.

183

When this project was announced, even the Beat Generation people were shocked. They joined forces with bums, artists, writers and family men in collecting a petition with 10,000 signatures demanding that the park be altogether closed off to traffic and that the highway be put underground.

But, again, progress has won the day and construction will probably get started as soon as Moses and Borough President Hulan Jack can agree on its size.

"I will not go along with a 48-foot (wide) road," Jack declares. "And, furthermore, no person (Moses) will be responsible for the treatment of the roadway other than this office." Jack is for limiting the highway's width to 36 feet.

"Thirty-six feet is ridiculously narrow and is, in fact, no better than the present roadway," Moses answers. "It ignores the new developments . . . and their traffic requirements."

WANT NO DADDIES FROM SQUARESVILLE

In the park itself, a goateed hipster who spends his days lolling around "digging the people and their dogs" and his nights in jazz joints on the East Side expressed his sentiments on the fracas.

"Aw, man, the park is the most. We don't want no daddies from squaresville barreling through and scaring the pigeons."

The change in the character of the Village can be seen in the rise of a new kind of coffee shop with clean floors and washed cups. Catering to the 9-to-5 crowd from uptown, they serve café espresso, cappuccino and cinnamon stick in a pleasant, conversational atmosphere.

"The only time I see one of those Beat characters," says Mrs. Gee, the attractive proprietress of the Limelight, a new coffee shop just off Sheridan Square, "is when there's a job open for a dishwasher. They'll come over for a few days to pick up enough money to go back to their flats on the 'Left Bank' [the Lower East Side].

"Once," she added with a smile, "a few came in to see our photography exhibition. They looked at the pictures, couldn't raise enough for one cup of coffee—and left."

RECALLS THE OLD, UNTRAMMELED, DAYS

At the Rienzi, a well-known meeting place of artists and writers, 72-year-old Romany Marie sips exotic coffee, smokes cigarettes and talks about the simple, untrammeled bohemianism in the days when she ran literary tea rooms and fed such starving artists as Eugene O'Neill, Sinclair Lewis, Maxwell Bodenheim, Edna St. Vincent Millay and Will Durant.

"Things will never be the same with my Village," said Romany Marie, shaking her head sadly.

"We have lost the most important thing—freedom. When Gene [Eugene O'Neill] and Harry Kemp lived and worked here, there were no tall buildings to block the sunlight and kill the trees and flowers and we used to sit till dawn over one bottle of wine without the owner worrying over his cash register.

"This Beat Generation," Marie continued sadly, "is truly sad. They have no dreams, no stars to follow and they live not to create but to destroy. They will soon destroy themselves. And there will be no one to take their place."

However, there is a group in the Beat Generation, according to Bill Seward, a Charles St. author, "which does care about what's happening with the world and is concerned with H-bombs and moral depravity."

"We believe," he added, "that people will need more than a nice apartment, a good job and a TV set to save themselves from the world's head-on rush toward complete destruction. Our group spends more time circulating petitions and writing articles than swilling booze or using a needle."

RENT PARTY'S BACK—ALL ARE INVITED

Rents may be cheap on the Lower East Side where the hipsters indulge in the delights of modern jazz and the snowballing affairs with Beat-women, but many of them have trouble raising the money.

On the first of the month word gets out that a certain cat is going to have a rent party and everyone is invited. Rent parties are a throwback to the depression days in Harlem, when whole neighborhoods chipped in to make up the rent of an unemployed friend.

To an outsider, the rent parties of the "Left Bank" would seem like a convention of Bedlam inmates let out of their straitjackets for a night. Arms flap in the air to the beat of the jazz on the phonograph, feet stomp and shuffle and everyone shouts.

In one small room about the size of a subway car, there may be as many as 100 people. In the morning, as they leave, those who have a dime or a quarter give it to the host, congratulating him that the party "swung way out."

But if the building boom continues—and most likely it will—even the Lower East Side is "doomed" to be rehabilitated. Where will the bohemians go from there?

During the past 10 years, San Francisco has attracted large numbers of offbeat artists to its hills and narrow streets and particularly to the North Beach section—the Greenwich Village of the West. Its lazy living, international atmosphere and famous jazz clubs—not to mention its cheaper rents—make it a desirable place to live for the improvident artistic type.

A TOWN WHERE THEY ALL COME TO BALL

"San Fran is a good-time town," said a high-priced call girl who nets over $250 a week working its innumerable conventions. "It's the town where everybody comes to ball, baby."

Roaming the country with empty pockets and bulging rucksacks in which they keep all their belongings, the Beat Generation isn't coming back to New York. In search of a place in which they can "dig," San Francisco, Denver and Chicago look better to them than the rapidly vanishing Village.

When the last one finally goes, he will be leaving a Village empty of bohemians but full of the legends of its offbeat days.

View of MacDougal Street looking north from Bleecker, October 1, 1959. Most of the establishments are long since gone, like the San Remo Café.

Poet Tuli Kupferberg, center, in front of the Gaslight Café, 116 MacDougal Street, March 8, 1959. Behind him are Sheila Bryant and, left, Sylvia Topp.

Rick Allmen's Café Bizarre, 106 West 3rd Street, June 7, 1959. The entire block was torn down in December 1983.

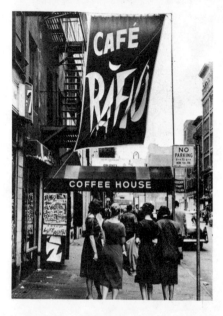

The Café Rafio, 165 Bleecker Street, was managed by Ronald Von Ehmsen, who was shot in front of the café by a tenant in the building.

Pacifist David McReynolds on MacDougal Street in front of 8th Street Bookshop in an anti-nuke speech, September 18, 1960.

Editor-writer Yaakov Kohn and John Mitchell in front of Gaslight Café, 116 MacDougal Street, being interviewed for Mike Wallace special on the beat generation, May 15, 1960.

Deane Dexter, Howard Hart, Bob Lubin, and Brigid Murnaghan with Mike Wallace TV show journalist Danny Meehan (with cigarette) in Washington Square Park, May 15, 1960.

Bob Lubin and William Morris in front of first Village Voice *office, 22 Greenwich Avenue. Cobblestones have since been removed. August 21, 1959.*

"Angel," a Brooklyn College student, was selected as the most representative "beatnik" of 1959. She is posing on MacDougal Street, June 16, 1959, in front of 1931 Chevrolet Independence wood-wheeled roadster owned by radio monologist Jean Shepherd.

Ted Wilentz's 8th Street Bookshop, corner of MacDougal Street. It opened in 1947 and lasted over thirty years.

William Morris, Bob Lubin, and Mimi Margeaux a the Gaslight Café, 116 MacDougal Street, August 21, 1959.

Washington poets making the scene on MacDougal Street. Left t right: Dick Munske, Pete Coonley, Bil Jackson, Dick Dabney, Bob Collins.

Provincetown Review *editor and poet* Bill Ward *with writer-anthologist Seymour Krim on East 10th Street, March 16, 1959.*

Ambrose Hollingsworth on MacDougal Street.

Louisiana poet Dick Woods in standard beatnik outfit on MacDougal Street, August 2, 1959.

Ted Joans in front of Café Bizarre, 106 West 3rd Street, August 25, 1959.

Rick Allmen of Café Bizarre and John Mitchell of Gaslight Café at 8th Street and Sixth Avenue, June 26, 1960.

George Preston of the Artist's Studio with writer-artists Turk La Clair and William Morris on MacDougal Street, May 3, 1959.

Rent-a-Beatnik entrepreneur Fred McDarrah on MacDougal Street being interviewed for Mike Wallace beat generation documentary by reporter Danny Meenan, April 30, 1960.

THE ANATOMY OF A BEATNIK

by Fred W. McDarrah

Saga, August 1960

Scratch a beard . . . find a Beatnik. It doesn't even make any difference whether you're actually a rabbi, a university professor, a concert musician, a real, live, honest to goodness poet, a grocery clerk or a bus driver. The beard symbol has become so strong that it doesn't matter what or who you are. If you've got a beard, you're a Beatnik.

This symbol system has become such a "thing" in this country that nobody knows what to believe any more, perhaps because nobody cares; everybody wants the fake, the phony, the spurious anyway. Here's a classic description of America's Beatnik taken from a major Negro magazine: ". . . Unwashed, bearded, free-loving, pseudo-intellectual, reefer-smoking, non-working, self-styled artists or writers living in protest of something or other."

Time magazine says Beatniks are "a pack of oddballs who celebrate booze, dope, sex and despair." The same magazine calls Allen Ginsberg "the discount-house Whitman of the Beat Generation." They also call Jack Kerouac the "latrine laureate of Hobohemia."

Time's poison pen sister, another four-letter-word magazine, was perhaps more successful in twisting the pliable minds of Americans. Last fall it published an incendiary piece called "The Only Rebellion Around." It was written by staff writer Paul O'Neil, who is apparently mixed up with fruit flies since he used the expression five times in one paragraph.

Carried away by College Composition I and II, O'Neil opened his remarkably twisted tale by saying: "If the United States today is really the biggest, sweetest and most succulent casaba ever produced by the melon patch of civilization, it would seem only reasonable to find its surface profaned—as indeed it is—by a few fruit flies. But reason would also anticipate contented fruit flies, blissful fruit flies, fruit flies raised by happy environment to the highest stages of fruit fly development. Such is not the case. The grandest casaba of all, in disconcerting fact, has incubated some of the hairiest, scrawniest and most discontented specimens of all time: The improbable rebels of the Beat Generation, who not only refuse to sample the seeping juices of American plenty and American social advances but scrape their feelers in discordant scorn of any and all who do."

The illustration of the "well-equipped pad" which accompanied the *Life* feature by O'Neil was so funny it was offensive. I happen to know the girl who posed for the photograph. I'm sure she needed the model fee. She is married to a struggling painter. Both are good people who mind their own business. Their two children are just about the most attractive kids anyone could imagine. Nevertheless, in the illustration she is pegged as "the beat chick dressed in black" surrounded by "naked light bulbs, a hot plate for warming espresso coffee pot and bean cans, a coal stove for heating baby's milk, drying chick's leotards and displaying crucifix-shaped Mexican cow bells." The real killer remark was "a beat baby, who has gone to sleep on the floor after playing with beer cans." You can imagine how that went over in Dubuque.

Gilbert Millstein of the New York *Times* told me, "We're the innocents." And I guess he's right. How incredibly innocent we must be to be not only fooled but also taken. O'Neil's *Life* article went on and on with cheap drivel, lies, phony stories, misquotes, slander and slaughter of some of my best friends. An apology for a malicious misquote between Allen Ginsberg and Dame Edith Sitwell did not appear in the magazine's Letters column until seven weeks after the original article was published.

Let me use just one more example of how this erroneous impression of the Beat Generation is perpetuated. Last winter the poetry editor of the *Saturday Review,* John Ciardi, wrote about the Beat Generation as "not only juvenile but certainly related to juvenile delinquency through a common ancestor whose best name is Disgust. The street gang rebellion has gone for blood and violence. The Beats have found their kicks in an intellectual pose, in drugs (primarily marijuana but also Benzedrine, mescaline, peyote, assorted goofballs, and occasionally heroin) and in wine, Zen, jazz, sex, and carefully mannered jargon. . . .

"The Beats wear identical uniforms. They raise nearly identical beards. . . . They practice an identical aversion to soap and water. They live in the same dingy alleys. They sit around in the same drab dives listening to the same blaring jazz with identical blanked-out expressions on their identical faces. And any one of them would sooner cut his throat than be caught doing anything 'square.' . . ."

It seems clear that the mighty U.S. press has caught on its journalistic meathook a new scapegoat, a whipping boy, a real live sucker, the so-called *Beatnik*. It doesn't matter if the facts are straight, after all, we need a little entertainment anyway. The hell with the Truth and down with the Facts. It's better to lay it on the Beatniks than to reflect too seriously on the headlines in the morning paper:

Whites Buy Out Gun Shop As Race Rift Widens in Africa . . . City to Intensify Battle on Crime . . . House Expands Inquiry into Federal Power Commission and Gas Industry . . . Child Kidnapped, Abductors Ask $100,000 . . . Militia Aids Castro in Hunt for Rebels . . . New Haven Asks Another Fare Increase . . . Mistress Stabs Wealthy Sales Executive . . .

I could go on and on. Allen Ginsberg puts it much better than I can. "Life is a nightmare for most people, who want something else. . . . People want a lesser fake of Beauty. . . . We've seen Beauty face to face, one time or another and said, 'Oh my God, of course, so that's what it's all about, no wonder I was born and had all those secret weird feelings!' Maybe it was a moment of instantaneous perfect stillness in some cow patch in the Catskills when the trees suddenly came alive like a Van Gogh painting or a Wordsworth poem. Or a minute listening to, say, Wagner on the phonograph when the music sounded as if it was getting nightmarishly sexy and alive, awful, like an elephant calling far away in the moonlight."

What Allen describes here are a few basic necessities of life, the things that make us what we are, Truth, Love and Beauty. As I see it there is very little else in the world that means anything. And this is what the real meaning of the Beat Generation is. This is what the so-called Beatnik wants. The Beat wants his life to mean something to himself. He is looking for an Order. Whether he finds it in poetry, painting, music, plumbing, carpentry, weight-lifting, selling shoes, or no matter what, he must find a meaning for his life.

He wants a hero he can genuinely believe in, not like the figure all too frequently presented today, a hero in the form of a professional soldier who won the Bronze Star and half a dozen battle stars, a soldier who carries in his wallet a souvenir photograph of a Red Chinese soldier he bayoneted.

Essentially, it's a matter of living, of awareness, of sensitivity to nature . . . that single miracle ingredient of life that is present when you stand on top of a hill and face the sunny sky and want to scream at the top of your lungs how wonderful it is to be alive.

The trouble is, most people don't have time for such luxuries of the spirit. They're too mixed up, as Jack Kerouac says, in "hustling forever for a buck among themselves . . . grabbing, taking, giving, sighing, dying, just so they could be buried in those awful cemetery cities beyond Long Island City."

In deciding what he is pursuing, Jack writes, in his fine book, *On the Road,* ". . . they danced down the streets like dingledodies, and I shambled after as I've been doing all my life after people who interest me because the only people for me are the mad ones, the ones who are mad to live, mad to talk, mad to be saved, desirous of everything at the same time, the ones who never yawn or say a commonplace thing, but burn, burn, burn like fabulous Roman candles exploding like spiders across the stars. . . ."

I talked to my friend Edwin Fancher about Beatniks and the Beat Generation as we were driving out to Brooklyn to a Methodist church where they were holding a "Convocation of Youth." The theme was "Man's Strength, Man's Distress." The program consisted of the Beat film *Pull My Daisy,* a lecture on "What Is the Beat Generation?" and a poetry reading by LeRoi Jones, the editor of *Yugen,* which is a pocket-sized literary magazine publishing many Beat writers. The lecture was to be given by Ed.

I first met Ed Fancher at a party nearly a dozen years ago on a snowy New Year's Eve. He was living in the Village and going to the New School for Social Research. He is about 36, a veteran of the war in Europe, has always worn a beard and is a practicing psychologist. Five years ago he started a weekly newspaper in Greenwich Village, *The Village Voice*. Ed's knowledge of Beatniks is solidly based on his experience and his background of being there when it all started.

Fancher says that "it is a movement of protest. The Beat looks at the world we live in, everything that is part of our way of life, including finding out what is holy. . . . They live in a world gone mad and no one cares but them. Not only is the Beat Generation interested in intellectual work, they themselves are very social people. It's an attempt to cry out that what we need is a sense of society. If it's necessary to be part of a crazy, offbeat group, all right, that's better than being detached.

"I think the Beats have achieved popularity in America because they correspond to a very deep sense of unrest in America. Americans don't want to think about the real issues of concern; they want to stick their heads in the sand and avoid anything important. They forget that the Beat Generation does confront some of these issues. Even the Beats who act nutty feel it's better to have vitality than to be dead at the core like the rest of America. Many Americans are dead at the core and don't know it. The Beats are interested in religion because they live in a society where no one is interested in it. They live in a hostile society and they are struggling to find the meaning of life outside of that dead society."

The religious theme that Ed Fancher talks about was brought up again by Howard Hart. I don't think it makes much difference that he's a Catholic. I've known Howard for about ten years, from the days when the up-and-coming literary set and the *Catholic Worker* crowd used to hang out in the White Horse Tavern and swill down steins of half 'n' half. Howard has been a drummer and has been writing poetry for a great many years. He's the same age as I and is represented in my picture book *The Beat Scene*. Howard says this about the Beat Generation:

"It's an obvious manifestation of the fact that the whole structure of American life is phony. The clothes and the manner immediately call attention to them (the Beats) because they are declaring something which is really a fact and they want to proclaim it. More than protest, there is an affirmative thing there . . . they are really looking for God . . . and after all, God is love. If they didn't have so much of a longing for God in their hearts they wouldn't come on so strong. It's a real search that gives them a kind of right to flaunt themselves even when they haven't got the talent or anything. . . ."

Bernard Scott is another who has some interesting comments to offer. Bud is 31 and is the associate minister of Judson Memorial Church in the heart of Greenwich Village. The church has an adjoining art gallery and sponsors a literary magazine called *Exodus,* which Bud edits. He says, "I always use the term Beatnik to designate a kind of part-time, imitation Bohemianism that was brought up to date with the Beat Generation. The definition of Beatniks rose out of the Beat Generation. It's really nothing more than a couple of dozen writers who helped to define what was happening to people consciously. In fact I remember when I was going to school right after the second war, I was hitchhiking across the country and I was doing a lot of things, writing poetry, staying up all night, doing all kinds of weird things. And when the Beat writers came on the scene, I found they were defining me and talking about the things I knew for the first time. They were the articulate spokesmen. I don't associate myself with the Beat Generation in an orthodox, stylistic sense any more, but I welcomed what I saw. They described experiences I knew and they were the first writers to do it.

"When you meet a Beat at a Village party he never asks you what you do because he's not interested in your economic definition. But what you do is one of the first questions you are asked on the outside. Our culture defines people in terms of their utility. The Beat wants to know what you are thinking, what's ticking inside of you, how real you are in your heart, what you've got to say, can you help me see anything, can you turn me on . . . ?"

Somewhat apart from the Beats are the Hipsters, devotees of a philosophy best expressed by Norman Mailer, the author of *The Naked and the Dead.*

I see Norman around the *Village Voice* newspaper office quite a bit since he was one of the paper's founders, and I frequently run into him at parties. At one party I heard him being interviewed for a Monitor radio broadcast so his comments on Hip were abbreviated:

"I would say that Beat is more idyllic than Hip; it assumes that finally all you have to do is relax and find yourself and you'll find peace and honesty with it. Hip assumes that the danger of the modern world is that whenever anyone relaxes that is precisely the moment when he is ambushed. So, Hip is more a philosophy of ambition, less destructive of convention than Beat. There is more respect for the accretion of human values. As an example, manners are important in Hip; the Beats say all manners are square. . . . The Beat writers seem to be getting better, more exciting. It may become a very powerful force in our literature. I think the Beat has opened the way to more excitement in our lives. . . ."

Another statement of the Hipster philosophy comes from Ted Joans, the 31-year-old poet and one of the more interesting characters living in Greenwich Village. He says, "I'm a hipster. I'm concerned with the moral revolution in America; revolution through peace and love; we're the richest people in the world and yet we don't have truth and love. It's not what's up front that counts, it's what's in your heart and brain. There is nothing wrong with material possessions. But you should use them and not let them use you. I think everybody wants to conform, but the future of the world lies in the hands of the nonconformists . . ."

It's difficult for me to remember when I first ran into Mimi Margeaux. Maybe it was at a party, perhaps in a coffee shop. I might have even been formally introduced to her, as unlikely as it sounds. Mimi is 25. She is a beautiful girl, with thousands of friends, has traveled on the road frequently between her home in Chicago and San Francisco, New York, Mexico City, a thousand places. Mimi has been associated with the Beat movement for a long time. She knows all the poets, the painters and all the rest. I was walking down MacDougal Street one day when I met her and asked if she would join me in a beer in the Kettle of Fish, one of the Village's staple Beat haunts. Her conversation was characteristically candid: "There really are two kinds of Beats, people like [Kenneth] Patchen, the jazz musicians, [Norman] Mailer, Jack [Kerouac], Allen [Ginsberg], they're really Hipsters. The Beatniks are younger kids who are taking advantage of the trend. They don't know what they're rebelling against. They just can't get along with their parents so they run away from home.

"I would say I'm a Hipster, but people think I'm a Beatnik.

"The longest I've held a job is about six months. In fact my whole working career is only about a year. Most of the time I've lived from saved money, unemployment, living at home, living with friends, and I was married . . . I get along."

Then there is John Mitchell, who has a coffee shop called The Gaslight, right next door to the Kettle. For a couple of years The Gaslight has been sponsoring Beat poets reading from their work. Just about every poet in New York has read there at one time or another, and the shop has gained a national reputation. Recently Mitchell published an anthology of poetry called *The Gaslight Review* which included the work of most of the poets who have read there. John is in his early 30s and is very well informed about the Beat Generation since he has lived in the Village for years and is right in the center of all the activity.

"I've been accused of being a Beatnik," he says. "Maybe it's the way I dress. Maybe I act peculiar and people become hysterical and anything that looks different to them is a Beatnik. Being Beat is really an attitude. I sympathize with these young people. I was raised during the Depression and I can have more fun with five cents than these kids can have with fifty dollars.

"With The Bomb and all, I don't blame these kids for flipping. They're rejecting the incredible mess that the adults have created in the world. Every time you pick up a newspaper you find another corrupt government official exposed. To quote Frank Lloyd Wright, this country went from barbarism to decadence without a period of culture in between. I think the Beat protest is a healthy thing.

"There is a difference between the Bohemians of twelve years ago and the Beats. Five years ago people who came here were rejecting society but they weren't raising hell; they were dejected and defeated. The old-time Bohemians were really beaten down by society. These kids haven't given up. It's a much healthier movement. The Beats aren't a formal movement but they know what they don't want. They don't want cold wars, hot wars, military service, all the rest. One of the things they reject is a political party in a group. Some good will come from all this. It's a healthy thing and a lot of people are involved. The American people put them down because they're afraid that they don't want change and these [Beats] might change their ways. The last big thing in this country like the Beat Movement was the marches on Washington during the Depression. This movement will be stronger."

I also talked to Jack Micheline, a poet, who is associated with the Beat Movement. Jack is in his early 30s and has put in his time on the road, so to speak. I'd call Jack a loner. He has a lot of friends but he pretty much sticks to himself and his writing, which is a spontaneous, brick-and-mortar, concrete, big-city type of writing.

"I want to get away from politics," Jack said. "I might have been politically active but it's all corrupt. I want to see better things happen that would help this country. I think the Beat is growing in all the arts. I've been told that the vitality of my work is identified with the Beat Generation. I'm anti-materialistic, the way I live, the way I feel, the way I think. I have no interest in becoming a millionaire. I'm interested in growing as a writer. Aside from my work I'm interested in girls.

"The Beat Generation is a way of life. All my life I've been rebelling against something or other. The reason for my rebellion is that I want to be able to be what I want, do what I want, without being restricted. I fight to remain myself. If my life means anything to me it has nothing to do with Beatniks. I've met a lot of people who weren't Beat who taught me a lot, who showed me things. A Beatnik is somebody running away from himself. Today they dress up in old clothes and hang around coffee houses. In the 1930s they joined the Communist Party. A Beatnik is the first stage of rebellion against society. Perhaps there will be an overthrow of the old order and not everything will be keyed to the machine age. You might say this is a rebellion against escalators."

The Beat Generation was practically founded in the East Harlem apartment of Mary Nichols, a 33-year-old mother of two children. Mary now lives in the Village and is a newspaper reporter and very active in politics. "I was a little girl out of Swarthmore College in those days," she says, "and I was terrified by that *Go* bunch, Clellon Holmes, Louis Simpson, Allen Ginsberg, all the rest. I moved to the Village to get away from all those Bohemians. Of course, they didn't have a name then. Everybody smoking pot, inviting me to wild parties, and I thought, my goodness, they are an amoral group.

"I'm not a Beatnik but I think I understand some of them. I'm really quite bourgeois myself. But if someone accused me of being bourgeois, I might say I was Beat. I don't care for labels. I suppose the way I'm living is Beat, but I'm not satisfied with it. In my wildest dreams I want to die in the Saint Regis Hotel.

"It's a question of anxiety, I think, that produces the Beat Generation. It may be an anxiety for order and security, which is a funny thing to say about them, but they want a security that's more cosmic than what the average square wants. . . . Beatniks are really very political in a strange way. I think there is a relation between their rejection of politics and their concern over the H-Bomb. You can't reject something unless you're involved in it.

"I think the security the Beat person wants is knowing that he's not going to be annihilated in the next ten years. When I really think about it I think it's possible that the human race will be destroyed in my lifetime. Perhaps that's why I always look so happy. There may be so little time, it doesn't seem worth being any other way."

Ted Joans's birthday party, painter Larry Poons, far right, July 25, 1959,

Poet John Brent, left, painter and manager of Epitome Café, Larry Poons and Joe Bolero, with toilet seat around his neck, at Ted Joans's beatnik birthday party, July 25, 1959. Brent's definitive poem "Bibleland" was published by John Mitchell.

Ted Joans's beatnik birthday party, St. Mark's Place, July 25, 1959. Sculptor Jackie Ferrara (gingham dress, left), earthworks artist Robert Smithson (in striped sport shirt), filmmaker Robert Frank (center) in white shirt and tie.

Ted Joans, striped shirt, at his beatnik birthday party given in his storefront railroad flat on St. Mark's Place, July 25, 1959. Dan List in straw hat to his left, earthworks artist Robert Smithson, painter Gene Kates, dancing in center.

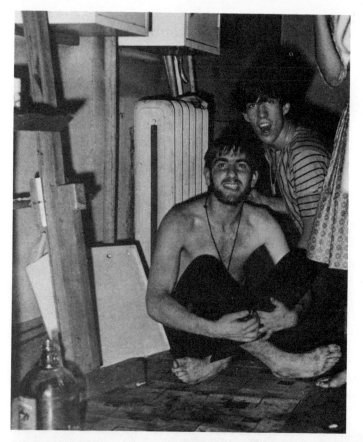

Bob Lubin and Steve Mildworf at Ted Joans's birthday party, July 25, 1959.

A beatnik party staged by Holiday magazine and photographed May 24, 1959, by Burt Glinn in painter Maurice Bugeaud's waterfront loft for benefit of Holiday article. Banjo, Danny Barker; clarinet, Ken Davern; bass, Ahmad Abdul-Malik; trumpet, Walter Bowe; trombone, Ephram Resnick.

Bob Sauers, Adele Mailer, Norman Mailer, and art dealer Carroll Janis at artist Steve Montgomery's loft for benefit of the March Gallery, 95 East 10th Street, April 4, 1959.

Paul Cummings with Exodus art editor Marc Ratliff, and poetry editor Howard Hart at a party for the first edition of the magazine, May 8, 1959.

Seymour Krim at a Judson Gallery party for Exodus *magazine, November 13, 1959.*

LeRoi Jones, Allen Ginsberg, anthologist Donald Allen, and Larry Ferlinghetti, at Ted Wilentz's party, October 9, 1959.

Herbert Gold and Jack Micheline at party given by publisher and 8th Street Bookshop owner Ted Wilentz, September 17, 1960.

Artist Edward Clark (rear), William Morris, in center with cigarette, Howard Smith (beard), A. B. Spellman, and Jim Spicer of the Living Theatre (rear, white shirt) at Ted Wilentz's party, October 9, 1959, 72 West 8th Street.

Jack Micheline, dancer/choreographer Cynthia Fancher, her Village Voice publisher brother Edwin Francher, David McReynolds, and Allen Ginsberg at a party given by Ted Wilentz for Ferlinghetti, October 9, 1959.

Publisher and bookstore owner T Wilentz with Allen Ginsberg at 38 We 8th Street, September 17, 196

LeRoi Jones, Maric Zazeela, A. B. Spellman, and Ray Bremser viewing th new Bremser baby Rachel, at party given by Ted Wilentz, September 17, 1960.

Sylvia Topp and Tuli Kupferberg at Bridgit Murnaghan's party, 772 Eighth Avenue, October 3, 1959.

YOUTH "DISAFFILIATED" FROM A PHONY WORLD

by David McReynolds

Village Voice, March 11, 1959

Discussions of the beat generation remind me very much of blind men trying to tell what an elephant is like. This is so because on the one hand so many of those discussing the beat generation really don't know what they are talking about, and on the other because the beat generation itself is a very complex animal. It is a generation which consists of jazz festivals, Zen Buddhism, peyote, a return to Catholicism, early marriage, no marriage, marijuana, street gangs, poetry, and general confusion. It is therefore both a safe and a dangerous subject to treat with. Safe in that anything you say will be partly true, and dangerous in that anything you say will be correctly termed an oversimplification.

To make my job easier I am limiting my comments to what might be called the "jazz-poetry section" of the beat generation.

The beat generation has withdrawn itself from organized society. Its drive is not a revolutionary drive toward a new society but simply a rebellious break from the existing society, a drive to discover personal reality and meaning outside of a social framework which the hipster finds unreal and meaningless. Mort Sahl, for example, devastates the existing social system with almost every word he speaks. The man is dynamite. But all he is really saying is NO. The disturbing thing about this younger generation is its refusal to even try changing the world—i.e., the world is phony and politics is a drag.

There are three reasons that help account for a generation of youth who have "disaffiliated" from society.

First is the Bomb. Young people all over the world are born and grow up knowing there may be no tomorrow. Not simply no "personal tomorrow," but no tomorrow for the human race. The last act is almost over, the curtain is about to come down, the play wasn't very good anyway, and now the younger spectators are getting restless in their seats. A recent poll of teenagers, being asked what they thought caused juvenile delinquency, turned up the fact that almost half felt the "world situation" was one reason—a feeling perfectly expressed by a young girl who said: "After all, the kids feel they have nothing to lose. We'll all be blown to bits anyway." We train our school children to hide under desks and flatten against walls in simulated bomb attacks, and then wonder that they lack a sense of social responsibility when they get a little older. Kids are too wise. Only adults—and only government officials at that—are foolish enough to believe in Civil Defense. The kids know better.

The second factor is that youth today emerges into a society that is in a state of profound and ceaseless change. This is the age of technology and the human race hasn't even begun to adjust to it.

The old patterns of culture, of family relationships, of regional ties—all are loosened or swept away.

Outside of our immediate circle of friends there is no real sense of community. Our relations with others fire a constantly shifting series of impersonal contacts. Things are too big or too far away. Politics is something in the New York *Times* or Washington, D.C. We are in a crowd in which no one is going anywhere in relation to anyone else. We do not know one another, our faces having become shifting masks and abstract shadows. Youth feels alienated from contemporary society. They emerge into it without being able to identify with it. In that same survey on juvenile delinquency, one student said: "We live in the world, yet we have no say as to what should or shouldn't happen."

The third factor is that in the midst of all this tremendous change in the social framework, we have lost our sense of moral values which might possibly have sustained us in a period of such profound upheaval. Both the U.S. and Soviet Russia are led by power groups which are patently dishonest, and every bright high-school student knows this. The "free world" of John Foster Dulles includes Franco, Chiang, Rhee,

Trujillo—and until very recently Batista and Jiménez. The "people's democracy" of the Communist bloc is a morbid farce underlined with the blood of tens of thousands of Hungarian workers.

Nor is this all. Students who know history begin to feel that the present governments don't even allow a decent interval between lies. For example, Russia was viewed as a brutal dictatorship until 1942, at which point Franklin Delano Roosevelt and Henry Luce discovered it was a democracy—a fact of which the Russian people were themselves totally unaware—and it remained a democracy until 1945, when it suddenly reverted to a dictatorship. On the other hand, Germany and Japan were, in 1945, so morally depraved that we vowed to reduce Germany to a land of farmers and wrote into the Japanese constitution a clause against Japan's ever having an army again. By 1950 our government was pleased to report that the Germans and Japanese had undergone a most wondrous spiritual transformation—they had not only become democratic but were now so peace-loving that we insisted they re-arm (over the vigorous protests, let it be noted, of the majority of both the German and Japanese public). On the Communist side of the fence we have Marshal Tito undergoing the fascinating metamorphosis from hero to counter-revolutionary to hero to deviationist.

These points simply illustrate the basic issue. In the nineteenth century we had substituted for faith in God a faith in the inherent goodness and rationality of man. This faith was mortally wounded by World War I, and then buried by the senseless murder of millions of Jews under Hitler and by the bloody miscarriage of the Russian Revolution. Having lost faith in God, we now lost faith in ourselves. Lacking any moral absolutes, we drift about in a tepid sea of "relative values." Youth is again wiser than adults—they know too well that a set of "relative values" which not only permits and tolerates but demands the building of hydrogen bombs is not a set of values at all, but a rationale for insanity.

The hipster is desperate to find some meaning in life. The social framework does not offer this meaning—he must conduct the search for real values on his own. The "future" having no meaning as a concept in a world preparing for suicide, the hipster can only define reality by actions in the present—by a series of personal and direct experiences. Seen thus, peyote, marijuana, and the series of disjointed and seemingly irresponsible actions of the beat generation take on a new meaning, for these actions are all part of the search for reality, all part of the effort to engage in conscious personal actions in a world where conscious personal actions become increasingly difficult. The only "real" reality for the hipster is the cool scene, the cool sound, and the ability to be aware of oneself and to prove one's existence by personal actions.

In a recent issue of the *Voice*, James Wechsler was appalled by the "flight and irresponsibility" of the beat generation. However in point of fact it is Kerouac and Ginsberg who are operating at the deeper level of reality. When Wechsler complained that life is complicated enough without turning it into a poem, the answer of the beat generation is that unless we can turn human life into a poem it has no meaning, no value. As Kenneth Patchen put it: "Gentle and loving, all else is treason." The beat generation has a better "sense of the times"—their fear of war is not an abstract fear of eventual conflict. It is an immediate concern, expressed by Lawrence Ferlinghetti, about "any stray asinine action by any stray asinine second lieutenant pressing any strange button anywhere far away over an arctic ocean thus illuminating the world once and for all."

But what meaning does the beat generation have for those of us who are not beat, who are politically involved, who conceive of a future and have faith in the ability of the human race to evolve beyond mass murder? And what of the beat generation itself—where is it going?

Taking the last question first I have a strong feeling that no sensitive person can remain sane if he believes in nothing but himself, his own immediate experiences and sensations. These members of the beat generation who as a consequence of rejecting the existing social system remain turned in upon themselves must ultimately become religious or go mad. Without a sense of values of some kind, life becomes impossible. This accounts, I think, for the surge of interest in the cult of Zen, and the attempt through religion to find meaning in life.

However, other members of the beat generation are taking a different and healthier direction. Some who began as rebels seem to evolve slowly into writers who want to do more than protest—who want to *change* society. There is an awareness that one can find an existential meaning to life through involvement in social struggle; a realization that even if "the issue is in doubt" regarding man's fate, the struggle itself has meaning.

The writers and poets of the beat generation begin to make political sounds. In Ferlinghetti's recent poem, "tentative description of a dinner to promote the impeachment of president eisenhower," there is a warning that even the hipster is about to leave the coffee table and engage himself in the task of changing the social order—particularly in the following lines: *And some men also despaired and sat down in Bohemia and were too busy to come/ But other men came whose only political action during the past twenty years had been to flush a protesting toilet and run/ And those came who had never marched in sports car protest parades and those came who had never been arrested for sailing a protesting Golden Rule in unpacific oceans.*

The beat generation itself may not be able to play a direct or responsible role in politics. For all the sophistication of its members, they are naive in political terms, too easily equating the necessary compromise of political action with the unnecessary betrayal of moral values which they sense so deeply in the present situation.

But the beat generation by its very existence serves notice on all of us who are political that if we want to involve youth in politics we must develop a politics of action. The beat generation can understand Gandhi much better than they can understand Roosevelt. They can understand Martin Luther King much better than they can understand Hubert Humphrey. They can understand the Hungarian workers much better than they can understand Mikoyan.

The beat generation is not yet political, but it knows what many of us who are political do not know—that neither the liberal nor the radical movements have any significance for human values if we do not learn to base our politics on the individual human being. The future has hope and meaning only if we learn to act with integrity in the present.

Artist's Club New Year's Eve party, 1958. Ginsberg, center rear; Tamara Bliss dancing with Village Voice co-founder John Wilcock, foreground; artist Robert Delford Brown, right.

A panel discussion held at the Artist's Club, 73 Fourth Avenue, on February 13, 1959. Subject was "A Little Room for Feeling, Symbolism, and Meaning in Abstract Art." From left to right: Daniel Schneider, Allen Ginsberg, Hubert Crehan (moderator), Sonia Gechtoff, Peter Selz, John Ferren.

Ginsberg and Corso after a panel discussion at the Artist's Club, February 15, 1959.

Jack Kerouac takes over the drums at the Artist's Club New Year's Eve party, 1958.

Neddie Jones (co-editor of Yugen with husband eRoi Jones) and Joyce Glassman (later ohnson) at Artist's Club, March 10, 1960. Glassman's experience with Kerouac was ublished under the title Minor Characters by Houghton Mifflin in 1983.

Kerouac's longtime friend Stanley Twardowicz with concert pianist Tamara Bliss at the Artist's Club Jazz Party, May 22, 195

Paddy Chayefsky, Seymour Krim, and Ted Joans at Artist's Club Jazz Party, May 22, 1959.

WHERE IS THE BEAT GENERATION GOING?

by Norman Podhoretz

Esquire, December 1958

Americans are very fond of rebels, at least at a distance and provided they aren't too subversive, so it was probably to be expected that the Beat Generation would become the object of a lot of journalistic ballyhoo. In the last year or two, Jack Kerouac, Allen Ginsberg & Co. have been more intensively interviewed ("Tell us, Jack, why do you hate the suburbs?"), more glamorously photographed (always looking spiritual as hell, of course), and more earnestly analyzed ("In this Age of Conformity when the Individual is Crushed . . .") than all the Lost Generation writers put together. They have been advertised as the spokesmen for all the hipsters, all the junkies and all the juvenile delinquents in America—as though it were some kind of special virtue to speak for a vicious tendency. They have also been related to the Angry Young Men in England, to the loosely connected group of under-thirty artists (made up of the novelist Françoise Sagan, the painter Bernard Buffet, and the director Roger Vadim) in France, as the American branch of an international movement of Youth rising up to protest against the Conformity, Collectivism, and Despair of the postwar years. Almost everything, in fact, has been done with the Beat Generation except to ask what its existence reveals about the state of our culture and what the pernicious spread of hipsterism, juvenile violence, and drug addiction among the young can be expected to lead to. In England and France, where the literary rebels have no Teddy-boy nonsense in them, no taste for violence and criminality, no *mystique* of "free," instinctual self-expression and where they are fighting not against civilization but against a strong traditional social and cultural order, the situation (both in life and literature) is not so alarming. But in America, we are witnessing a revolt of all the forces hostile to civilization itself—a movement of brute stupidity and know-nothingism that is trying to take over the country from a middle class which is supposed to be the guardian of civilization but which has practically dislocated its shoulder in its eagerness to throw in the towel.

There isn't any question, I think, that the rebels in America, England, and France are products of a similar mood, but we can't begin to understand what in fact has been happening throughout the world until we look behind the slogans that have been flying so noisily through the air since Allen Ginsberg's *Howl* brought the Beat Generation into public view. The best way to begin is to ask what attitudes the Beat boys, the Angry Young Men, and the French group have in common, and since it is in literature rather than music or painting or the movies that these attitudes are most explicitly expressed, the best place to look is in the books they have produced. Probably the most general thing we can say is that they show very little interest in, and want as little as possible to do with, the public world—the world of politics, social problems, and large-scale action. Where the Cold War is concerned, for instance, they tend to be apathetic and resigned, or to take a more or less pacifist position. "Go f—— yourself with your atom bomb," shouts Allen Ginsberg in a poem addressed to America. John Osborne, both in his plays and in an essay he contributed to the symposium of Angry Young Men called *Declaration,* denounces Britain's hydrogen tests without so much as considering whether they may be a hideous political necessity. Kingsley Amis, whose first novel *Lucky Jim* has become the classic source-book of the Angries, stigmatizes devotion to anything other than self-interest in politics as "romantic," and says that intellectuals have no interests as a class and therefore no "respectable" motive for being politically active. And Françoise Sagan—in sharp contrast to all the older French writers—never even glances sideways at the political turmoils of her time.

What the young rebels mainly care about is the private life—love, personal relations, problems of the self. The same

emphasis on love and the same attribution of supreme importance to personal relations mark every word written by Kerouac, Ginsberg, & Co., and love is, of course, the only subject
that Françoise Sagan ever bothers with. For her, the alternatives seem to be ennui or a grand passion, and for Jack Kerouac it is always a choice between boredom and kicks. A kick is
anything that stimulates sensation and therefore enables you
to get into contact with others. The great thing is contact, communication, intimacy, sex, and let the rest of the world go by,
preferably at ninety miles an hour.

It's easy enough to understand why this mood of retrench-
ment, this impulse to shrink back into oneself, this feeling that
any involvement in the affairs of the great world is bound to
corrupt a decent man, should have become so powerful in the
writing of young people everywhere. In itself it is a perfectly
sensible reaction to a political stalemate on the international
front and the absence of any deep social disturbances on the
domestic scene. Being apathetic about the Cold War is to admit
that you have a sense of utter helplessness in the face of forces
apparently beyond the control of man—for all we know the
guided missiles will start firing themselves one of these days of
their own malignant volition and save our governments the
trouble of declaring war. And it is both reasonable and justifia-
ble to feel that there is no point in getting overly ambitious and
competitive in a world where the possibility for great careers in
the old style is so severely limited by the Welfare State or the
American Organization, and where action on a heroic scale has
become inconceivable and even a little ridiculous ("I suppose
people of our generation aren't able to die for good causes any
longer," says Jimmy Porter, the hero of Osborne's play, *Look
Back in Anger.* "If the big bang does come, and we all get killed
off, it won't be in aid of the old-fashioned, grand design. It'll
just be for the Brave New-nothing-very-much-thank-you").

This increasing apathy was forecast by the writers of the so-
called "Silent Generation," who were supposed to be the con-
formists but who have expressed pretty much the same impulse
to wash their hands of the world of affairs and to concentrate
on love, friendship and self. The novels and poems of the "Si-
lents" exhibit the same indifference to politics and society, the
same bias against ambitiousness and competition, the same in-

clusive concern with personal relations and love. And to make matters still more curious, the sociologists tell us that, for the same reasons, even the junior executives in industry these days suppress the urge to go after power and wealth, settling instead for modest careers that do not engage their deepest responses and giving themselves over whole hog to problems of marriage and family. In what sense, then, are the rebels rebellious? What are they protesting against? What do they stand for? And most important, what do they mean for the future?

At this point we have to look more closely at the particular situation in each of the three countries under discussion. France presents the interesting case of a society in a state of unprecedented economic boom that continues to produce an art of despair and bitterness. There is the "nausea" of Sartre's work, the deserts and plagues that dominate Camus' fiction, the grim, emaciated figures of Buffet's paintings, the stark amoralism of Sagan's novels. There are, too, Vadim's movies in which his former wife Brigitte Bardot often stars and in which she has become the very incarnation of unbridled sexuality and the attempt to intensify every passing moment by a pursuit of pleasure without regard for consequences. (Incidentally, one of those rare moments of symbolic history was made some months ago when Bardot offered to act as godmother to Vadim's illegitimate daughter by another woman a day after her divorce from him became final.) But the melancholy of the older writers should be distinguished from the mood of the younger group. In the bitterness of Sartre, Camus, Simone de Beauvoir, and others of their generation we can detect a reaction to the cultural decline of France since World War II, the loss of its age-old position as the leader of Western civilization—a reaction so powerful that it remains unaffected by the new optimism of the general population. And here we have the link between the Sagan-Buffet-Vadim group and the economic boom. One of the main effects of this modernization of France's economy has been to create a mass of young people who have grown up in an atmosphere very unlike the curious combination of national self-esteem and wartime demoralization of their elders, and who, as one observer has put it, are "almost un-French" in their interest in technology and their indifference to the ideological passions of their parents. The young generation, that is, has been "Americanized," and not only because it cares more about machines and technology than witty conversation and a glorious national destiny. Along with this modernization of the economy, a mass popular culture similar to our own and perhaps based on it has begun to emerge—cars, jazz, movies, picture magazines, and the like. If Françoise Sagan and her circle are rebels, it is in the sense that they participate in and support this invasion of French life and culture by a kind of Americanizing spirit. Sagan's novels, in fact, are full of the feeling that traditional French education is irrelevant—Bergson is a bore because as a philosopher he demands close attention and mental discipline, Stendhal is someone once read in school, intellectual discourse is tiresome.

Actually England too is involved in a process of Americanization, but the causes are social and cultural rather than economic. As a result of legislation passed by the Labor Government after 1944 which opened the doors of the universities to more and more children of the lower classes, the upper-class monopoly on education has been broken, and a new type of Englishman (born in the provinces, raised in a relatively poor milieu, educated, if he was bright enough to win a scholarship, at Oxford or Cambridge or one of the "red-brick" universities, and typically holding down a job as a teacher or a librarian somewhere in the Midlands) has come into prominence and begun to demand his cultural rights. The Angry Young Men are either of this class themselves or spokesmen for it. In general, they welcome the forces that are turning England into an egalitarian society, and they have directed their wrath against the upholders of the established culture, who are known simply as "The Establishment." The Establishment includes the rich and fashionable who live in Mayfair and make the rounds of Epsom and Ascot: the graduates of the old public schools like Eton and Harrow and Oxford and Cambridge, the people who control the BBC, *The Times,* and *The Observer.* In the style and tone of The Establishment, the Angry Young Men hear the voice and see the values of an obsolete ruling class, the class that proved its bankruptcy in the Suez fiasco of 1956. When John Osborne denounces the "posh" Sunday papers, or when Kingsley Amis sneers at "filthy Mozart" and T. S. Eliot says that he would be happiest if the low-brow picture magazines could come out "once an hour instead of once or twice a week, without impairing the rigor of their standards," we know that they are attacking the effete highbrows of The Establishment in the name of something more honest, more vigorous, and more masculine in British life.

The Establishment more or less dismisses America and Americans as vulgar, but John Osborne and Kenneth Tynan are forever praising American movies and plays and books (whose excellence, they seem to think, is America's reward for believing in equality), and Kingsley Amis intimates that his real interests in life are "films, drinking, women's breasts, American novels, jazz, science fiction."

But here again, as in France, the pull of the established culture is strong enough to keep the rebels from flying off into space. Amis, for instance, stays strictly within the main tradition of English social comedy; even his theme—the rise of a new class into "polite society"—is the theme of much eighteenth-century English fiction which was preoccupied with the effects of the growing power of the *bourgeoisie* as against the aristocracy. The point to remember about Lucky Jim Dixon is that he has a pathetic desire to make it in a world where Mozart and T. S. Eliot and elegant manners are necessary, and because he really is an intellectual himself, we can imagine him, ten years after the novel closes, beginning to sneak off into a secret room where he can listen to records of *Don Giovanni* without being exposed to the charge of artiness and affectation from one of his drinking buddies in the pub down the road. As for John Wain, he was attacked not long ago by the Angry movie-director Lindsay Anderson for saying that The Establishment, after all, has the virtue of having acted as a bulwark against the corruptions of "the entertainment industry and the cheap press." "At this rate," Anderson comments, "he will soon be writing speeches for the Queen."

THE REBELS: RULES ARE NOT THEIR VIRTUE

If the rebels in France and England both represent and stand for the "Americanization" of their native countries and are critics of the traditional social and cultural order, what about the Beat Generation? Does it represent and stand for anything comparable over here? Only, I think, superficially. Like the Angry Young Men, who are attacking the kind of airy-fairy gentility that passes for cultivation in The Establishment and who are asserting that there is nothing "crude" or "vulgar" about the tone and attitudes of provincial lower-class life, the Beat boys have turned their fire on the standards and style of the educated American middle class and they have claimed to be introducing a new vigor, based on the language and experience of the mass of the people. To some extent, it would be accurate to say that the San Francisco writers represent an attempt to challenge the cultural dominance of the big cities (or, rather, of New York) and the major universities. But what is the challenge founded on? Who are the grass-roots constituents of the movement? What social forces are being expressed in Kerouac's novels, in Ginsberg's and Philip Lamantia's and Lawrence Ferlinghetti's poems? The answer they themselves would probably give is: all the economic failures (poor farmers, bums, vagrants, and the lumpen of the cities), all the victims of social injustice (colored people and people who can't find work), and especially the suffering adolescent, the juvenile delinquent, and the hipster. As usual in such movements, the underprivileged, the dispossessed, and the snubbed—the types who haven't for one reason or another been able to make it in the world—are declared to be the source and fountainhead of all things good and true, including (in this particular case) culture itself. Do the outcasts and the adolescents have trouble in articulating their feelings and ideas? This must mean that there is something wrong with the power of articulation; to speak and think coherently isn't "true" intellectuality but "pretentiousness"; "true" intellectuality is in the soul and since the outcasts and the adolescents are considered in our culture to have greater purity of soul than the so-called intellectuals, they must be the "true" intellectuals. Or again—does the stuff Kerouac writes seem to you careless, confused, and chaotic? This must mean that you are a conformist, upholding the standards and values of those creeps who (in Ginsberg's image) are burning to death in their gray flannel suits on Madison Avenue. The Beat Generation writers, it seems, are trying to redefine culture so as to include themselves in. You can't criticize their work by calling it careless and confused, banal and aesthetically undernourished, because they don't admit that coherence and careful thought and precision are virtues. They are like a baseball team that has no hitters and therefore insists on changing the rules so that to swing at the ball three times and miss will be scored as a home run.

THEIR LINE IS ZIGZAG,
BUT THEY CAN THROW A CURVE

Listen to Jack Kerouac's prose:

"I was coming down the street with Larry O'Hara old drinking buddy of mine from all the times in San Francisco in my long and nervous and mad careers I've gotten drunk and in fact cadged drinks off friends with such 'genial' regularity nobody really cared to notice or announced that I am developing or was developing, in my youth, such bad freeloading habits though of course they did notice but liked me and as Sam said 'Everybody comes to you for your gasoline boy, that's some filling station you got there' or say words to that effect—old Larry O'Hara always nice to me, a crazy Irish young businessman of San Francisco with Balzacian backroom in his bookstore where they'd smoke tea and talk of the old days of the great Basie band or the days of the great Chu Berry—of whom more anon since she got involved with him too as she had to get involved with everyone because of knowing me who am nervous and many leveled and not in the least one-souled—not a piece of my pain has showed yet—or suffering—Angels, bear with me—"

And so on and on for another twelve lines until the sentence ends. You certainly need the patience of an angel to "bear with" this prose. Not only does it fail to "break through" into new vitality, but it is a style a thousand times more "literary" and derivative and academic than the writing produced by the most anemic instructors of English in our colleges. It is an inept imitation of Faulkner and Joyce done by a man who thinks that to be a Faulkner or a Joyce all you have to do is sit back and pour out anything that pops into your head—and the more mixed-up the better.

But the Beat Generation is a significant phenomenon for all that, and it can't be disposed of by showing up its literary fakery or even by pointing out that its "protest" finally comes to nothing because it stems from nothing and leads to nothing (except perhaps the irresponsible Western interpretation of Zen Buddhism). There *is* meaning in the fact that these writers have attracted so much attention. The San Francisco "renaissance" and the spread during the last few years of hipsterism, juvenile delinquency, and drug addiction among the young arise from the same central cause: the flabbiness and spinelessness of contemporary American middle-class culture. What I mean by middle-class culture here is not only the books written by respectable people and for respectable people, but the way of life, the values, and the attitudes shared by the majority of college-educated Americans. For all practical purposes, this is the class that runs America, just as surely as the aristocracy ran France before the revolution of 1789: it controls industry, dominates the best universities, and has a monopoly on the professions, and because it is a prosperous group, it also embodies the American notion of how to be "high class." Anyone moving up in American society has to learn how to fit into this group: he has to like Martinis (very dry), he has to be interested in (but not too earnest about) good books, good music, serious ideas. Most sociologists agree that this class is largely liberal and "enlightened" in its view of the world. On the whole, it tends to believe in reason and science as opposed to preserving the *status quo;* unlike the lower-middle and working classes, it sets great store by civil liberties and "Internationalism"; it is indifferent or even hostile to religion; it favors greater freedom in sexual matters than the older middle class did (in principle it has nothing against premarital affairs for men or women, and though its members get jealous like anyone else, most tolerate the idea of infidelity in marriage or at least don't absolutely condemn adultery, and of course they have a much higher rate of divorce).

When I say that middle-class culture is flabby and spineless, I mean that it has grown defensive and timid about its (liberal and "enlightened") values and has therefore proved unable to assert its authority over the young. The causes are too complex to go into here, but we can see the kind of timidity I am talking about almost anywhere we look. Take the much-publicized religious revival, for example. What has actually been revived is not piety and spirituality (even most clergymen are willing to admit that), but the influence of the anti-secularist forces in our society who were temporarily routed during the Thirties and Forties.

HOWLING AT RANDOM

Today we inhabit a society where parents are only too happy to let the children "decide for themselves" because they don't have enough faith in the soundness of the principles and values that are the driving force of their own way of life—I mean their *real* principles and values, not the pieties they mouth. And what has come along to fill this power vacuum? Only the conservative drivel that the fears and insecurities of the Cold War period have dredged up again—the slogans of rugged economic individualism preached incessantly by politicians and propagandists who themselves know perfectly well that the day of rugged individualism is long since gone; the pretense that we are a pious, God-fearing nation, when every ten-year-old recognizes that religion plays about as important a role in the actual way of life of this country as the regulations of medieval chivalry; worst of all, perhaps, the insidious attempts by clerics in psychiatric clothing to make the freer sexual mores of a whole population seem disreputable and unhealthy by calling them "immaturity." Does anyone expect the obsolete morality—disguised or not—of the new Victorians who have come to the fore in the Eisenhower era to impress a creature even so impressionable as a child? We are not so different, really, from those Englishmen who go around pretending (in Lindsay Anderson's phrase) that "it's *Great* Britain" still, or who (as John Osborne describes it) suggest that "fatuity, so long as it is hallowed by tradition, is acceptable and admirable." No wonder that young writers everywhere and of every stripe are so obsessed with hypocrisy and so sure that to be an adult is to be a phony. The combination of hypocrisy with a paralysis of parental authority is beautifully contrived to turn the children loose to make their own rules. And the rules they make are invariably the rules of the street.

The disobedience of a child with a weak father often takes the form of a tantrum, an explosion of undirected, incoherent, inarticulate rage and aggression. This, plus the need to organize the world by setting up authoritative standards in the absence of any provided by adults, is what much juvenile delinquency amounts to. And what juvenile delinquency is to life, the San Francisco writers are to literature—howling at random against they don't know what and making up aesthetic rules of their own that are a rough equivalent in literary terms of the rules of the street gang, where control and discipline are "chicken," and subtle or complicated ideas are a lot of bull. Exactly the opposite is true of England, where The Establishment plays the role of a very strong parent indeed, and where the young rebels are forced to *argue,* rationally and passionately, instead of simply whining and then being patted on the head.

Where will it all end?

The pall of conservatism and hypocrisy that has been hanging over America for the past decade can only get blacker and fouler in the next few years, and the liberal middle class will probably react by sticking its head deeper into the sand and by growing mushier and globbier by the hour. This means that American youth will persist in believing that the only two alternatives in life are Zen Buddhism and drug addiction on the one hand, and wholesome suburban boredom on the other. We already have some of the results before our eyes, and anyone who isn't screaming in horror at them deserves what he gets— which will be plenty. The main result so far has been the development of what Robert Brustein (one of the few effective screamers-in-horror around) has called "America's new culture hero." This hero appears in many guises: he is the brutal Stanley Kowalski in Tennessee Williams' *A Streetcar Named Desire,* whose vicious animality and mindlessness (especially as Marlon Brando played the role) have become the image of masculinity and—God help us—sensitivity for the rank-and-file of the Beat Generation; he is also Jimmy Dean, whose inability to speak is taken as the mark of spiritual superiority, just as inarticulateness in Jack Kerouac is proof positive of saintliness and virtue; and he can be heard in the orgiastic mumblings of every Elvis Presley record ever made. All these phenomena, to quote Brustein, "prophesy the ruin of culture. . . . In the hero's inarticulacy, we find represented the young American's fears of maturity, for to speak out—to be a speaker—is to be a man."

Exactly.

There you have the whole point.

Isn't the Beat Generation a conspiracy to overthrow civilization (which is created by men, not boys) and to replace it *not* by the State of Nature where we can all romp around in free-and-easy nakedness, but by the world of the adolescent street gang? Maybe our own civilization demands too high a price in repression from the individual spirit, but it is sheer madness to think that the answer lies in never getting beyond the age of seventeen. The San Francisco writers, in their hatred of intelligence, their refusal to respect the requirements of artistic discipline, their contempt for precision and clarity are a perfect reflection of "the fear of maturity," the fear of becoming a man that Brustein finds in American youth at large. We all know what happens when a human being grows up without achieving maturity—he continues to need someone to make decisions for him, to run his life, to lead him. If the guardians of our civilization allow themselves to be bamboozled and intimidated by the arrogant clamor of the crippled young, what will be the political consequence? For what begins as culture always ends in politics, and it is dreadful to contemplate a situation in which nothing exists to stand up against the Beat brigades except the fuddy-duddies informing us that "a family that prays together stays together."

Living Theatre founders Julian Beck and Judith Malina celebrate an anniversary, November 28, 1960. The theater was the gathering place for the beat generation.

The Living Theatre company at the Village Voice *Christmas party, December 19, 1959. From left to right: Garry Goodnow, Jack Gelber, Judith Malina, Julian Beck, Malka Safro, Jerome Raphel, Lester Schwartz, Jock Livingston, James Spicer (on floor).*

Beat & Hipster
Fortune Cookies
by
Beck
Berkson
Burroughs
Corso
Ginsberg
Goodman
Koch
O'Hara

Girl Scout cookies were not as popular as Beat & Hipster Fortune Cookies sold in the lobby of the Living Theatre by Cynthia Robinson.

Poet-author Paul Goodman with Allen Ginsberg at the Living Theatre, January 26, 1959.

Lawrence Ferlinghetti reading from Coney Island of the Mind *at Living Theatre, October 5, 1959.*

Living Theatre poetry benefit for Yugen Press, November 2, 1959. Frank O'Hara, Ray Bremser, LeRoi Jones, Allen Ginsberg.

San Francisco poet Bob Kaufman at the Living Theatre, August 27, 1960.

Editor Jonathan Williams, publisher Ted Wilentz, and writer Paul Goodman in the Living Theatre lobby during party for Charles Mingus and Kenneth Patchen, March 13, 1959.

Intermission in lobby of Living Theatre—Totem Press poetry reading, November 2, 1959. John Fles (glasses), Clint Nichols, novelist Hubert Selby (white sweater), Ted Wilentz (tie), Diane DiPrima, and Joel Oppenheimer (back to camera).

Jargon Society publication party at the Living Theatre, November 13, 1959. Gilbert Sorrentino, Joel Oppenheimer, Tony Weinberger, Max Finstein, Irving Layton talking to Paul Goodman (with pipe), Denise Levertov (center rear), playwright Jack Gelber, Ted Wilentz talking to Allen Ginsberg (far right), Julian Beck (right foreground).

Ginsberg and Orlovsky at the Living Theatre benefit for the Jargon Society, November 13, 1959.

Margaret Randall, Bill Ward, Seymour Krim, and Taylor Mead, from left to right, at Living Theatre for Lawrence Ferlinghetti poetry reading, October 5, 1959.

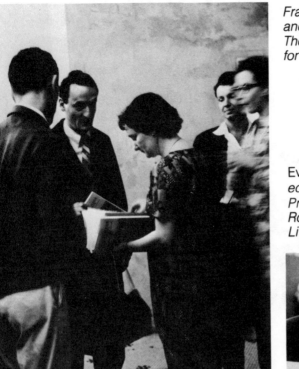

Frank O'Hara, Larry Rivers, and Daisy Alden in Living Theatre lobby, benefit reading for New Folder, June 12, 1959.

Evergreen Review managing editor Dick Seaver with Grove Press publisher Barney Rosset, April 12, 1960, at the Living Theatre.

Intermission at Living Theatre Totem Press poetry reading, November 2, 1959. Bob Lubin, filmmaker Ken Jacobs (rear wall), Clint Nichols, E. Wilentz, William Morris (with cup), Donald Allen, Ted Joans, Gandy Brodie talking to Allen Ginsberg, John Fles, Jim Spicer (right foreground), Willard Mass, and Kenward Elmslie (left foreground).

Lawrence Ferlinghetti and Brigid Murnaghan at Living Theatre publication party for Seymour Krim's The Beats, April 5, 1960. Her poem in the anthology was "George Washington: A Dialogue Between Mother & Daughter."

Norman Mailer and Jack Micheline at Living Theatre book party for Seymour Krim's *The Beats, April 5, 1960. Micheline's "streetcall new orleans" was included in the anthology.*

New York Post *reporter Al Aronowitz, Hubert Selby, and A. B. Spellman at the Living Theatre, November 28, 1960.*

Poet John Fles, editor Irving Rosenthal, filmmaker and critic Jonas Mekas at Edward Dahlberg and Josephine Herbst poetry reading, Living Theatre, March 23, 1959.

BEATNIKS FOR RENT

by Joseph Morgenstern

New York Herald Tribune, May 1, 1960

From operational bases in and around Greenwich Village, intrepid poets of the Beat Generation are going forth to beard the materialist lion in his den. They're bringing the Word to the fat cat in his posh pad. The beatniks are chanting their caveats and beating their bongos in enemy territory. They're renting themselves out, at "reasonable rates," to lecture at clubs and read at parties.

"Badly groomed but brilliant," they advertise themselves. For $25 an evening and up, published poets and their acolytes can be hired through a newly organized talent service in the Village. They come fully equipped with beard, frayed shirt, sneakers or sandals (optional), black sweaters, and berets. Beardless models are available upon request. All of them are guaranteed to shed light on the beatnik movement, a phenomenon that they concede to be "the most significant literary event of our time."

"We play the honesty scene," says their impresario, Fred McDarrah. "We provide legitimate poets for parties, and we can even supply five or six cool guys and girls who show up for atmosphere." McDarrah is a 33-year-old photographer specializing in pictures of beat poets and artists.

His efforts have endeared him to the beatniks, who feel he has a real love for his subject. "He doesn't run to *Life* with his pictures," one poet says. McDarrah is bringing out a book called *The Beat Scene,* and contributes to the *Village Voice,* a Greenwich Village weekly newspaper where his Rent Genuine Beatniks advertisement appears.

This venture was conceived last December, when McDarrah got a call from a suburban acquaintance, Laurence Barken of Scarsdale, New York. Mr. Barken wanted to know if he could obtain the services of a practicing beat poet for a party.

Immediately McDarrah thought of Ted Joans, an ebullient Negro bard and painter who came to New York from Indiana and still prides himself on the fact that he was the third customer at the Rienzi when the Greenwich Village coffee shop opened its doors in 1953.

He discussed the idea with Joans. "Like let's go up to this thing in Scarsdale," he said, "and pick up some dough." The evening, McDarrah recalls, was a "classic, and I figured like this is it, boy; maybe we can really do something."

Barken also has fond recollections of the party. "Joans turned out to be the guest of honor, although he didn't do much reciting. Everyone had been doing some drinking, and when the time came for him to read, the natives were too restive. But he was there, resplendent in his beret and his slightly torn black sweater. It worked out wonderfully. People in Westchester are still talking about it."

Spurred on by this success, McDarrah devised an advertisement and ran it in the *Village Voice*. "We got legitimate answers from everywhere, mostly from young people who live on the other side of the tracks and need to be clued in. We get some very high-class inquiries, like one from a Vassar Club."

From one young woman came this letter: "We're a group of young mothers, all with growing children, and feel we're never too old to learn."

Another request reached New York from Rockford, Illinois, but the ensuing correspondence ended on this note:

"Dear Mr. McDarrah: I've just received your postcard stating that it would obviously be impossible to send a beatnik to Rockford unless I send the carfare in advance. If this is a genuine beatnik, as advertised, he obviously wouldn't object to coming on a freight train. There are many good freight trains from New York to Rockford, so he obviously could make good connections."

Not only were there requests *for* beatniks, but requests *from* them. "Dig your idea," one letter announced. "Wish to be screened for possible inclusion on list of talents at liberty and on tap. Age—36; eyes—brown; weight—150; beard—black."

As engagements presented themselves, the stable of rentable beatniks grew. Today it includes a girl who calls herself Mimi Malraux (available when she isn't touring the provinces in an aged station wagon), and an intense, beardless New

Yorker of 29 named Jack Micheline, who says it's "sad that a poet of my reputation has to do a whole lot of gigs just to make a buck."

One of Micheline's appearances was at a party given by students at the Cornell University School of Nursing in Manhattan. Girls in bare feet and pseudo-beatnik costumes were tiptoeing around cold tile floors, and the room was lit by candles planted in Chianti bottles.

Spurning a microphone, Micheline sat in a chair in the middle of the floor and declared, in a matter-of-fact voice, "All right, we'll begin the poetry reading now. I'm very glad to be here, and very glad to read my poetry."

Suddenly his voice changed. It mounted to a plaintive plateau, faintly reminiscent of Dylan Thomas's readings, and Micheline read,

> Rise up, O choking city, rise . . .

and

> . . . sing your sadness in the sewers . . .

and

> . . . bleeding gutters with crutches . . .

and

> You never had a chance,
> standing on a corner
> in the belly of Harlem
> and the horns are blowin' crazy, Jenny Lee.

His audience was consistently respectful, and there were a few moments of enthrallment when nothing could be heard but the voice of the poet and the occasional click of a cigarette-lighter cover.

Only once before had Micheline appeared under Fred McDarrah's auspices, at a party given by Dorothy Arrigo, an advertising copy writer. Evoking the memory of that engagement, Micheline says, "They were really moved."

Miss Arrigo concurs. "He was received with some amazement. His poetry was better than we thought it would be, and it wasn't at all like looking at animals in a zoo. He had something to say to the guests, they had something to say to him, and we hit it off very well. It was a lovely party."

While the beatniks may hurl their shafts at any number of recondite targets—the authenticity of Dave Brubeck's jazz or the virility of Mr. Clean—their favorite target is materialism, to which they are unalterably opposed. And thus it was that Ted Joans accepted an assignment recently that brought him face-to-face with a group of young Wall Street executives.

They'd come together to fete one of their own number in a large, extremely well-heated apartment in Sniffen Court, midtown Manhattan's answer to the charms of Greenwich Village. Certainly they qualified, in McDarrah's words, as "young people who live on the other side of the tracks and need to be clued in."

Most of the guests tried to out-beatnik the beatnik. There was a girl in leopard-skin Bermuda shorts, another in a Princeton sweater with 1947 on the back, and still another wan creature carrying an enormous lily. There were men with beards painted on, hung on, and glued on. One man sported a real beard, which was tugged by all present.

In contrast to these caparisons, the poet's garb was solemn—black beret, black sweater, nondescript scarf, and sunglasses to protect his eyes against the light from a single 60-watt bulb inside a Japanese lantern.

As the evening wore on, the room became super-heated and the guests became incandescent. Their noise prevented Joans from reciting at any great length, but he made his way among them, offering books of his poetry and sketches for $5 the set. "I'm selling these," he explained, "because I'm trying to get Con Edison to turn my heat back on."

After the party had collapsed of its own weight and the guests had dispersed, Joans reflected on the evening and decided he still enjoyed renting himself out, in spite of the clamor, the often strange surroundings, and the occasional blank stares that greet his blank verse. "Why should I sit in a coffee house and read to my constituents who already know?" he reasoned. "I gotta get out and tell it to the squares."

McDarrah's ad in the Village Voice, 1959 and 1960.

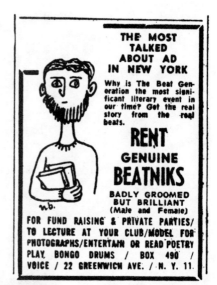

Fred McDarrah as a Village Voice photographer and genuis of Rent-a-Beatnik, January 24, 1960. His book The Beat Scene, *published in 1960, was a collection of photographs and poems by the beat generation.*

Ted Joans at a Rent-a-Beatnik party in Scarsdale given by Joyce Barken, 60 Old Lyme Road, on December 19, 1959. Guests dressed in their idea of beatnik garb.

Young ladies at a Rent-a-Beatnik party given by stockbroker Douglas A. Campbell in his townhouse, 10 Sniffen Court, April 1, 1960.

Ronald Von Ehmsen on his way to a Rent-a-Beatnik party for radio executive Joe Given of 7 Roberts Road, Englewood Cliffs, New Jersey, April 30, 1960.

Ronald Von Ehmsen at a Rent-a-Beatnik party for Joe Given in Englewood Cliffs, New Jersey.

Rent-a-Beatnik party given by Seymour Winuk, 1177 East 56th Street, Brooklyn, April 9, 1960. Payment was $40 plus $20 for each additional beatnik.

Ronald Von Ehmsen in his St. Mark's Place basement apartment, May 12, 1960.

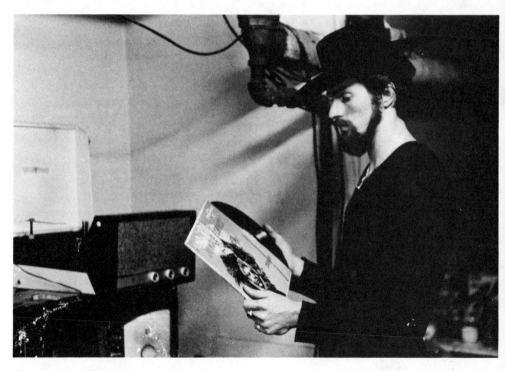

Ronald Von Ehmsen in his basement apartment on St. Mark's Place, May 12, 1960.

Edwin Fancher, publisher of the Village Voice, *giving a talk on the beat generation to convocation of youth at Hanson Place Central Methodist Church, Hanson Place, Brooklyn, April 2, 1960.*

EPITAPH FOR THE DEAD BEATS

by John Ciardi

Saturday Review, February 6, 1960

It wasn't much fun as rebellions go. Heaven knows the young need their rebellions. And let it be said of the Beats that there was a time when they might almost have been taken as an intellectual uprising. By now, however, it seems clear enough that the rebellion has gone for kicks, that what offered itself as an intellectual refreshment has turned out to be little more than unwashed eccentricity, and that one more Parnassus has turned out to be a grimy dive not much different from the speakeasy or the back room of the Communist cell meeting.

The fact is that the Beat Generation is not only juvenile but certainly related to juvenile delinquency through a common ancestor whose best name is Disgust. The street gang rebellion has gone for blood and violence. The Beats have found their kicks in an intellectual pose, in drugs (primarily marijuana, but also Benzedrine, mescaline, peyote, assorted goofballs, and occasionally heroin), and in wine, Zen, jazz, sex, and a carefully mannered jargon.

There is in all of them an innate fidget. As high-priest Kerouac tried to dramatize—at least to the extent that monotony can be drama—the Beats talk endlessly about serenity, detachment, and mangled Zen, but the last thing they know how to do is sit still. Were it not for the fact that the narcotics squad drives them to secrecy, and that few of them can afford fast cars, they would be off racing from roadhouse to roadhouse in an excellent imitation of their once-flapper and once-flaming parents. The impulse to run away from convention (while remaining close enough to it to flaunt it) is the same as it ever was. Nor is the search for "kicks" finally distinguishable from "making whoopee" back in the supermelogorgeous days of the cat's pajamas.

And like every essentially adolescent rebellion, that of the
Beat Generation is marked by an orthodoxy as rigid as the blue
laws. The Beats wear identical uniforms. They raise nearly
identical beards (now beginning to disappear in reaction to the
crop of beards being raised on campus by would-be beat-
nikoids). They practice an identical aversion to soap and water.
They live in the same dingy alleys. They sit around in the same
drab dives listening to the same blaring jazz with identical
blanked-out expressions on their identical faces. And any one
of them would sooner cut his throat than be caught doing anything "square."

It is clearly in the nature of all our rebel youth movements
to need a touch of the illicit. The flappers and their plastic-age
boy friends made a ritual of drinking rotgut, less because the
human nervous system is naturally attracted to bad alcohol
than because drinking it was against the law. The Young Communists plotted in secret meetings with dramatic precautions
against undercover agents and dramatic fears of being raided,
or they distributed pamphlets and howled from soap boxes in
ecstatic defiance of "the Cossacks." The G.I. generation had its
potential rebellion largely blurred by army restrictions and
could do little more than grumble or go AWOL on a binge, but
that much at least they did manage regularly enough. The
Beat Generation has marijuana and the ritual of dodging the
"narcos"—the narcotics squad.

The need to be illegal in some way is a simple enough need
to thumb one's nose at society. The need to make a ritual of the
illegality is as juvenile as the basic gesture itself. Let four
Beats gather in a desert to fire up some marijuana and at least
two of them will mention the narcos and look carefully in all
directions before they bring the stuff out of hiding. It is exactly
the ritual of four high school pals about to sneak a smoke in
the boys' room.

The Beats have carried their little drama a step further by
adding to it their special argot. The marijuana is "tea." The
rolled cigarette, looking very much like a paper-wrapped tooth-
pick, is a "joint." The butt is a "roach." You light up, take a
deep drag, and pass it on, holding the smoke in your lungs as
long as possible. You save the roaches when they get too small
to hold, wad them up, pick the tobacco from the end of a

"straight" (a regular cigarette), put in the wadded roach, crimp in the end of the straight, and fire it up for one last drag. Meanwhile, the chicks stare off glassy-eyed into the Ultimate-All and keep saying "Yeh! . . . hyeh! . . . hyeh!"—long drawn out, ecstatic, and aspirate. I mean like real cosmic, man.

Ideally, the Beat plays it cool, talking a great deal about a serene detachment from the materialism of the square and the corniness of the hot hipster. But put him on wheels and he instantly becomes a raging hot-rodder, distinguishable from the leather-jacket boys only by his volubility in discoursing on "the magnitude of the risk" as he spins his way around a tricky curve.

Speed is, of course, another drug, the illusion of one more escape. In the kind of Beat who most resembles the late Jimmy Dean (who was most nearly a middle ground between the Beats and the leather-jacket hoods, and who finally found the big crack-up he had long been looking for) speed is some sort of death wish.

It is, simply enough, a child's game without the easy freshness of the child's imagination. To the Beat, anyone over thirty is "The Enemy." One trouble, of course, is that by now most of the boys and girls Father Kerouac celebrated in "The Subterraneans" are over the line into enemy territory.

But whatever its foibles, and whether "Beat" is taken to mean "done in," as most people seem to understand it, or "beatific," as Kerouac has been insisting, the separation of the Beat Generation from "square" society was conceived as an intellectual and spiritual revolution. The Beat is a Krazy Kat longing to be stoned by the Mouse he loves, who, in his turn, always manages to fling his brick despite the worst Officer Pup can do. He is Charlie Chaplin ridiculously in love and being chased by cops. He is the jazz-man blowing his soul out in a dive, or wailing through the jail bars. He lives in skidrow-under-the-stars in the company of other "personal madmen poets"—the phrase is Kerouac's. He is a soul rescuing its identity from square conformity. His object is to escape the blindness of the square not only by disassociation, but by a systematic flouting of all square values. The rationale of this disassociation, or so he insists, is Zen.

Zen is an ancient way of life whose ends can be achieved

only through a lifetime of rigorous spiritual discipline, and I certainly have no notion of posing as an expert on it. Yet, though its method and discipline are profoundly complicated, Zen is profoundly simple in its basic Buddhist goal of achieving absorption into the All. Zen has been called a religion without a creed; yet it has a priesthood and its candidates must undergo a training as demanding as that imposed by any other religion. Its rituals are basically rituals of purification from the dross of matter and of identification with the ultimate life-force.

But though the Beats have cried loud the name of Zen, the boys and girls have never been close to adopting Zen discipline. The last thing they want on earth is a discipline. They have, rather, raided from Zen whatever offered them an easy rationale for what they wanted to do in the first place. What they seem to have found most attractive in Zen is the idea of the holiness of the personal impulse, and the dramatic role of the Zen lunatic.

By ritual detachment from materiality, and by ritual meditation on the All, the Zen disciple prepares to achieve that point at which all trace of the world's dross will be purged from his mind. At that point there is left only the pure, the spiritual, the holy, and the eternal. The self will have been absorbed into the All. And at that point, whatever speaks to the consciousness is ultimate and true. That goal achieved, every impulse of the soul is an impulse of holiness.

The idea is not, of course, uniquely Zen. It is, in fact, common to all religions whose goal is the surrender of reason to faith after proper purification. At the top of the Mount of Purgatory, Dante achieves an identical state of purification wherein he is free to act entirely on impulse, since his every impulse has become holy.

To the Beats, however, Zen purification has been reduced to little more than "get high and let it spill." Drugs, alcohol, long hours of voodoo sessions with jazz or bongo drums, plus a very eager self-hypnosis, make up the way to a "flip," which may be anything from an epileptic seizure to an inner illumination.

Most Beats are careful not to flip too far out. The really cool ones do not want to flip at all, nor even to get too high. What they want is a "low-high," a kind of serene marijuana-float that will induce a heightened awareness of sounds, smells, colors, and time. They are, that is to say, sensation seekers on the trail of a mildly "mystical" experience. I am surprised, in fact, that they have systematically overlooked the possibilities of laughing gas as a stimulus to semi-mystical hallucination, and I recommend that they look into William James's *The Varieties of Religious Experience* for some interesting details on this point. With the narcos sending in bearded, poetry-writing undercover men to make the scene and raid the tea parties—as they did recently in New York—it might be useful to know that there is, or so I am advised, no law against the inhalation of nitrous oxide.

On this level, Beat ritual is no more than sensation-seeking, which is itself the mark of an overcomfortable and sterile generation. The Beats like to claim the obsessive violence of Rimbaud as theirs, but too much of what they do is much closer to the raveled nerve-ends of a Huysmans. For the Beats are sprung of a generation that had it easy. When someone accused Kenneth Rexroth (an *hombre,* may I say) of being Beat, he answered: "Beat, Hell!—I've been beaten." And certainly the Beats would not be out on their particular limb of the nervous system had they had to face a tougher problem of basic subsistence or of basic survival. Had the Beats reached their early twenties in time for the Depression bread lines or for the army's dreary combination of foxholes and boredom, they would certainly have found other business than the elaborate cultivation of their sensations and of their purified sacred impulses.

The second aspect of Zen upon which the Beats have seized most avidly is the Zen-lunatic. The holy madman is a figure to be found in many religions. In Zen, as nearly as I understand, the lunacy is cultivated as part of the long discipline of detaching oneself from the material appearances of reality and from the conventions of material rationality. As with Rimbaud, the goal is the deliberate derangement of all the senses in order to open oneself to the larger reality to which convention is blind. One plays the fool for God.

There is an innate nobility in the idea of playing the fool for God. David, as an example of humility, put by his majesty and danced before the Ark (II *Samuel* vi, 14). But these boys and girls come closer to playing the fool for the fun of it, drawing upon the Zen-lunatic as a sanction for their antics. Shedding one's clothes in public, for example, is a well-established Beat prank (the point of which is probably to prove one's purity of all traces of soap and water). Allen Ginsberg has even made the point by stripping naked in the course of a public lecture. Another kind of antic was demonstrated by three beat poets at the end of a long radio interview in Chicago last year. Closing out the program, the announcer (Studs Terkel) asked if they had anything more they wanted to say. They replied that, yes, they had a message for the world, and they were, of course, invited to give it. Their three messages were, in order: "Fried shoes." "Meow." And "Chicago is a wose" (i.e., a "rose" with a lisp).

So much for the intellectual revolution. To the extent that the Beat Generation can be thought of as a literary movement, it has been systematically vitiated by this insistence on the holiness of the impromptu and by the urge to play the lunatic. Whether or not Jack Kerouac has traces of a talent, he remains basically a high school athlete who went from Lowell, Massachusetts to Skid Row, losing his eraser en route. His method of composition, as he himself has described it, is to put a roll of paper in the typewriter and to bang out eight or ten feet a day. Nothing must be changed because "whatever you try to delete . . . that's what's most interesting to a doctor."

I take Kerouac's particular phrasing of that point as symptomatic of a narcissistic sickliness in all Beat writing. "This is important," it says, "because it happened to sacred me." The object seems to be to document one's own psyche on the assumption that every reader will find it as interesting as your psychiatrist does. Sorry, boys: I find it zany without illumination, precious rather than personal, and just plain dull.

For the Zen-spill turns out to be simply a license to write without revision. "It's a new method of composition," Allen Ginsberg told me over the phone a while back. He was assuring me that the first part of "Howl" was written entirely without revision. He had, he confessed, tinkered a bit with the second part.

Ginsberg, for all his carefully cultivated (and natural) zaniness, is a writer far above Kerouac in my estimation. I find that first part of "Howl" a compelling piece of writing. I also find it impossible to believe (though I may be confessing my own square blindness in saying so) that any man could put together without revision as tight a catalogue as I find there. By a "tight catalogue" I mean a piling up of specific details that are intimately related, that maintain interest despite lengthy enumeration, that move at a reader-compelling pace, and that mount to a unified effect that is somehow greater than the sum of its parts. Perhaps it was written exactly as Ginsberg says it was. Or perhaps he had prepared a great deal of it in his mind before committing it to paper. Perhaps he is simply making a claim for effect. All I can do here is record both my doubts that the catalogue was entirely impromptu, and Ginsberg's insistence that it was.

But whatever the truth of the matter, and ready as I am to admire that first part of "Howl," I cannot find that Ginsberg has written anything worth reading since "Howl." Nor can I find any vein of poetic gold in Ferlinghetti, in Corso, or in the odds and ends of the less well-known Beats. As the literary heritage of the Beat Generation, I conclude, we are left the unreadable un-novels of Kerouac and the first part of "Howl." Add in the Beat influence on a few writers such as Norman Mailer who were on their way before the Beats, but took some of their later direction from behind the beard. It still seems a thin enough achievement for what has been the most talked-of "literary" movement of the last decade. Its very paucity serves to underline the fact that even the literary leaders of the Beats have made their careers primarily in personal eccentricity rather than in writing.

There remains William S. Burroughs, whose *Naked Lunch* is a powerful empathetic descent into the Hell of dope addiction. But though Burroughs has been claimed by the Beats and has been featured in collections of Beat writing, he is, in simple fact, his own kind of madman, a lost soul who has skidded through every mud at the bottom of the world in his journey from one addiction to another. A writer of careful horrors, Burroughs certainly has admitted revision as part of his craft. His literary ancestry may perhaps be best described as a combination of surrealism and Henry Miller. The point is that he would have written exactly as he does write had there never been a Beat Generation. And though many readers will find Burroughs's writing revolting, the revulsion is from reality. Its passion has been suffered rather than theorized.

Aside from the frivolity of depending upon improvisation as a method of composition, it is exactly in its tendency to be theorized rather than suffered that Beat writing seems thinnest. It tends too readily to become not intellect but exhibitionism posing as intellect. It talks endlessly about itself (like those endless dull movies about making movies). And it claims even to be a revolution in human values, but the fact is that the Beat Generation is basically the product of a false dilemma.

There is always reason enough for the young to rebel from the patterns of American complacency. Up at 6:30 to punch an eight o'clock time card, and home at five to watch TV on the installment plan can hardly be expected to recommend itself to the young as a romance with the universe. Nor are the patterns of two-car and swimming-pool success much more attractive when it all comes down to sitting around on the patio and small-talking the world from martini to martini.

The young may be blatant, but their rebellions are always essentially noble. At the core of the Beat rebellion there lies a single, simple, all-embracing distinction between what is "square" and what is "hip." It is, in fact, all but impossible for a Beat to speak ten consecutive words without using one or both of those terms. They define the center of his world. By "square" the Beat means "complacent, stodgy, sterile, spiritually dead." By "hip" he means "aware"—aware of the life force, of reality, of the universe.

And were it a simple choice between going Madison Avenue and going Beat, I should certainly insist that the Beat has all the merit on his side.

The Beats have permitted themselves the ignorant assumption that they have stumbled on ultimate answers. What they have ignored in their youth and insolence is the simple fact that the human position has always been a middle term between good and evil, and that the simple continuity of man and woman born of man and woman, and seeking to transmit through every confusion a sense of the value of that continuity, is the one human position there is. It is an imperfect position, but it is the enduring one, and it will survive every doctrinaire fad.

What the surviving Beats have yet to learn is that they, too, must in time peter out into a random Bohemianism (as they have, by and large, already done) or take their own places within that continuity, to be accused in time, and with reason enough, by the confusions and rejections of their own young.

Bless their fling. May every child in his mad adolescence find parents who can remember their own madness. Perhaps the Beat Generation's dabble in Zen will even teach that detachment that leads to mercy and compassion. Even had the rebellion of the Beats lacked all theory, the very fact that the young will yet find their rebellion is itself a cause for hope, the point of which seems to become remarkably clear when we lost souls on the faculty wander into a fraternity house for an evening session with our pink-scrubbed future corporation idiots.

And still, as rebellions go, this Beat jazz wasn't really much fun. As a literary movement it began and ended just about nowhere. As a set of antics, it still has a bit of mileage in it. They are still playing at it in the Village, out there at North Beach, and at Venice West. Certainly there is no problem in coming by marijuana in Chicago. In Denver, I noted recently, a joint that bills itself as a Beat dive runs night after night with a fifty-foot line of high school and college kids waiting to get in. But if the Beats had any sort of rebellion going once, there seems to be little enough left of it now beyond a fad for hip-talk and blare-jazz in crumby dives. That's dead enough, as the man said waving away the buzzards, let's bury it.

I hope the next time the young go out for an intellectual rebellion, they will think to try the library. It's still the most subversive building in town, and it's still human headquarters. And even rebels can find it useful to know something, if only to learn to sit still with a book in hand.

A writers' and poets' meeting to discuss "The Funeral of the Beat Generation," held on January 23, 1961, in Robert Cordier's railroad flat at 85 Christopher Street. De Hirsh Margules, Shel Silverstein, Sylvia Topp (seated left), Bill Godden, Gloria McDarrah, unidentified women, Robert Cordier, James Baldwin, Howard Hart, Norman Mailer (back to camera), Ted Joans, Lester Blackerstone.

Robert Cordier greets William Styron at his flat, 85 Christopher Street, January 26, 1961. Poet Sandra Hochman (in ski sweater), Lester Blackerstone, Ted Wilentz (seated).

Seymour Krim, left, at a second writers' and poets' meeting to discuss "The Funeral of the Beat Generation" at railroad flat of Robert Cordier (center), 85 Christopher Street, January 26, 1961.

The so-called Funeral of the Beat Generation, listening to Norman Mailer, January 26, 1961.

Susan Sontag, Alfred Chester, and Edward Field at the Provincetown Review *benefit symposium at the Mills Hotel, 160 Bleecker Street, December 2, 1962.*

A symposium on sex for benefit of Provincetown Review *held in the atrium of the Mills Hotel, 160 Bleecker Street, December 2, 1962. Left to right: Edward Field, Susan Sontag, Alfred Chester (sunglasses), William Gaddis, Bill Manville, Bill Ward, Rona Jaffe, Sam Kramer, David Amram, John Williams, Jack Micheline, William Saroyan, John Roebert, Seymour Krim, Rick Carrier.*

BEGONE, DULL BEATS

by Ralph J. Gleason

New Statesman, June 2, 1961

A full U.S. Grant beard, luxurious and flocked with gray, provided Bill the Beatnik with a supplementary income during his several years in San Francisco's North Beach neighborhood, home of the original Beats.

Photographed—for a fee—by a tourist against the wall of the Co-Existence Bagel Shop, the Coffee Gallery or any telephone pole on Grant Avenue, Bill was the living symbol of modern American urban dissent, proof positive to the folks back home that the tourist had seen a Beatnik in the flesh.

Last year Bill went to Veterans Hospital for repairs. He came back to the Beach this spring, his beard a hospital casualty. But it didn't matter really because, for Bill, North Beach is now a strange and lonely land. The tourists still throng the streets, but the regulars have gone like the ferries from the Bay. 'What happened? Everybody's split,' Bill complained on his first night back On the Scene: 'All the joints are closed. Where's everybody?' Now beardless, Bill is no longer even in demand as a model. 'There's nothing to do but sit in somebody's car and dig the tourists,' he says resignedly.

Bill's dilemma symbolises what has happened to North Beach, locale of Beat Generation literature from Kerouac and Ginsberg to *The Connection*. The Beatnik in his native form has all but disappeared from its alleys and cafes, like the Model T Ford from the roads of the U.S. When you see a Model T now, it's owned by a vintage car club member. Any surviving Beatnik on the Beach belongs to the entrepreneurial minority making a living off the tourists, selling sandals or running guided tours for Little Old Ladies from Dubuque. Or they are amateur Beats, fleeing part-time a dull office.

The situation illustrates a sort of Gresham's Law of sociology which was once articulated by a New Orleans madame named Countess Willi Piazza. Some 40 years ago she dramatised a not entirely different amateur-professional dichotomy when she remarked: 'The country club girls are ruining my business.' Madame Piazza's territory of nonconformity, Storyville, and Beatnik-land met the same fate. They attracted too much publicity and too many amateurs—and the cops closed them down. The weekend commuters to Bohemia and the tourists increased in strength until the San Francisco police reacted. North Beach, like Storyville, had, in the words of the Beat hipsters, 'blown its cool.'

The great diaspora began like chunks of ice slipping away from an iceberg entering warm waters, a few at a time and then a grand rush. They went to Big Sur, to Monterey, down the coast to Santa Monica and Venice: westward. They moved to other neighbourhoods in San Francisco—the Fillmore, Potrero and Russian Hills. They went up-coast to Bolinas and inland to the Sierra. Mostly they went to New York.

Kerouac and Ginsberg had already left by the time the tourists and the amateurs took over (though both returned for brief visits in 1960). Bob Kaufman, known as Bomkauf and author of the Abominist Manifesto, went to New York; Pierre deLattre, the Beatnik priest, whose Bread-and-Wine Mission was a landmark but is now a laundromat (Pierre got tired of being a housemother to the Beats, on call any hour of the night), went to the country to write a novel. Grant Avenue now is as dark and lonesome at night as any neighbourhood street. The Cassandra (Zen soup—20 cents) is a record store; The Place is an art-goods shop; the Coffee Gallery is open only occasionally ('They have events now,' an old-timer says disgustedly); the Co-Existence Bagel Shop is a sandals-and-jewelry shop, and the Jazz Cellar is dark and empty.

The end was really heralded when the whole of Grant Avenue burst into brief flame last year with a series of tourist traps. The Surplus Store added berets and turtleneck sweaters to its staples of sweatshirts, blue jeans and GI clothing. A leather-goods shop offered 'sandals for beatnik dogs'. Henri Lenoir hired Hube-the-Cube Leslie, one of the authentic originals, who in recent years had existed at survival level by serving as a human guinea-pig at hospital laboratories, to sit in the window of the Cafe Vesuvio, an earnest of the cafe's authenticity.

The City Lights Bookstore, owned by poet-businessman Lawrence Ferlinghetti, and featuring an extraordinary collection of paperback books and magazines, began to remain open to two and three o'clock in the morning. 'The tourists buy books all night,' says Shig Mauro, whose corduroy jacket and full beard behind the counter fit the late-night bookstore mood.

The Place, which originated Blabbermouth Night, where the customers could rise and speak at will, was the first to topple. Leo Kerkorian, the owner, recalls it as 'the kind of a joint where I had a bartender once took off his pants and worked all night with no pants. Some places he couldn't do that but in my place it was all right.'

The Co-Existence Bagel Shop lasted until this winter when, under continual police harassment (once a cop even ripped down a poem from the window), its proprietor, Jay Hoppe, universally known as Jay Bagel, gave up. Jay Bagel is only one of the colourful names of Beats. Others are Reverend Bob, Dr Fric-Frac, Linda Lovely, Barbara Nookie, Mad Marie, Lady Joan, Big Rose, Groover Wailin', Taylor Maid and The Wig.

'I'm tired of dealing with a psychopathic police department,' Hoppe said when he closed the Bagel Shop and left town. Hoppe also credits the police with being the basic cause of the others leaving. 'Bob Kaufman gave up when he was arrested on his birthday,' Hoppe says. 'Everybody got tired of being rousted by the cops. In New York City, San Francisco poets are treated like visiting celebrities.'

But the tourists still come; and Bill the Beatnik, a vestigial remnant of a departed era, alternates between parked cars in the day and the window of the grocery store on Broadway, across from the Expense Account Row of restaurants, at night. 'They got TV in here,' he says, 'and I can watch it with one eye and catch the Passing Parade with the other. But it's not like it was. All the old-timers are gone and the cops never bother the tourists.'

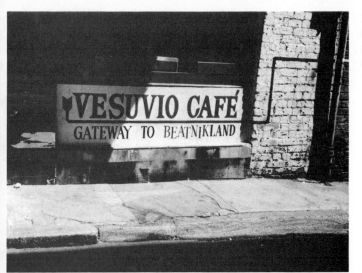

"Gateway to Beatnikland," North Beach, San Francisco, June 1, 1960.

Famous City Lights bookstore, 261 Columbus Avenue, San Francisco, June 1, 1960.

Lawrence Ferlinghetti in his
City Lights bookstore, San
Francisco, June 1, 1960.

Mural by Aaron Miller
in Co-Existence
Bagel Shop, North
Beach, San
Francisco, June 1,
1960.

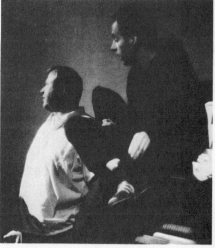

Six-foot-seven, 300-pound Eric Nord,
manager of North Beach Co-Existence
Bagel Shop, San Francisco, with Taylor
Mead, June 1, 1960.

THE LAST WORD

by Jack Kerouac

Escapade, February 1960

The history of the world is bloody and sad and mad—The First Crusade was nothing but Peter the Hermit spreading the word and leading a ragged horde of unarmed poorfolk who thought they could walk all the way to Jerusalem, Walter the Penniless strode in front of them with a big long staff, they never made it, they were all insane—Emperor Frederick Barbarossa arrived at a river and wanted to show his troops how to get across safely on horseback, so with all his armor he spurred the horse into the stream and drowned before their very eyes—The Children's Crusade was two little boys named Stephen of France and Nicholas of Germany who wandered barefoot along the gray mist roads of Medieval Europe gathering children to follow them and ended up perishing in the snows of the Alps and what was left of the pitiful ragged army was sold into slavery in Mohammedan markets—Every phosphorescent fish in the sea worries me like the Children's Crusade—History is a vast inexplicable tale that seems to make no sense—The Chalcedonian Patriarch of Alexandria was torn to pieces by a crowd on Good Friday in his own church—Francis Bacon sat in the snow with a dead chicken in his lap to prove the home freezers of today but died of pneumonia—No wonder Voltaire laughed!—The Danes of the 8th Century were led by King Harold Wartooth—Krum was the Khan of the Bulgarians and Yah Yah the Sage of Baghdad—Harold Fairhair killed Eric Bloodaxe on a big rock for reasons even Ida Graymeadows'll never dream—In 896 the corpse of Pope Formosus was propped up on a chair and put on trial—Mazoria the Senatrix went to bed with Popes, gave birth to Popes, and murdered Popes—At the Nicean and Chalcedon Councils eastern priests sitting on both sides of the church suddenly began screaming insane accusations across the holy nave—The bones of John Wycliffe the first English translator of the Bible were dug up and burned—Huss burned a Papal Edict and himself was burned—Luther nailed the ninety-five Theses on the door of the Cathedral of Wittenberg and promptly married a nun while Henry the Eighth got mad at Luther in a political fit and joined the Roman Catholic Church but promptly broke from the Roman Church to marry Anne Boleyn but got sick of her too and cut off her head—Ancient sailors caught in enormous storms at sea were only afraid of Sea-monsters—Peter the Great the six-foot-nine giant Tsar of Russia executed people with his own hands—When Russia finally got enlightened Tsar Alexander II was assassinated by bomb-throwing nihilists—Later when a group of workers and a priest wanted a few words from the Tsar affectionately known as "The Little Father of All The Russias" they got rifle fire in the kisser—Catherine de Medici the Queen Mother of France threw a royal wedding at the church of St. Bartholomew and invited all the Huguenots and had them all massacred in their pews—The Thirty Years War was concluded by Richelieu who was jealous of the Hapsburgs and had many people killed for nothing, a Catholic Cardinal leading a Catholic country against a Catholic King and a Catholic Emperor all so's Richelieu can slaver his lips in midnight chambers—The early cure for fever was swallow a live spider in syrup—Semmelweis was well-nigh crucified for suggesting that doctors wash their hands at childbirth—Man—Highest perfect fool, the wisdom of the two-legged rat—The great Habeas Corpus law was only passed in Parliament because a funny clerk decided to note down ten votes for a fat member of the House who weighed 350 pounds—John Randolph said that Edward Livingston "shines and stinks like rotten mackerel in the moonlight" and Napoleon called Talleyrand "a silk stocking full of mud"— Napoleon's soldiers crowded so hysterically around bonfires in the cold Russian winter that the nearest men were pushed in the fire and burned to death—The terrible war of 1870 was deliberately connived by Bismarck who changed the wording of a peace telegram and during the Siege of Paris that followed Gambetta magnificently escaped in a BALLOON—The history of the world is full of olives. When the hell will people realize that all living beings whether human or animals, whether earthly or from other planets, are representatives of God, and that they should be treated as such, that all things whether living or inanimates and whether alive, dead, or unborn, and whether in the form of matter or empty space, are simply the body of God?

Kerouac.

THIS IS HOW THE RIDE ENDS

by Jack McClintock

Esquire, March 1970

Like a little boy, an eternal innocent, he had no defenses. He seemed neither to need them nor to care for them, although he was sensitive enough to understand that many people do, and in beery conversation Jack Kerouac was like a one-man T-group. He always, in the phrase of Ken Kesey (whom he didn't like), brought it all up front.

The innocence in his last months made him do things that appeared simply foolhardy. A few weeks before he died in St. Petersburg, Florida, he and a friend went out (as he rarely did), drank too much and were beaten up by several angry blacks in a ghetto bar. I think it never occurred to Kerouac that he was not wanted there, not in these times. It hadn't been like that on the road.

But he had not been on the road in a long time. "You can't do what I did anymore," he said one evening about two weeks before he died. "I tried, in 1960, and I couldn't get a ride. Cars going by, kids eating ice cream, people with hats with long visors driving, and, in the backseat, suits and dresses hanging. No room for a bum with a rucksack."

For that reason and others he had lived in obscurity for at least the last eight years, many of them in St. Petersburg, perhaps the last place in the world one would expect to find Sal Paradise. It is an appallingly typical Florida city, with palm trees by the roadside, pastel concrete-block houses with plaster-of-Paris marlins pasted on their facades, sprinklers whirling silver pellets onto green lawns, polluted bays to cross when you go for a drive. Kerouac, ironically enough, never learned to drive, but somehow as he grew older he wound up here, in a town trying valiantly, if vainly, to throw off its old-fogy image. His paralyzed mother lived here (and I will indulge a maudlin impulse and say that I'll never forget her wailing over his gray face in its casket: "Oh my little boy. . . . Isn't he pretty? . . . What will I do now?" as Jack's wife Stella stood in a black dress and gripped the handles of her wheelchair). It was Stella, mostly, who cared for Mrs. Kerouac, getting up and gliding toward the back of the house whenever the little bell rang.

A few months before his death, Kerouac had written a magazine article, "After Me, the Deluge," in which he castigated no less than the 1960's, and tried to assess his own feelings on being credited in large part with the development of the hippie "movement."

"It's about the Communist Conspiracy," he said of the article—in deadly seriousness, it must be added.

The article was selling well to newspaper Sunday magazines and the *Miami Herald* asked me to visit Kerouac and dispatch a short profile to publish along with it. I had been thinking of approaching him anyway, and was glad to have an excuse for overcoming my reluctance to bother a man who I knew valued his privacy.

He lived in a suburb. The house was concrete block with a partial fake-brick facade and palm trees flanking the sidewalk. You had to shove the fronds aside to get on the front porch. I knocked on the door and met Stella.

She is a gray-haired woman in her early fifties, with a wide, bitter-sad smile and a deferent manner. She said, "He's not here," when I asked for Jack Kerouac.

He was, though. A shadow moved in the dim room behind her and then a face peered over her shoulder. The only photographs I had seen of Kerouac were old Associated Press biog shots in the files of the St. Petersburg *Times*. They show a young man, lean and handsome, with chiseled features, dark eyes, and rakishly tousled hair. Such pictures were still appearing on the dust jackets of his books, and Jack told me once, later on, "I'm always getting letters from girls who think I'm still twenty-six."

This was a different face. It had red-rimmed eyes and a day's growth of salt-and-pepper whiskers. But the hair was tousled and he wore a brightly colored sport shirt. He always wore a brightly colored sport shirt, and the only time I saw him with his hair combed was in his casket.

"Jack Kerouac?"

"Yeah," said the face. "You want to come in?"

Although the sun was two hours away from setting in the Gulf of Mexico, ten miles to the west, the house was dim inside. The drapes were all drawn tightly shut. Early American furniture, cherry wood and print cushions tied on with little bows. An oil painting of Pope Paul, almost cartoonlike with big blue eyes. Gray images dancing on the screen of a television set in the corner across from an Early American rocker, but no sound coming from the speakers. The sound was Handel's *Messiah* lifting itself mightily from stereo speakers in another room.

Kerouac planted his feet in the carpet, tilted his head in a characteristic, little-boy way, offered a bellicose glower and said, "Are you gonna take my pho-to? If you try to take my pho-to I'll kick your ass."

No, I assured him, I just wanted talk. I told him why, and, when he learned that a magazine had bought the article, he became more friendly. He was pleased.

He dragged up another rocker, found an ashtray to go with it, and then slumped into the dim corner in front of the television set.

"I like to watch television like that," he said, then turned his head to call out: "Stella. *Hey!* Turn the music up!" Stella went and turned the music up.

He was wearing unpressed brown trousers, a yellow-and-brown-striped sport shirt with the sleeves rolled to the elbow. The shirt was unbuttoned and beneath it the T-shirt was inside out. His belly was large and round, oddly too large for the stocky body. He pointed to it.

"I got a goddamn hernia, you know that? My goddamn belly button is popping out. That's why I'm dressed like this. . . . Well, I got no place to go anyway. You want a beer? Hah?"

He picked up a pack of Camels in a green plastic case. "Some whiskey? I'm glad to see you 'cause I'm so lonesome here."

We sat there and drank and talked for the rest of the evening. It was the first of perhaps a dozen such visits, and there was never a time until the last one or two visits when he didn't mention his loneliness. When I left that night about midnight he said, "Are you coming back to see me?"

I said yes, and would phone before dropping in if he would give me the number.

"I don't have a phone," he said. "I don't have anybody to call. Nobody ever calls me. Just come. I'm always here."

The visits seldom varied. Sometimes I brought a friend. We would pick up a dozen half-quart cans of Falstaff, his favorite beer, and shove aside the palm fronds and knock on the door. Stella would greet us with obvious and touching gratitude. "Jackie needs company," she would say in her quiet way.

We would push and pull the chairs around, find ashtrays, crack open the beer. There would always be a couple of books on the table next to what we came to think of as Jack's chair, usually classics. Once there was Boswell's *Life of Johnson,* another time a volume of Balzac, on whom he doted. There was always a stack of *National Review* magazines somewhere, for if Kerouac had a hero, it was William F. Buckley, Jr.

In addition to this paraphernalia, there was invariably a half-quart can of Falstaff, a pack of Camels, and a little two-ounce medicine vial with one of those white plastic caps that snap on and off. The medicine vial mystified us at first until we learned that it contained nothing more exotic than Johnny Walker Red.

"Call me Mister Boilermaker," Jack said, and when I ventured to ask why he drank the Scotch from that tiny container, he looked at me as though I were an idiot, as though I had disappointed him, and said, "So I won't spill it."

And then we would talk for hours. I think he could have been an actor. He loved to read aloud and was exceptionally good at it. Boisterously he'd say, "Wheer the divil are me glawsses?" and pick up something with type on it and read with broad, wild gestures of self-parody, grinning and mugging and dipping into a cornucopia of foreign accents for just the right one. The voice would go along, swoop up high, drop confidentially low. It sped, it dragged portentously. It understood the words and brought them alive. These times were altogether astonishing performances from this man with bare feet, whiskers, and a Kennedy half-dollar taped over his navel hernia.

Kerouac was forty-seven when he died. He had been out of the house very few times since he came to St. Petersburg the last time eleven months before, blaming his seclusion variously on illness, laziness, fear of "the niggers," lack of transportation, or merely joking it off as meaningless.

Once a professor asked me to invite Jack to speak to his class, and Kerouac answered, "Naw. I'd just get drunk." Then he illuminated the diminishing room with one of his astonishing little-boy grins. Now and then in the silver television light he seemed to become very young again until you remembered how this ravaged face looked in the harsh light of the refrigerator. The way it looked sometimes gave me a chill I couldn't attribute to the draft from the icebox.

It was almost as if Kerouac, in the last years, had burrowed farther and farther back into his own personality, back into the dense-packed delights and detritus of a life, and then turned around, and was peering out at the thronged world through the tunnel he made going in. Perhaps being back there clarified his sight in some ways, focused it more clearly on the things he could see. Perhaps it just gave him tunnel vision. I don't know.

You got the impression that, unlike his occasional friend Allen Ginsberg, who adapted slickly to the Aquarian Age by becoming one of its gurus and Om-ing his way from coast to coast, Kerouac was determined to remain out of fashion, or at least to appear that way.

He would rant for hours about the Jewish literary mafia that he believed had placed a moratorium on publication of his work. Once, when the real Mafia came up, he said: "The Mafia? The real enemy is the Communist, the Jew."

The notion that he started out a freethinking leftist and moved to the right later on was one he resisted. "I'm not a Beatnik," he said once, "I'm a Catholic."

"The Communists jumped on my movement and turned it into a Beat insurrection. They wanted a youth movement to exploit."

His rancor toward the left and his ultra-patriotism had come close to splitting him away from Ginsberg, whom he hadn't seen for years. Kerouac told us once of a party of Ken Kesey's in New York, at which Ginsberg came up and wrapped Jack's shoulders with an American flag—with obvious satiric intent.

"So I took it [he showed how he took it, and the movements were tender] and I folded it up the way you're supposed to, and I put it on the back of the sofa. The flag is not a rag."

The names and faces of his youth had grown away from

him, Kerouac said, and it made him frankly sad. He didn't whine, he merely allowed himself to feel that way and never tried to hide it.

The death of Neal Cassady bothered him the most. Sometimes he denied that Neal had died. "They *say* he's dead," he would mutter. "But I don't believe it. I don't want to believe it." But other times he would tell how he had heard Cassady met his end, walking down a Mexican railroad track in a T-shirt, in the middle of the night, stoned on grass and drunk on beer, and finally freezing to death.

It was Cassady, in fact, who was the pivot on whom Kerouac's opinion of Ken Kesey rotated: "I don't like Kesey," he said, "because he ruined Neal."

Four or five of us had been visiting Kerouac regularly for a couple of months when, one night, I showed up with the beer and another friend, the writer Richard Hill. We stowed the beer in the refrigerator, dragged the chairs around and were hardly seated when Kerouac burst out:

"Hey! I finished a book! *PIC*. I finished it yesterday and sent it to Sterling [Sterling Lord, his agent]. I started it in 1951 and finished it yesterday, what do you think about that? Only took me nineteen years!" And he laughed and laughed, and we laughed, too. He had a copy of the manuscript and I glanced at the first page. The protagonist was a ten-year-old black boy in the South, Pictorial Review Jackson, writing his own story in Negro dialect.

"Is it a story of prejudice?" Hill asked, mostly for something to say.

"Shit," said Kerouac. "It's a story of life. Of people living."

That was a week and a half before he died. A few evenings later, after we had opened beers, Stella said, "Look, Jackie's lost weight."

"About twenty pounds," Kerouac said, and leaned back in the rocking chair and sang: "I'm romantic,/And strictly frantic,/I love those old-fashioned times."

That evening, the last time I saw him alive, we just drank and talked as usual. He was the perfect drinking buddy: uninhibited, creative in conversation, inventive in mimicry, erudite in the range of his knowledge. Some of what he said was trash, but some was the fruit of his erratic genius. I remember only a little of what we talked about that particular night. It was, as usual, mostly about his boyhood, and about writers and writing.

"Who was the greatest American writer?" he asked, leaning forward and adding his bellicose challenge: "Hah?"

I was about to toss out Melville for lack of anything better to say, but he couldn't wait. "Wolfe! Thomas Wolfe. After me, of course."

Somehow that led to talk of autograph-seekers, whom he detested. "What do they want my damn name for?" He once wrote a fan and said he charged five dollars apiece for signatures. I jokingly said I wanted his autograph and would be glad to amortize it at a dollar down and a dollar a week, but the subject was boring and conversation skipped razzle-dazzle onto other things.

Cassady again: "I really loved that guy. He looked like Kirk Douglas, you know that? A little. He didn't have the dimple. He said, 'Douglas may have dimples but I've got pimples.'"

Football, and music (he played piano a little), and women (Stella's presence did nothing to impede talk on that topic), and painting (it was Kerouac himself who had painted the picture of the Pope on his wall, and he loved the way the blue eyes seemed to follow you). All that evening, a week before he died, he seemed extra cheerful.

The subject of the autograph never came up again, but a few days later the mail turned up a small envelope addressed in block letters. Inside it were a three-by-five card with Kerouac's name signed on it, and a piece of notebook paper on which was scrawled: "Jack Mac—Sorry I forgot—Would you like a piece of my toenail too, with Scotch tape?—Come on over—St. George." There was a cross drawn on the paper next to the signature.

"I just sneak into church now," he had said, "at dusk, at vespers. But yeah, as you get older you get more . . . genealogical."

There is one more thing to tell. Jack Kerouac died on a Tuesday. On the Sunday before that, Al Ellis, a law student, had dropped by to return a book he had borrowed from Jack. Jack had something to show him. He led Al to the kitchen and pointed. On the wall was a telephone. And on the table beside it was a telephone book, with four or five names and phone numbers carefully circled in ink.

Kerouac.

MAD Magazine, September 1960

! Xo "He's pretty sure of himself, isn't he?"

There have been many magazine articles written *about* the Beat Generation in an attempt to defend the movement. Now MAD presents its version of a magazine written *by* the Beat Generation which *really* defends the movement . . . the movement to *abolish it!* See if you don't agree after reading . . .

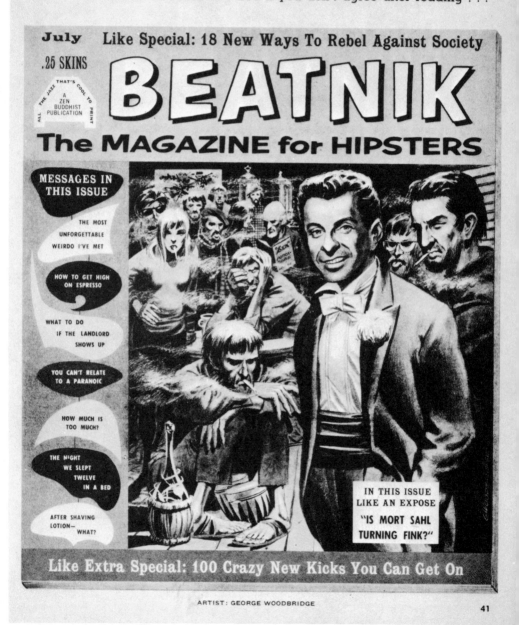

July

Like Special: 18 New Ways To Rebel Against Society

.25 SKINS

A ZEN BUDDHIST PUBLICATION

ALL THE JAZZ THAT'S COOL TO PRINT

BEATNIK

The MAGAZINE for HIPSTERS

MESSAGES IN THIS ISSUE

THE MOST UNFORGETTABLE WEIRDO I'VE MET

HOW TO GET HIGH ON ESPRESSO

WHAT TO DO IF THE LANDLORD SHOWS UP

YOU CAN'T RELATE TO A PARANOIC

HOW MUCH IS TOO MUCH?

THE NIGHT WE SLEPT TWELVE IN A BED

AFTER SHAVING LOTION— WHAT?

IN THIS ISSUE LIKE AN EXPOSE

"IS MORT SAHL TURNING FINK?"

Like Extra Special: 100 Crazy New Kicks You Can Get On

ARTIST: GEORGE WOODBRIDGE

41

THE INQUIRING HIPSTER

by Seymour "Psycho" Getzoff

QUESTION:
Like, how come you became a Beatnik?

WHERE ASKED:
Various coffee houses and wild parties.

SIDNEY SFORTZ,
Free-Lance Philosopher

I became a Beatnik because I had-da get out of the "rat-race", Man! I mean, I got fed up with the way things are these days . . . with everybody running around, trying to out-do everybody else. Like, a "competitive society" is a drag! You dig me? You get the message? Crazy! Because I gotta split now. I gotta cut down to the coffee shop and grab me a table, before them other hipsters get there.

GERALD ZENN,
Poet and Push-Cart Peddler

I became a Beatnik because I wanted to maintain my individuality in a world sick with conformity. I didn't want to act, think, and feel the way everybody else acts, thinks, and feels in order to be accepted. I wanted to be a person in my own right. Listen, Man! Ask any of the other beats around here! They know what I'm talking about . . . because they all act, think, and feel exactly the way I do!

KERR U. ACK,
Part-Time Intellectual

I joined the movement because I wanted culture. Not the commercial Madison Avenue kind of culture. Not the trite Bourgeois kind of culture. I wanted real culture. I was always on the intellectual kick, and I knew that this was the scene for me. So like, now, every night, there's beer, and chicks, and wild parties…and I tell you, Dad, this culture is the end!

WANDA KUHL,
Full-Time Emotionalist

I used to sit around at home nights, with nothing to do and nowhere to go. I was vegetating, that's all! Vegetating! It was getting on my nerves. I wanted adventure! I wanted action! I wanted thrills and kicks and excitement! So I became a Beatnik. Now, every night, I go out to some coffee shop, and I sit around, and I listen to jazz records, or poetry. I mean, I'm leading a real wild life now!

MELVIN COWZNOFSKI,
Metaphysician and Waiter

Like, I became a Beatnik because I don't dig money. Money is a drag. It's nowhere. Money is the root of all evil. Money corrupts the incorruptible, and causes more misery in the world than all diseases. Man, like money stinks! That's why I became a Beatnik. And now that I've answered your question, Pops, hows about helping me out with fifty cents for a cup of espresso?

SAL VAN CLUTZ III,
Hanger-On and Part-Time Fink

Man, once I was a real "square". I mean once I was a real cornball. I lived with my folks in this 17-room house in Connecticut, with my own car, servants, flashy wardrobe and plenty of loot. And then, one day, I decided I had to find something meaningful in life. So I moved into a dingy cold-water walk-up pad in Greenwich Village, and I grew a beard, and I became a Beatnik. And suddenly, everything became crystal-clear. Suddenly, I realized what I had been searching for. But, like, it was too late to go back home!

Man, like we'd seen plenty of wild kicks
in our time, but this one was the end...

Prize-Winning Beatnik
Confession Story

The Night "Wild Harry" Flipped His Lid

By Irving Neudnik
author of
"Zen Buddhism and All That Jazz"
"The Story Behind My Shock Treatments"
and other cool tomes

*Like we couldn't put
our finger on it, but
somehow, "Wild Harry"
was acting strangely.*

We knew Harry was heading for
Doomsville right after he blew
back into town from Frisco. Like
it wasn't the "Wild Harry" we all knew
back in the old days. The "Wild Harry"
who would run through the streets at four
in the morning, yelling "Chloe!" at the
top of his voice. The "Wild Harry" who
could swing from chandeliers at parties.
The "Wild Harry" who once "fixed" a
Russian Roulette game; who once hitchhiked to Chicago in the nude, who once
went berserk in a subway; the old "Wild
Harry" we all had grown to love and respect.

The first sign that Harry was cracking
up came last week, when he stamped out
of our coffee shop screaming, "I hate espresso!" We thought nothing of it, then.
We figured it was just another of Harry's
wild kicks, and we all grooved it. But
later that same night, when he said, "Let's
all take a walk down Madison Avenue!",
we suddenly saw the handwriting on the
wall.

After that, he got much worse. The next
day, one of the cats waltzed in and told
us he got a line that Harry was seen at a
baseball game. That same night, Harry
came around with his *beard shaved off.*
And when the word got out that Harry
was seen at a party, drinking beer *out of
a glass;* when he was spotted walking with
a *chick from the Bronx;* when he didn't
bat an eyelash after somebody mentioned
"Kerouac", we all knew for certain . . .
Harry was turning into a "square"!

But we thought there still might be a
chance to save him. So, last night, we cut
over to his pad in the wild hope of
straightening this poor sick cat out. And
that was when we gave up on "Wild
Harry"! Because no sooner had we opened the door, then we dug the most terrifying bit of all.

There was "Wild Harry" . . . *taking a
BATH!*

Man, like then we knew! As a Beatnik,
"Wild Harry" was *all washed up!*

43

PERSONALS

AT LIBERTY
Poet—Artist—Philosopher—Metaphysician seeks job cleaning windows. Write Box 76

TWO CONGENIAL Beatnik Psychotics seek third to share padded apartment. Own closet and bongo drums. Like we mean you supply 'em yourself. Box 81

BIG AL—Like make it back to the pad. All is cool. We still dig you. MOTHER

I am no longer responsible for any loot owed by my chick. She left my pad and like bored. "Hard Luck" Milton, Bench 3, Central Park.

MOTHER—Like I can't make the scene. I'm hung up in this crazy hotel in Lexington, Kentucky. BIG AL

ANYONE HAVING INFORMATION as to the whereabouts of Charlie "Hip" Grammis—like keep it down, hear! The fuzz is on his tail. A FRIEND

DEAR DADDY-O
Advice to the Love-Bugged

If any of you cats or chicks are hung up or put down by some love problem, clue me in on the deal, and I'll hip you on how to come on swinging again. Just send your blues note to "Daddy-O", Beatnik Magazine, Table No. 5, Psycho Coffee Shop, Greenwich Village, New York

Dear Daddy-O,
    This chick left my pad over four years ago on the pretext of going out to buy some pretzels for the beer, and she never came back. Like what should I do?
                                    Still Wailing

Like finish the beer yourself, Man! It just don't make it when it's warm!

Dear Daddy-O,
    I got big eyes for this chick, see. But like she's 86 years old, and I'm only 22. Clue me in, Daddy-O. Should I marry the broad?
                                    Rattled

Why not? But make sure first that it's not just a physical attraction you feel, Man!

Dear Daddy-O,
    My chick is a masochist, and I am a sadist. Everything was cool in our relationship until last week, when she pleaded with me to beat her, and I said "No!" What's happening?
                                    Torturer

You're winning, Man!

Dear Daddy-O,
    What does a Beatnik like me, who is interested in more intellectual pursuits, do with a beautiful blonde chick who wants to kiss you and hug you and love you all the time? Like what do I do?
                                    Gassed

Like you send me her phone number, that's what you do!

Dear Daddy-O,
    I'm at my wit's end. You see, I'm madly in love with this big ape, and all he does is treat me rotten. I guess it's my own fault for falling in love with him, but I couldn't help it. I was terribly lonely, and I needed a relationship badly. Any relationship! So the minute I saw him, I fell. My problem is: I want him to move downtown to my pad, and he wants to stay where he is in his cage at the zoo! What should I do?
                                    Kookie Annie

Forget him! He sounds like a real "square"!

Dear Daddy-O,
    I started going with this Beatnik artist a few weeks ago, and now he wants to paint me in the nude. What do you think?
                                    Shy Selma

Until you get to know each other better, I think he should at least wear a bathrobe when he paints you!

Dear Daddy-O,
    I'm a real square, and I'm miserable. I want to be Beat, but I don't know how to go about it. Can you help me? Tell me the quickest way to be Beat.
                                    Square Jack

The quickest way to be Beat is to pick on somebody much bigger than you!

Dear Daddy-O,
    I'm crazy about this chick who digs Lawrence Welk and cowboy pictures and Vogue Magazine. Like what do I say to her?
                                    Hung-up

You say to her like "Goodbye!"

Dear Daddy-O,
    I'm going with this crazy-looking chick, but she keeps bugging me with all her wild bits. Like last night she locked me in this Pizza Pie oven, and turned it on. How do you relate to action like that, hah, Man?
                                    Steamed Up

Just keep cool, hear!

Dear Daddy-O,
    The chick I'm married to is the most, but like sometimes she's a little too much. For instance, every night she insists upon going to bed wearing her sweater, black stockings, blue jeans and purple beret. She says it's wild, and I say it's real cornball. Who's right?
                                    Hassled

Like she's the square, Man! No one cool wears a beret with jeans!

Dear Daddy-O,
    All of the hipsters always break up when I make the scene. They keep laughing at me, and I don't know why. Enclosed is a snapshot of me with some of my beat friends. I'm the one in the middle with the beard. Can you clue me in on what's so funny about me?
                                    Puzzled

It beats me too. I just can't figure it. Like I think you're a pretty cool-looking chick.

THE COOLEST SQUELCH

    Like one day, the police were tipped that the members of a certain jazz combo were taking dope while playing. So they assigned a young undercover man, disguised as a high trumpet player, to sit in with them, and gather evidence. Right in the middle of the first set, the undercover man saw a sideman passing the junk. But he played along to make sure, so he could nail every cat involved.
    Long about closing, when everybody was feeling woozy, the undercover man leaped to his feet and announced, "I'm a police officer! You're all under arrest!"
    To which the drummer looked at him glassy-eyed, and said, "Man, you are really high!"

WILD NEW BEARD STYLES

by SAM OSSZEFOGVA, Fashion Editor

A couple of years ago, a beard was a "must" for a real Beatnik. These days, unfortunately, many "squares" are wearing beards. It's getting so bad, you can hardly tell the difference between them and us. So we Beatniks have got to do something about it. We've got to make our beards more distinctive. We've got to adopt wilder-looking beard styles, so we can continue to stand out as the anti-social, sensationalist clods that we are. Here, then, are BEATNIK Magazine's suggestions for new beard styles:

SINGLE HAIR BEARD

Just the thing for those who only want to "suggest" a beard. Allow it to grow real full, and then clip off all the hairs but one.

FULL FACE BEARD

Ideal for the Beatnik who wants to remain anonymous. Effect is achieved by letting beard grow long, and combing it up over the face.

SIDEBURN BEARD

Simply let your sideburns grow until they're so long they hang beautifully down to your chest. Ideal for the arty-type of Beatnik.

UPSIDE DOWN BEARD

A startling new effect is achieved by growing heavy beard to resemble head of hair, and shaving head of hair to resemble a goatee.

ONE SIDED BEARD

A gay new gimmick in beard styles, designed for those Beatniks who have been unable to decide whether or not to grow a crazy beard.

FAR OUT BEARD

Full appreciation of this new beard style comes when onlookers realize that its owner has accomplished an impossible task for a girl.

INITIALED BEARDS

The best new style suggestion of all is the "Personalized Beard"... just the thing for the Beatnik who wants to maintain his own "individuality."

A Glossary Of Square Terms

Man, there's a big hassle going on now that the uptown tourists have moved in to rubberneck us cats. Like ever since they started making our cool scene, it's gotten harder and harder to tell the "squares" from the Beatniks. Mainly because the "squares" seem to be using "hip talk" words and phrases, too. But don't be fooled! These words and phrases aren't "hip talk" at all! They mean something completely different. So if you ever get hung up with some of these aliens, and you want to dig just what it is they are saying, here's a glossary of their jargon.

AX—The horn a square woodchopper swings with.
BLUES—Like colors, mostly on square suits.
BREAD—What you scoff on a feed-bag kick.
BUG—That nowhere creature that crawls in your pad.
CAT—That beast who's got nine chances for kicks.
CHARGED-UP—When they stack the loot on your tab.
CHICK—That crazy stud that comes on from an egg.
CHOPS—A kind of ribble you scoff with "Bread".
COOL IT—When you stash some action in the refrigerator.
CRAZY—When a square is like too far out to come back.
DADDY—The tag a square pegs his old man with.
FUZZ—What squares wash out of their belly-buttons.
GEORGE—The real tag on some squares.
HIP—Where all the action is during a square Cha-Cha.
HUNG-UP—Like when you stash your rags.
KICK—Like when you're hung up, and put up a beef.
LEFT FIELD—A part of the scene in some square game.
LICK—An action when you're scoffing with your chops.
LIKE—When you got big eyes for some cat or bit.
PAD—The action you write on.
POPS—The bits that Good Humor cat pushes.
PUSHER—A cat who leans on you with his mitts.
SCENE—The action in a square play.
SCOFF—Like when you put down some cat or bit.
SCORE—What the deal is when squares compete.
SPLIT—Like when two squares get unhitched.
SWING—What small studs in parks get their kicks on.
THE END—Like the finish of a square bit.
WAY OUT—The route when you split from the scene.
YOGI—The tag on some square cornball idol.

The Beat Beat

Goings-On Around The Scene

BY EARL E. BYRD

WHO'S MAKING IT WITH WHO . . . **Myrna Loyola** and **Dennis Finster** holding hands under the chess table at The Way-Out Espresso Shop…gin rummy hands, that is…**Lance Sturdley** and **Selma Klotz** a twosome in a doorway on The Bowery . . . **John Miltown** relating well to **Audrey Blech** on a bench in Central Park . . . before being mugged.

* * *

LIKE WHAT'S HAPPENING . . . **Ernie "The Psycho Kid" Highbutt** planning to commit suicide again next summer . . . **Max Nodiffrance** threw a wild party down his cellar last Monday . . . the wild party was named **Felix Twinge**…A stork for the **Melvin Cowznofskis** last weekend . . . not a baby, just a stork . . . **Tony Globb** writing a new volume of Beat Poetry . . . with his feet . . . **Sally Mudge** painted a mural on the side of a Mack truck . . . while it was in motion . . . **Sol Plotzi** carving a bust of **Jack Kerouac** out of a 3-ton block of Halavah . . . **Augie Van Dam** composing a symphony without any sound . . . just various shadings of silence . . . **Sammy Whackoe** flew to Frisco last week . . . swears he'll take a plane next time . . . **Herman Grunch** planning poetry readings at the all-night Automat . . . **Randolph Slatztzt** evicted from his pad for falling behind in his boozing . . . now living atop the Washington Square Arch . . . **Zelda Slofkis** exhibited her latest painting technique . . . she roller-skates across her palette and onto a blank canvas.

* * *

WHAT THEY ARE SOUNDING…**Fenwick Creeppe**, while banging his head against an Eighth Street parking meter: *"Man, I put down all the squares as sick, sick, sick!"* . . . **Quaz E. Moto**, to a Taxi driver who told him a bridge was washed out: *"Fake it, Pops! Fake it!"* . . . **Kermit Koones**, seeing the tightrope walker fall to his death at the circus: *"Like that's show biz!"* . . . **Sol "Schizo" Snerd**, at the Village Dump Coffee Shop: *"My analyst just doesn't understand me!"* . . . **Ted Slumpf**, while sweating out a cold turkey treatment at the City Jail: *"Arrrgh-h-h-h-h-h-h-h-h-h-h-h-h-h-h-h-h-h!"*

* * *

NOBODY CLUED ME, BUT . . . Cats who wear heavy woolen sweaters over their black leather jackets are odds-on to sweat . . . Chicks who make it in purple jeans are usually named *"Shirley"*…It's all over if your chick starts reminiscing about her old boyfriend from the **Bronx** . . . For some strange reason, I'm suspicious of squares who come downtown to the Village carrying **switch-blade knives** . . . It's all over between you if your broad runs off to the **Belgian Congo**, makes it with the natives, and doesn't even send you a card . . . If I'm sixth in a game of **Russian roulette,** and it comes my turn, you can count me out!

* * *

The KICK of the Month

Each month, we offer a thermos of espresso to the hipster who sends in the most original idea for a crazy new kick. This month's new kick comes from Bernard G. Zitzlaffbath.

This kick is a wild bit you can pull on that cat who's always looking for a party to go to, and who keeps bugging you to clue him in on where the action is.

If you really want to hang this creep up, tell him there's a real wild party at a certain pad, and give him the address. But before you do, have your buddy at the pad stick a note outside his door, saying the party has been moved to a new address. Then, when the cat gets to the new address, like he finds another note telling him the party's been moved to still another address. All you gotta do is clue your friends to leave these messages on their doors. So now you got this crazy cat running all over the city, looking for this wild party. The last note he hits gives him the address of your pad again. So like it's around six in the morning when he comes staggering to your door. All you do is open it, and you greet him cooly with:

"Man, how come you're so late? You just missed the wildest party of the year!"

LIKE ETIQUETTE

The Cool Thing
by Thelonius Monkey

Man, like it's THE COOL THING in beat circles to never get excited and flip your lid, no matter what happens!

This month's contribution sent in by Felix Fleagle, brother of the late Constantine Fleagle, beloved Philosopher, Poet, and part-time Co-Existence Bagel-Baker, who lost his life in the Barefoot Espresso Shop fire two weeks ago.

What's WRONG With This Picture?

ANSWER: Man, *everything* is wrong with this picture!!

BIOGRAPHICAL SKETCHES

Daisy Aldan, publisher, editor, translator, edited the celebrated anthology series "A New Folder," which published avant-garde poets and painters of the New York School. She won an NEA grant and was nominated for a Pulitzer Prize in poetry for *Between High Tides*. Her latest works are *A Golden Story, The Art & Craft of Poetry*, and *Poetry and Consciousness*. She conducts workshops, translates books from French, Spanish, and German, and runs the New Folder Editions Press. She lives in New York and Switzerland.

Donald Allen published the anthology *The New American Poetry: 1945–1960* (Grove Press, 1960), launching the careers of many of the American postmodern writers and poets and giving wide significance to their work. Allen was also first co-editor of the original *Evergreen Review*. He lives in San Francisco.

Rick Allmen, who came from the Lower East Side, started the Café Bizarre with $100. It became one of the most colorful coffeehouses in Greenwich Village in the late 1950s. The entire block where the café stood was demolished in 1983. Allmen was on the committee that battled City Hall and the police department to permit poetry readings in coffeehouses. Allmen is now in real estate and still lives in the East Village.

David Amram, the Renaissance man of American music, is a composer, conductor, musician (French horn) and actor who played in the famous beatnik film *Pull My Daisy*. Following Kerouac's vision, Amram bases his work on "the natural sounds of people and life." He is one of America's most performed composers of concert music and has composed for both Hollywood and underground films and Broadway theater. He lives in Greenwich Village with his wife LoraLee and three children.

Alfred G. Aronowitz was the first print journalist to write seriously about the beat generation as a literary movement. He is also credited with introducing many pop stars to the public. Bob Dylan once joked that Aronowitz was the only man who could save the world. His latest work is *Blacklisted Masterpieces of Al Aronowitz*. He is now completing a book on Murray the K and lives in Bearsville, New York.

Fernando Arrabal was born in Spanish Morocco, moved to Madrid after the Spanish Civil War, and later moved to Paris. His literary heroes are Beckett, Kafka, De Sade, St. Teresa of Avila, and W. C. Fields. He writes novels and plays in French; his best-known works here are *Baal Babylon, The Automobile Graveyard,* and *The Two Executioners,* all published by Grove Press.

James Baldwin, novelist and playwright, is one of this country's most respected and successful writers, even though he has been living in Paris for two decades. Born in New York, he is the author of such memorable works as *Go Tell It on the Mountain, The Fire Next Time, Nobody Knows My Name, Nothing Personal, Little Man, Little Man,* and *The Devil Finds Work.*

Julian Beck and Judith Malina, *Voice* Obie Award winners, began the Living Theatre in 1951 with a series of one-act plays in their living room by Brecht, Lorca, Stein, and the American writer Paul Goodman. They have performed all over the world and have caused riots, police busts, and a seizure of their loft theater in New York City by the IRS, which forced them to leave the country in the early 1960s. The Living Theatre became a wandering nomad tribe, performing mostly in France and Italy, but returned after 15 years to New York in 1984 to present new plays and a retrospective of its work at the Joyce Theatre.

Bill Berkson is a poet and art critic. His books include *Blue Is the Hero: Selected Poems 1960–1975, Red Devil, Start Over,* and *Parts of the Body*. He lives in Bolinas, California, and was the editor and publisher of *Big Sky* magazine. With the playwright and novelist Joe LeSueur, he edited the extraordinary, touching *Homage to Frank O'Hara,* a collection of essays, memoirs, poems, and other works by many of O'Hara's friends and associates.

Paul Blackburn came from Vermont and was a Fulbright scholar as well as a Guggenheim fellow. Poet, translator, and contributing editor of *Black Mountain Review,* Blackburn lived in Spain in the mid-1950s. *The Dissolving Fabric,* his first book, was published in 1955. Altogether he wrote 19 books. He died at the age of 41 in 1971. The Paul Blackburn Archive is at the Archive for New Poetry, University of California in San Diego.

Tamara Bliss was born in Moscow and educated in Canada and at Barnard College. She is a composer, arranger, and concert pianist and teaches regularly at the New School. She has written the music for three off-Broadway plays as well as the score for the famous de Kooning documentary film. Miss Bliss is the musical director of the Downtown Theatre Project and divides her time between Cuernavaca and New York. Presently she is writing a cantata on contemporary New York street scenes.

Ray Bremser was born in Jersey City, got involved in armed robbery, and did six years at Bordentown Reformatory, where he wrote his first poems at age 18. He later married Bonnie Frazer and, again in trouble with the law, fled to Mexico. Much of Bremser's writing—*Angel, Drive Suite, Blowing Mouth/The Jazz Poems 1958–1970*—was done at Rahway State Prison. Plagued by drugs and alcohol, Bremser eventually moved to Utica, New York. He participated in the Jack Kerouac Conference at Naropa Institute in Boulder, Colorado, in 1982.

Art Buchwald is a syndicated humor columnist from Mount Vernon, New York. He lived in France in the 1950s, where he wrote *How Much Is That in Dollars,* and *Art Buchwald's Paris.* His best-seller *While Reagan Slept* was published in 1983. He lives and works in Washington.

William S. Burroughs, legendary beat figure born in St. Louis and a graduate of Harvard, met Kerouac and Ginsberg in 1944. He worked as a private detective, exterminator, and bartender. Burroughs chose drugs as a way of life and settled in Tangiers in 1953, the year he published *Junkie: Confessions of an Unredeemed Drug Addict.* His knowledge of addicts, criminals, and sexual deviates was the basis of his famous 1959 book *Naked Lunch. The Place of Dead Roads* was published in 1984 on his 70th birthday. Burroughs acted in many films and was the subject of a feature film shown at the New York Film Festival.

Paul Carroll, one of the patriarchs of the Chicago poetry world, came from a banking and real estate family, attended the University of Chicago, and was editor of *Big Table.* A poet and literary critic, Carroll is professor of English at the University of Illinois and founding president of the Poetry Center of the Art Institute of Chicago. His works include *Odes, The Luke Poems, New and Selected Poems,* and *The Young American Poets,* an anthology.

Neal Cassady, legendary folk hero in the beat movement, was born in Salt Lake City to a life of hardship, married three times, was immortalized as Dean Moriarty in *On the Road,* and died in Mexico in 1968 presumably of alcohol and drugs, four days before his 43rd birthday. *The First Third,* his autobiography, was published in 1971 by City Lights Books. His wife Carolyn, now living in England, wrote about their relationship in *Heart Beat,* published in 1976 and later made into a movie starring Nick Nolte as Neal, Sissy Spacek as Carolyn, and John Heard as Kerouac. William Plummer's definitive book on Cassady, *The Holy Goof,* was published in 1981.

Paddy Chayefsky, a native New Yorker and a City College graduate, was a World War II veteran with a purple heart. He was best known for his 1955 television and film drama *Marty* and his Oscar-winning film *Network,* which popularized the phrase "I'm mad as hell and I'm not going to take it anymore." His other credits include *The Americanization of Emily, The Hospital,* and *The Passion of Josef D.* He died in 1981.

Alfred Chester was born in Brooklyn and went to NYU. He was an expatriate for most of his adult life. He wrote *Jamie Is My Heart's Desire, The Exquisite Corpse* (a surrealist novel), and *Behold Goliath* (a collection of short stories). His essays and criticism appeared in *The New Yorker, Commentary, Evergreen Review,* the *New York Review of Books,* and the *New York Times Book Review* as well as the literary magazines, *Sewanee Review* and *Botteghe Oscure.* He was twice a Guggenheim fellow. In the mid-1970s he went to Jerusalem, where he died.

John Ciardi, from Boston, was known for his scolding reviews and denouncements of Kerouac and the beats in the *Saturday Review.* A onetime Harvard professor, Ciardi is an established poet, essayist, novelist, translator, anthologist, and literary critic. His books have been published widely. He lives in New Jersey.

Marvin Cohen was raised in Brooklyn and now lives in Manhattan. He has published eight books, including *Fables at Life's Expense, The Self-Devoted Friend, The Inconvenience of Living, Baseball the Beautiful, The Monday Rhetoric of the Love Club,* and *Aesthetics in Life and Art.* His two plays, *The Don Juan and the Non-Don Juan* and *Necessary Ends,* were presented at the Public Theatre and in London. He's now conducting writing workshop courses at C.W. Post College on Long Island.

Robert Cordier, poet, stage and film director, was born in Belgium, came to New York in the fifties and directed plays by Adamov, Artaud, and McClure, etc. His feature film about New York and the rock scene, *Injun Fender,* won several major awards in international film festivals. He is now living in Paris, where he heads a theater company and acting school, and writes and reads poetry. His last published play, *Hattie's Song in Babylone so Cold,* won France's Ministry of Culture award.

Gregory Corso was already interested in writing before becoming an inmate in Clinton State Prison, where he read all the books in the library. Corso's famous poem "Bomb," as well as "Gasoline," was published in 1958 by City Lights. Corso, with Ginsberg and Orlovsky, lived poorly in Paris at the famous beatnik hotel at 9 rue Git-le-Coeur until 1961. The anxiety of waiting for money at American Express offices apparently led to the title of his only novel, *American Express,* a work of surrealist episodes. Corso taught at the State Universities of New York at Buffalo and attended the 1982 Kerouac conference in Boulder, Colorado.

Paul Cummings is adjunct curator of drawings at the Whitney Museum of American Art and the president of the Drawing Society. He was founder and publisher of the *Print Collector's Newsletter* and for a decade the director of the Oral History Program of the Archives of American Art and the editor of its journal. His books are *American Drawings: The 20th Century, Dictionary of Contemporary American Artists,* and *Artists in Their Own Words.* In 1984 he organized and wrote the catalogue of the drawing show of Willem de Kooning's retrospective at the Whitney.

Dick Dabney, raised in Rappahannock County in Virginia, earned a master's degree from American University and a doctorate in American civilization from the University of Virginia. During the beat era he wrote for the *Washington Post Weekly,* an underground paper. Later he was an Op-Ed page columnist for the *Washington Post* and contributor to *Washingtonian* magazine. He wrote *Old Man Jim's Book of Knowledge, The Honor System,* and his best-known book, *A Good Man: The Life of Sam J. Erwin,* published by Houghton Mifflin. In November 1981 Dabney died at 48 of a heart attack, leaving a wife and three children.

Richard Davidson was born in Chicago and settled in New York's Upper West Side in 1954. He gave numerous poetry readings at the Gaslight as well as other coffeehouses. He continues to write and read his poetry in public. His work has appeared in many literary magazines, and he is the author of four poetry books. Davidson is finishing a two-act play, *The Shattered Image*.

Fielding Dawson was born in New York, grew up in Missouri, and attended Black Mountain College. An artist and illustrator as well as poet and author, Dawson's paintings, drawings, and collages have been exhibited widely. He was contributing artist for Daisy Aldan's *New Folder* and Sorrentino's *Neon* and is author of the famous memoir of Franz Kline published by Pantheon in 1967.

David Dempsey was born in Pekin, Illinois, and became a book critic after serving with the Marine Corps in World War II. Formerly with the *New York Times,* he has written numerous short stories, articles, and books, his latest being *The Way We Die* (Macmillan). Dempsey lives in Rye, New York, with his wife.

Diane DiPrima, one of the outstanding authors from the beat era, published her first book, *This Kind of Bird Flies Backwards,* with LeRoi Jones's Totem Press in 1958. DiPrima has more than 15 books to her credit, including her famous *Memories of a Beatnik.* Many of her plays were performed by the Living Theatre. Born in Brooklyn, she has five children and has been living and teaching in California.

Kirby Doyle became prominent in San Francisco in the late 1950s but it was not until 1966 that *Sapphobones,* his first collection of poems, appeared. His best-known work, *Happiness Bastard,* written in 1958, is an autobiographical work dealing with his struggle to survive out of jail, with poverty, drug addiction, and unhappy love affairs. Doyle stopped writing for over ten years and lived alone in the wilderness of California before returning to North Beach in 1982 to finish his epic trilogy, *Pre-American Ode.* Green Light Press in San Francisco brought out his *Collected Works* in 1984.

Robert Duncan was born in Oakland. He edited the *Experimental Review,* one of the first magazines to publish postwar American poetry. He has done over 35 books since the late

'40s and has been at the heart of literary activity in the San Francisco Bay area. Duncan broke ground in 1944 by publishing the controversial essay, "The Homosexual in Society," on a topic rarely discussed then in public.

Kenward Elmslie, a 1950 Harvard graduate, is a librettist, poet, playwright, and novelist who now lives in Vermont. His librettos include *Lizzie Borden, The Sweet Bye and Bye* and *The Seagull.*

Edwin Fancher, a practicing psychologist, was cofounder with Daniel Wolf and Norman Mailer of the *Village Voice* and was its publisher for its first 19 years. In the 1950s and early '60s the *Village Voice* published more articles, criticism, poetry, and photographs on the beat generation than any other newspaper or magazine in America.

Bruce Fearing, the son of the famous Chicago novelist Kenneth Fearing, was graduated from Harvard and at one time was a science writer. His cryptic poetry appeared in many of the beat literary magazines. He now lives in Seattle and corresponds with old friends by sending out photocopied letters filled with beat humor, referring to himself as bruce goose, son of mother goose, and referring to Gregory Corso as Gregory Kerchoo.

Lawrence Ferlinghetti, born in New York, attended Columbia and the University of Paris, where he received his doctorate. He moved to California and began City Lights Press and bookstore in San Francisco. After more than 30 years it is still one of the most influential and successful presses and bookstores in the United States. Ferlinghetti published Ginsberg's *Howl,* Corso's *Gasoline,* and Kerouac's *Book of Dreams* as well as books by Charles Bukowski and Sam Shepard. Ferlinghetti's best-known books are *A Coney Island of the Mind,* with over a million copies in print, and *Endless Life: Selected Poems.* His latest work is *Leaves of Life: Fifty Drawings from the Model.*

Edward Field, born in Brooklyn, was an Air Force navigator flying missions over Germany. His first book of poetry, published by Grove Press in 1963, was awarded the Lamont Poetry Prize. Other honors include the Shelley Memorial Award and a Prix de Rome. He has also edited an anthology of poetry for Bantam Books and collaborated on the novel *Village,* published by Avon, under the pseudonym Bruce Elliot.

John Filler wrote the script for the mythic film *Don Peyote* and worked for John Mitchell constructing the Gaslight Café, the seminal coffeehouse that gave rise to a generation of beat poets and folk singers. Filler free-lanced in writing and film-making. Looking back on that social matrix, he says that "the creative process was a spiritual trip, the most compelling high of all."

Stanley Fisher was an enormously talented, underrated creative artist whose paintings, poetry, and writings had a wide underground reputation. Along with his wife Anita Fay, now working on an autobiographical novel, he edited *Beat Coast East,* an exceptional collection of beat writings. Charles I. Levine and Paul Morrissey based *Peaches and Cream,* a short impressionistic film, on Fisher's paintings. Another film, *Doomsday,* made by Ray Wisniewski, documented his 10th Street painting show, described as a "dark bleeding poem." Stanley Fisher died in 1980.

John Fles was managing editor of the *Chicago Review* and contributing editor of *Kulchur* and has had poetry in all the literary beat magazines. He edited a collection of pieces by Artaud, Genet, and Solomon called *The Trembling Lamb.*

Robert Frank began photographing in Switzerland in 1945 and arrived in New York in March 1947 on the S.S. *James B. Moore.* His enormous success as a still photographer was based on *The Americans,* which he did on a Guggenheim fellowship in 1955. Kerouac wrote the preface. Later they collaborated on *Pull My Daisy.* Written and narrated by Kerouac, it was shot in co-producer Alfred Leslie's loft and starred Ginsberg, Corso, Orlovsky, Larry Rivers, Alice Neel, David Amram, Dick Bellamy, Delphine Seyrig, and Sally Gross. Some of his other films are *Me and My Brother, Life-raft-Earth,* and *About Me.* Frank lives in Nova Scotia and New York.

William Gaddis was born in New York, went to Harvard, and is the recipient of a grant from the National Institute of Arts and Letters and the National Endowment for the Arts. His highly successful novel *The Recognitions* is his best-known work. Another book, *JR,* was published in 1975. Gaddis won a Guggenheim fellowship in 1981 and most recently a fellowship from the MacArthur Foundation in Chicago.

Jack Gelber is the author of the famous Obie-winning play *The Connection,* produced by the Living Theatre. Gelber's other plays include *The Apple, Square in the Eye, The Cuban Thing, Sleep, Rehearsal, Starters,* and an adaptation of Mailer's *Barbary Shore.* He also wrote a novel, *On Ice.* Among the many plays he has directed are Kopit's *Indians* and Coover's *The Kid,* which was awarded an Obie for directing. Gelber lives in Brooklyn with his wife Carol and his two children.

Allen Ginsberg, born in Newark, New Jersey, attended Columbia College, and later sailed in the Merchant Marine. In 1955 he went to San Francisco. His first book, *Howl and Other Poems,* published by City Lights, created a sensation and a court case for obscenity. Ginsberg has been a leading American spokesman for international peace. In 1974 he won the National Book Award for *Fall of America;* in 1982 he won the *Los Angeles Times* award for poetry for "Plutonian Ode." Ginsberg organized the Naropa Institute and the Jack Kerouac School of Disembodied Poetics' *On the Road* conference in Boulder, Colorado, 1982.

Ralph J. Gleason journalist, critic, columnist for the *San Francisco Chronicle,* cofounder and consulting editor of *Rolling Stone,* and a member of the editorial board of *Ramparts,* was born in New York and went to Columbia in the 1930s. He contributed numerous articles on pop music to *Down Beat, Esquire, Show Business,* and *Saturday Review* and produced a number of anthologies and books, including *Celebrating the Duke,* published in 1975, the year Gleason died.

Burt Glinn, a native of Pittsburgh, graduated from Harvard before establishing himself in photography. He collaborated with Laurens van der Post on *A Portrait of All the Russians* and *A Portrait of Japan*. Glinn's reportage includes the Sinai War, the Marine invasion of Lebanon, and Castro's takeover in Cuba. Glinn lives in New York with his wife and son.

Herbert Gold, two years younger than Kerouac at Columbia, frequently criticized the beats in his articles, which appeared in several national magazines. Gold characterized some of Kerouac's work as a "flood of trivia," but praised the novel *Big Sur*. Gold has written numerous articles, stories, and books, which include *Fathers, The Man Who Was Not with It,* and most recently *True Love*. He lives in San Francisco.

Paul Goodman was a writer and social critic and lived in New York. He wrote criticism, fiction, poetry, and works on urban planning and psychotherapy. *Growing Up Absurd, Speaking and Language,* and *Defense of Poetry* are among his best-known works. He died in 1972.

Barbara Guest was born in North Carolina and raised in California. After graduating from UCLA she came to New York, where she was associated with the poets and painters of the New York School. She has published five volumes of poetry and a novel, *Seeking Air,* and collaborated with painters on lithographs and paintings. Her works have appeared in *Partisan Review, Paris Review, Poetry, Commentary,* and *The Nation.* Her latest book, *Herself Defined,* published in 1984 by Doubleday, is a biography of the poet Hilda Doolittle. Barbara Guest lives in New York City and Southampton.

Howard Hart, jazz drummer and free-spirited Catholic poet, shared an apartment with Kerouac and Philip Lamantia in the same building where Micheline lived on the Lower East Side. After sleeping on Hart's floor among girls, musicians, editors, and junkies, Kerouac would take off every morning at 8:00 A.M. sharp. Hart, Kerouac, and David Amram did the first poetry-and-jazz readings in New York at the Brata Gallery, 89 East 10th Street, and at the Circle in the Square. Hart was poetry editor of *Exodus* and author of several books of poetry. He now lives in San Francisco.

Nat Hentoff writes about jazz, civil liberties, politics, and education and for 25 years has been a staff writer for the *Village Voice* and *The New Yorker*. Among his books are *The First Freedom: The Tumultuous History of Free Speech in America* and the novel *Blues for Charlie Darwin*. He lives in New York City.

Sandra Hochman, born in New York and educated at Bennington, is one of America's most successful poets. She is also a screenwriter, novelist, and playwright and has written fiction for children. Her 24 books include *Manhattan Pastures, Earthworks: Selected Poems 1960–1970, Walking Papers, Jogging,* and *Playing Tahoe,* as well as a new novel, *Affairs.* She lives and works in New York.

Ambrose J. Hollingworth appeared briefly in the beat coffeehouses reading his hit poem "Mental Toilet": "During the day I work in a mental toilet. Cardboard box and floor unsweepings, Dull possessors of paralyzed minds. Good 'company men' Not really. Casual lounging brains Which couldn't care less for thinking. Riding around tax free In sometimes physically fit bodies. Rock'n'Roll through process. This daily worker clod worker Doesn't know how much he depresses me Actually refusing to accept knowledge or culture. 'Do not throw rubbish into the toilet bowl.'"

John Clellon Holmes was born in Holyoke, Massachusetts, and attended Columbia. He introduced the term "beat generation" in an essay in *The New York Times Magazine* in 1952, the same year he published his first novel, *Go.* Holmes also wrote *The Horn, Get Home Free, Nothing More to Declare,* and *Death Drag: Selected Poems.* He won a Guggenheim fellowship in writing and is now a university professor of creative writing in Arkansas. Holmes was among those at the Kerouac Conference in Boulder in 1982.

Leonard Horowitz, who was born in Brooklyn and went to the Art Students League, was a popular figure on the scene at beat parties and art openings and in the coffeehouses. He was an art and film critic for the *Village Voice* and the *Soho Weekly News.* He has lived in the same Broadway loft for over 25 years and has been involved in avant-garde filmmaking, photography, and painting.

Harold (Doc) Humes, educated in science and chemical engineering at MIT and Harvard, was one of the founders and consulting editors of the *Paris Review*. When he lived in New York he crusaded against police licensing of poetry readings in cafés and music playing in the public parks, both criminal offenses in the 1950s. Humes is the author of *Underground City, Men Die,* and *Reflections on the Epitaph of Bernoule*. He now lives in Cambridge, where he is in unfunded detoxification community work researching the physical and psychological problems of drug addiction and "combat neurosis."

Herbert Hunke, legendary figure of the beat movement, is Elmo Hassel in *On the Road,* Herman in *Junkie,* Ancke in *Go.* Hunke met Burroughs in the 1940s around the time he acquired a habit for writing and for drugs, eventually spending five years in Sing Sing. In the 1950s Hunke moved into Ginsberg's East 2nd Street building for $30 a month. He was first published in Diane DiPrima's newsletter, *Floating Bear.* His latest book, *The Evening Turned Crimson,* a collection of autobiographical pieces, came out in 1980.

Rona Jaffe began her writing career at the age of two and a half when she dictated her first poem to her mother. Since then she has written a dozen best-sellers, which have sold more than 20 million copies worldwide. After graduating from Radcliffe at the age of 19 she went to work as an editor at Fawcett and in her spare time wrote magazine articles and short stories. Her first book, *The Best of Everything,* published in 1958 when she was 26, was a best-seller and a film. She followed this success with *Class Reunion, The Fame Game, Family Secrets, The Last Chance, Mazes and Monsters, The Other Woman,* and *Mr. Right Is Dead.*

Ted Joans, born on a riverboat on the Fourth of July, is a jazz fanatic and surrealist painter, writer, poet, and world traveler. His friendly presence was ubiquitous during the entire beat era. He gave and went to more parties, poetry readings, and art gallery openings than anybody else. He has at least 29 books to his credit. He went to Africa and Europe in the early 1960s, and lived in Timbuktu. He now lives in West Germany.

Joyce Johnson, née Glassman, met Kerouac through Allen Ginsberg on a blind date in 1957 when she was 21 and became his on-and-off lover. She recounts her story in her brilliant 1983 book *Minor Characters*. Joyce Johnson is now executive editor at the Dial Press and lives in New York. Her two other books are *Bad Connections* and *Come and Join the Dance.*

Hettie Jones, born in Brooklyn and raised in Queens, left home in 1951 for college and eventually hit the Village in 1956. She married LeRoi Jones in 1958, had two children, and got divorced in 1965. She worked on the *Partisan Review,* co-edited *Yugen* and Totem Press books, and has edited and written numerous books for children, including *Big Star* and *Fallin' Mama—Five Women in Black Music.* Her poetry and stories have been in *Sunbury, Infinite #,* and *Ikon.* The latest book she has edited is *Memory Babe* for Grove Press and her most recent publication is *Having Been Her.*

LeRoi Jones became Amiri Baraka in the 1970s. He attended Rutgers, Howard, and Columbia, served in the Air Force, was co-editor of *Yugen* and Totem Press Books and music editor of *Kulchur,* and has been a seminal force in Afro-American literature. Poet, musician, critic, essayist, dramatist, novelist, and political activist, Baraka has won a Long View Award and John Hay Whitney and Guggenheim fellowships as well as an Obie from the *Village Voice* for his classic play *The Dutchman,* later made into a film by Shirley Clarke. He has seven children and 30 books to his credit and lives and works in Newark, New Jersey, with his present wife, Amina Baraka.

Bob Kaufman, known in France as the "Black American Rimbaud," is the author of *Solitudes Crowded with Loneliness* (New Directions), *The Golden Sardine* (City Lights), and *The Ancient Rain* (New Directions). He cofounded *Beatitude* magazine in 1959 with Allen Ginsberg, John Kelly, and Bill Margolis. Kaufman costarred in the Ron Rice film *The Flower Thief,* which won the Spoleto Film Festival award.

Jack Kerouac was born in Lowell, Massachusetts, attended Horace Mann and Columbia University on a football scholarship, and was a World War II Merchant Marine. His first novel, *The Town and the City,* was published in 1950. *On the Road,* the quintessential beat novel, published in 1957, spoke for an entire postwar youth generation and was his most famous and successful work. Some of the others were *Dharma Bums, Doctor Sax, Maggie Cassady,* and *The Subterraneans.* Altogether 22 of his books were published. In 1969 he died of hemorrhaging esophageal varices, the classic drunkard's death, in his mother's house in St. Petersburg, Florida. The best biographies of Kerouac are by Gerald Nicosa, Ann Charters, Barry Clifford, and Lawrence Lee.

Edward Klein began his career as a copy boy, then feature writer, for the *New York Daily News.* He is a graduate of the Columbia School of Journalism, spent three years in Japan on the *Japan Times* and as a correspondent for UPI, and later was *Newsweek*'s foreign editor, winning two Page One Awards for the magazine. In 1977 he became editor of *The New York Times Magazine.* Klein's novels include *If Israel Lost the War,* published by Coward-McCann, and *The Parachutists,* published by Doubleday and selected as a feature alternate by the Book-of-the-Month Club.

Franz Kline, one of America's foremost abstract painters, was born in Wilkes-Barre, Pennsylvania, studied art in Boston and London, came to New York in 1938, and had his first show in 1950. His teaching at Black Mountain College brought him in touch with numerous poets with whom he drank at the Cedar Street Tavern, Joel Oppenheimer among them. Kline was the subject of writings by Frank O'Hara and Fielding Dawson, who wrote *An Emotional Memoir of Franz Kline,* published by Pantheon. On May 13, 1962, Kline died in New York.

Kenneth Koch was born in Cincinnati, Ohio, went to Harvard, and is a professor at Columbia University. Along with numerous volumes of poetry, Koch has published three books of plays, a novel, and several books about teaching children to write poetry. His plays have been performed on and off Broadway. He has been a Fulbright and Guggenheim Fellow. Koch's recent works are *The Art of Love* and *The Burning Mystery of Anna.*

Jaakov Kohn was the famous editor of the *East Village Other* and the *Soho Weekly News*. Before that he was one of the best jewelry makers in Greenwich Village (along with Sam Kramer). When he gave that up he moved to suburbia with his wife and five children only to return to Lower Manhattan when his house burned down. Kohn, who emigrated from Czechoslovakia to Israel, was a patriot in the underground there, had a run-in with a British tank in 1948, and then came to the U.S.A. for medical treatment. As a result of his war wounds, Kohn is now crippled and wheelchair-bound.

Seymour Krim has been published in the *Washington Post Book World*, the *New York Times Book Review*, the *New Republic*, the *Village Voice*, the *Provincetown Review*, the *New York Herald Tribune*, the *Partisan Review*, *Exodus*, and *Commentary*. His criticism, essays, and the anthology *The Beats* earned him a reputation as an authority on that generation of writers. He teaches at Columbia and lives in New York.

Tuli Kupferberg, offbeat pamphleteer, writer, poet, publisher of *Birth*, and author of 20 books, in particular *1001 Ways to Beat the Draft*, *1001 Ways to Live Without Working*, and *1001 Ways to Make Love*, lives in Greenwich Village. He was founder, songwriter, and tambourine player of the Fugs, the notorious satirical radrock group. He is also director of the Revolving Theatre and a singing cartoonist. His latest book is *Was It Good for You Too?*

Philip Lamantia was identified as a surrealist poet by André Breton as early as 1943. He worked as an editor on *View*, the famous surrealist magazine of the 1940s edited by Charles Henri Ford. Later associated with the San Francisco beats, Lamantia was identified as Francis DaPavia in Kerouac's *Dharma Bums*. Lamantia's important works include *Erotic Poems*, *Ekstasis*, *Destroyed Works*, and *Becoming Visible*. He is still on the road out west.

Alfred Leslie was born in New York and studied art at NYU. He was coproducer with Robert Frank of the famous film *Pull My Daisy*. In 1960 he edited and published *The Hasty Papers,* a compendium of avant-garde art and literature. He was a Guggenheim fellow in 1969. Leslie is still a successful artist whose works are in the Whitney Museum and the Museum of Modern Art collections.

Denise Levertov, writer, teacher, poet, translator, was born in Ilford, Essex, England, worked as a London nurse during World War II, and later married the American writer Mitchell Goodman. Since 1946 she has published over 25 books of poems, essays, and translations. She is a Fannie Hurst Professor at Brandeis University, a member of the American Academy and Institute of Arts and Letters, and a winner of the Elmer Holmes Bobst Award in 1983. Her latest work is *Babylon,* published by New Directions. A bibliography of Denise Levertov was compiled by Robert A. Wilson. She now lives in Massachusetts.

Stephen Levine, born in New York, coordinated some of the Gaslight poetry readings. His first collection of poems, *A Resonance of Hope,* was published in 1959 and reviewed in the *Village Voice* by William Packard, who called Levine "a poet of loneliness." He participated in the editing process on the anthology *Writers in Revolt* with Alex Trocchi, Terry Southern, and Richard Seaver. Among Levine's other works is *Synapse—Sutras, Myths and Visions of the Retinal Circus.*

Lawrence Lipton, poet, novelist, lecturer, and beat chronicler, was born in Poland and died in 1975 at the age of 76. He is best known for *The Erotic Revolution* and *The Holy Barbarians*. The original cover featured two men with one woman in bed. The copy read: "The complete story of that hip, cool, frantic generation of new bohemians who are turning the American scale of values inside out." He wrote six books and co-authored 22 books of mystery fiction under the pseudonym Craig Rice.

Daniel List, onetime U.S. Navy flight meteorologist, settled in Greenwich Village right out of service, supporting himself by building picture frames and working in a coffeehouse. He was a sports car collector and repairman, which led to his writing career as auto columnist for the *Village Voice* in the early days.

More recently, List has been publisher's consultant for *Industrial Design, Harper's Bazaar,* the *Soho Weekly News,* and the *East Village Eye.*

Bob Lubin ran away from Brooklyn at the age of 16 with the poet's gleam in his eye to live the bohemian life in Greenwich Village. He ran the poetry circle at the Gaslight Café in the '50s, later gave up writing altogether, and is now involved in architectural design. He has lived in various Soho lofts for over 25 years.

Jack McClintock, a free-lance magazine writer, first visited Kerouac on assignment for the *Miami Herald's* Sunday magazine, *Topic,* to do a brief interview. He returned for many subsequent visits along with friends Richard Hill and Al Ellis. Knowing he would die soon, Kerouac asked them questions about funeral homes and embalming, concerned that the undertaker treat his body with dignity. After Kerouac's death, McClintock wrote *Esquire's* valedictory reminiscense, "This Is How the Ride Ends." McClintock lives and works in Miami.

Michael McClure was born in Kansas and in the early 1950s settled in San Francisco, where he became part of the beat renaissance. He has written nine books of poetry and 20 plays, which include *The Beard,* a winner of two *Village Voice* Obie Awards, and *Josephine and the Mouse Singer,* an Obie winner for best play. McClure and his wife Joanna, also a poet, were prominent participants in the Boulder, Colorado, Kerouac Conference held in 1982, the same year McClure's essay collection *Scratching the Beat Surface* was published. His latest work, published by New Directions, is *Fragments of Perseys.*

Fred W. McDarrah, born in Brooklyn, made an early and important contribution to beat literature with his photos and poems he collected for *The Beat Scene,* published in 1960 by Corinth Books. He won a Guggenheim fellowship in photography as well as two Page One awards from the Newspaper Guild of New York for spot news. His photographs have been published widely and he is the author of several books. McDarrah has been picture editor for the *Village Voice* for over 25 years.

Gloria Schoffel McDarrah, born in the Bronx, has lived in Greenwich Village since graduating from Penn State, where she majored in Latin and French. She worked on the editorial development of *The Beat Scene* and wrote the text for *The Artist's World,* coproduced with her husband. She is now a travel book editor for Simon & Schuster and is currently writing travel articles and editing a book devoted to exotic trips taken by prewar figures in literature. She has two sons, Timothy and Patrick. Her latest book is a guide to Atlantic City.

Thomas McGrath, born in North Dakota, went to Louisiana State University, worked in the shipyards in Kearny, New Jersey, shipped out during World War II to the Aleutian Islands, became a Rhodes Scholar at Oxford University, taught at Los Angeles State College, was called before HUAC, was subsequently fired and blacklisted, and went on to write documentary films and produce 20 volumes, including a novel and two children's books. McGrath won an NEA grant, a Guggenheim fellowship, and an Amy Lowell Travel Poetry Scholarship. His latest titles are *Passage Toward the Dark, Letter to an Imagined Friend,* and *Echoes Inside the Labyrinth.* McGrath is now professor emeritus at Moorhead State University in Minnesota.

David McReynolds, a native of Los Angeles, graduated in political science from UCLA, works full-time for the War Resistors League in New York, was a Socialist Party candidate for President in 1980, and has written extensively on politics, art, culture, and the history of the pacifist movement. His essays are collected in *We Have Been Invaded by the 21st Century.*

Norman Mailer, Harvard-educated, was an overnight success with his famous novel *The Naked and the Dead,* published when he was 25. He was among those who launched the *Village Voice.* In 1957 he wrote the classic essay "The White Negro," in which he compared hipsters to Negroes. He has written over 30 books, ran for mayor of New York with Jimmy Breslin, and twice won a Pulitzer Prize, for *The Executioner's Song* and *Armies of the Night.* Mailer has produced and acted in both underground and Hollywood films. His *Ancient Evenings,* published in 1983, was among his most successful books. He lives in Brooklyn Heights.

W. H. (Bill) Manville, magazine writer and novelist from Brooklyn, worked in an advertising agency before he went to the *Village Voice* to write the "Saloon Society" column, which eventually became the title of his first book. He has written numerous magazine articles, especially for *Cosmopolitan,* and is the author of *Breaking Up, Goodbye,* and *The Palace of Money*. He is married to the writer Nancy Friday and lives in Key West and in New York City.

Edward Marshall came from rural New Hampshire, was raised by an aunt and uncle, went to New England College, and studied religion and culture at Columbia when he came to New York in 1953. He published his work in *Black Mountain Review, Measure, Mulch,* and *Yugen* and in Donald Allen's historic anthology *The New American Poetry: 1945–1960,* in which he had the longest single poem. Marshall was essay editor of *Exodus,* read mostly at the Seven Arts and the Gaslight, and published three works, *Hellan, Hellan, Transit Gloria,* and *Leave the Word Alone,* his 1955 epic poem, an outpouring of consciousness focused on the poet's mother. Marshall last read his poems at the St. Mark's Poetry Project in New York in 1975.

Taylor Mead, born in Detroit, son of a powerful politician, is better known for his comic acting roles than for his literary accomplishment. In 1984 he played Broadway. The star of Andy Warhol's 1968 film *Lonesome Cowboy,* Mead also played in Ron Rice's *Flower Thief* and *Queen of Sheba Meets the Atom Man* and Jonas Mekas's *Halleluja the Hills* and *Babo 73,* and he won an Obie Award for his performance in Frank O'Hara's play *The General Returns from One Place to Another*. Mead's poetry notebooks have been compared to the works of Kerouac and Ginsberg.

Danny Meenan has been the best street reporter in New York for over 35 years. He grew up on the West Side of Manhattan, went to Columbia College, and became a reporter for the *New*

York Daily News in 1946, covering the police beat for $24 a week. He then became a reporter for the Mike Wallace television show and in 1960 joined WMCA Radio.

Jonas Mekas was a film critic for the *Village Voice* and is known as the guru of American underground film. He filmed the Living Theatre production of Kenneth Brown's *The Brig,* which was the grand prize winner of the Venice Documentary Film Festival in 1964. His *Documents of the Sixties,* released in 1983, was the subject of a retrospective at the Collective for Living Cinema. He lives in Soho with his family.

Jack Micheline, Bronx-born author and playwright, has ten volumes to his credit. Micheline is well established in the great bohemian tradition as a street poet-balladeer. His poetry is meant to be read. Micheline's collection *North of Manhattan* includes poems from 1954 to 1975. His latest book, *Skinny Dynamite,* was published in 1980. He was a central figure in the 1982 Kerouac Conference and was then given an award for his poetry. Micheline now lives in San Francisco.

Gilbert Millstein assigned John Clellon Holmes to write "This Is the Beat Generation" for *The New York Times Sunday Magazine* in 1952; it was the first article on the subject. Millstein later wrote the first important review of *On the Road* for the *New York Times,* when he was a staff writer. He was an early organizer of jazz and poetry readings that featured Kerouac. Millstein now writes books and is a news editor for television. His best-seller *New York* was published by Harry Abrams. His latest book is *God and Harvey Grosbeck.*

Charles Mingus, born in Nogales, Arizona, was America's premier composer and bass player and among the first to introduce jazz and poetry. He won Guggenheim fellowships in 1971 and in 1978. Mingus's autobiography, *Beneath the Underdog,* was published by Knopf in 1971. He died in 1979.

John Mitchell ran the Gaslight Café, the most successful coffeehouse in Greenwich Village in the 1950s. All the great poets read there. Later the café was devoted to folk music and after that was the first place the new comics started. Mitchell published an anthology of beat generation poets and along with Emanuel Roth, the Rev. Howard Moody, Roderick MacDonald, Rick Allmen, and lawyers Edward Koch, Mark Lane, and Leonard Bodine fought the police and won the right to have poetry readings in cafés without a cabaret license. Mitchell lives in New York City and is at work writing his autobiography.

Barbara Moraff went to Columbia and had her first book, *Four Young Lady Poets,* published by Corinth Press in 1962. She lives in a Vermont farmhouse and has a son born in 1971. She resumed writing poetry in 1976 and since then has published *The Life, Learning to Move,* and *Telephone Company Repairman Poems,* and her journal excerpts appeared in *Ariadne's Thread,* published by Harper & Row. Moraff works as a potter and cofounded a crafts co-op school in the town where she lives.

Joseph Morgenstern has been a foreign correspondent for the *New York Times,* a theater critic for the *New York Herald Tribune,* and a movie critic for *Newsweek.* An Emmy Award nominee for *The Boy in the Plastic Bubble,* Morgenstern now lives in Los Angeles and is a columnist for the *Los Angeles Herald Examiner.*

William Morris, from Los Angeles, a pupil of William Carlos Williams and Joan Miró, was among the most ubiquitous MacDougal Street coffeehouse poets. He was also an accomplished artist who once had an exhibit consisting of one painting which took up the entire four walls of the gallery. He painted a picture using a truck tire instead of a paintbrush and also painted with his bare feet. His offbeat antics were often in the media. He once rode a motor scooter from Barcelona to Denmark. He moved to England some years ago and has not been heard from since.

Brigid Murnaghan, born in the "Holyland of the Bronx," moved to MacDougal Street in Greenwich Village in 1948 and by 1984 had moved one block away to Bleecker Street. She was the first film critic for the *Village Voice* and wrote terse, lucid, incisive reviews which immediately earned her a reputation.

She has been a central figure on the beat scene for three decades, writing and reading her poetry, running a weekly salon in a Bleecker Street tavern, working on a dramatization of "a book by Harold Lyden who was a radio operator on the *Exodus,* a ferry boat that went from Norfolk to Baltimore and was put into service across the Atlantic." Now an "American Mother," Murnaghan has two grown children.

Eric Nord, whose real name was Harry Hilmuth Pastor, started a coffeehouse in Venice, California, called the Gas House, where, as *Time* magazine put it in 1959, "the jukebox blared the beatniks 3 B's: Bach, Bartok and Bird." His famed "party pad" was an old produce warehouse where he threw bottle parties and poetry readings and charged $1 admission. Nord's eccentricities, scrapes with the police, and defense of the beats made him the high priest of the San Francisco scene. He later became the entrepreneur of North Beach's most successful rendezvous, the Co-Existence Bagel Shop.

Frank O'Hara, art critic and poet, was born in Baltimore, raised in New England, and educated at Harvard. He was a curator at the Museum of Modern Art from 1951 until his sudden death in 1966 when he was struck by a Fire Island beach taxi. He was one of the founders of the New York School of Poetry, a clique of mostly non-beat Harvard poets and second-generation abstract painters. He produced 14 books and is eulogized in *Homage to Frank O'Hara,* edited by Bill Berkson and Joe LeSueur.

Joel Oppenheimer comes from Yonkers, New York, went to Cornell, the University of Chicago, and Black Mountain College, and is an accomplished poet, novelist, and playwright as well as a sports writer *(The Wrong Season)*. He has been a columnist for the *Village Voice* for many years and resident poet at City College. Oppenheimer is now teaching journalism and creative writing at New England College.

Peter Orlovsky posed nude with Allen Ginsberg for a full-length photograph by Richard Avedon in 1963. Circulated widely as a poster, it helped raise the public awareness of gay unions. The poets met in 1954 in North Beach. Three years later, while in Paris, Orlovsky began to write poetry. His latest work, *Straight Hearts Delight: Love Poems and Selected Letters*, was published in 1980. Orlovsky won a grant from the National Endowment for the Arts. In addition to owning an apartment in New York, Orlovsky lives on a farm in Cherry Valley, New York, that he shares with Ginsberg.

Grace Paley, writer, political activist, and teacher, lives in Greenwich Village and became a cult figure with her enormously successful book *The Little Disturbances of Man: Stories of Men and Women at Love,* published by New American Library. Her other recent book is *Enormous Changes at the Last Minute.* She has devoted much of her career to the peace movement and in counseling young people of draft age. She has been for many years a faculty member of Sarah Lawrence College in Bronxville, New York.

Kenneth Patchen, who died at 60 in 1972, was an elder statesman to the San Francisco beats. In the 1950s he launched a new image of the poet as a swinging public spokesman by combining poetry and jazz. He performed in nightclubs, in concert halls, on college campuses, on radio and TV. In addition to more than two dozen books, Patchen made several records of his readings with jazz accompaniment.

Norman Podhoretz became the editor-in-chief of *Commentary* in 1960, a position he still holds. Among his important books are *Making It, Breaking Ranks,* and *Why We Were in Vietnam.* Some of the best critical articles about the beats were written by Podhoretz and appeared in the *Partisan Review* and *Esquire.*

Larry Poons, whose father was in business in Kobe, Japan, was born in Ogikubo near Tokyo. He went to the New England Conservatory of Music but became a painter, moved to New York, and took a Front Street loft in 1958. Poons ran the Epitome, 165 Bleecker Street, one of the liveliest poetry cafés of the beat period. Poons is now a world-famous artist whose work has been shown in numerous galleries and museums all over the world. He is represented by André Emmerich.

George Nelson Preston had a storefront "Artist's Studio" at 48 East 3rd Street where he orchestrated the most important poetry readings ever held in New York. One historic program on Sunday, February 15, 1959, included Kerouac, Ginsberg, Corso, Orlovsky, LeRoi Jones, Jose Garcia Villa, Edward Marshall, Ted Joans, and others. Both a poet and an artist, Preston went to Music and Art High School and CCNY and got his Ph.D. from Columbia University. He is now an associate professor in art history at CCNY. He has traveled and lived in Africa and is a widely published, world-renowned authority on African art. His new book is *Akon Commemorative Terra Cottas.*

Dan Propper graduated from P.S. 18 in Brooklyn. He received his first recognition as a poet with "The Fable of the Final Hour," published in Seymour Krim's *The Beats.* Propper participated in jazz readings with Dizzy Gillespie and Thelonious Monk and was on CBS television with the Jazz Quintet. His most recent work, *For Kerouac in Heaven,* was published in 1980. He lives in California.

Margaret Randall was a central figure on the New York beat scene and moved to Mexico City in 1961, where she edited *El Corno Emplumado* for eight years. In 23 years outside the United States, she lived in Mexico, Cuba, and finally Nicaragua. In 1984 she returned to her homeland. She now lives in Albuquerque, New Mexico, writing poetry and oral history and doing photography. Among some 40 books are *October, Part of the Solution, Cuban Women Now, Inside the Nicaraguan Revolution: The Story of Doris María, We, Carlota, Cuban Women: 20 Years Later, Sandino's Daughters, Spirit of the People: The Women of Vietnam,* and *Christians in the Nicaraguan Revolution.*

Marc Ratliff moved from Cincinnati to New York in 1955 to go to Cooper Union, and later attended Yale University. He lived at the Judson Student House and was one of the founders of the famous avant-garde Judson Gallery, as well as the beat magazine *Exodus,* where he served as art editor. Jim Dine, a hometown chum, Claes Oldenburg, who worked in the library at Cooper Union, and Tom Wesslemen were discovered by Ratliff and had their first shows at the Judson Gallery. Ratliff went to England to work for Studio International, then returned to New York to run his design studio. He now lives in Rockland with his British wife and two sons.

Kenneth Rexroth, poet, painter, dramatist, critic, translator, editor, and mentor of the San Francisco beats, was 76 when he died in 1982. Winner of numerous awards, including a 1948 Guggenheim fellowship, Rexroth published nearly 25 books in his lifetime. Rexroth organized the famous reading "Six Poets at the Six Gallery" in San Francisco, but only five poets actually read: McClure, Lamantia, Snyder, Whalen, and Ginsberg, whose first reading of *Howl* resulted in the famous censorship court trial.

Larry Rivers, poet and saxophone player, originally tried to seek his fortune as a musician. Instead he became one of the most famous painters in the country. He read poetry at the Living Theatre and portrayed Milo, the Neal Cassady character, in Robert Frank's *Pull My Daisy*.

Hugh Romney was among the best-dressed younger beat poets in Greenwich Village in the late '50s. He once teamed up with the blind musician Moondog and the falsetto singer Tiny Tim and played at the Fat Black Pussy Cat, 13 Minetta Street. He was an organizer of the 1968 "Pigasus for President" election campaign, and was emcee at the Woodstock Music Festival the following year. Later Romney became "Wavy-Gravy," the nonsense guru of the Hog Farm, a vagabond traveling commune. He was among the most vociferous antiwar activists during the Vietnam era and was the star of Robert Frank's film *Life-Raft-Earth,* a documentary. Romney lives in Berkeley and leads a circus called Camp Winnarainbow.

Irving Rosenthal was editor of the Spring and Autumn 1958 issues of *Chicago Review,* each of which contained a controversial chapter from *Naked Lunch.* The columnist Albert Podell, writing in the *Chicago Daily News,* attacked the publication and called it "Filthy Writing on the Midway," which resulted in the University of Chicago's banning the issue containing the second installment of Burroughs's book. Rosenthal then became the editor of Volume 1, Number 1 of *Big Table,* which was later impounded by the Post Office. Rosenthal now lives and works in San Francisco.

Barney Rosset, founder and president of Grove Press, was the publisher and editor, along with Fred Jordan, Richard Seaver, and Donald Allen, of *Evergreen Review,* the most prestigious avant-garde publication of the beat generation. Over 95 issues were published from 1957 until 1967. The works of many of the best-known composers, writers, poets, playwrights, painters, and photographers appeared in *Evergreen Review.* Rosset's Grove Press brought out Gerald Nicosia's *Memory Babe* in 1983, the definitive biography of Kerouac.

Rosemarie Santini, the author of *The Secret Fire* and *Abracadabra,* lectures on fiction at New York University and is now working on a miniseries for television. She was born in Greenwich Village and at a young age was given a special pass to the inner circle of San Remo writers, who were to change her life forever and form her artistic aesthetic. When she became a writer during the '60s sexual revolution, she "remembered their courage and missed them."

William Saroyan was the prolific author of several dozen volumes of stories, novels, and plays, including *The Time of Your Life,* for which he won a Pulitzer Prize. He was one of the earliest influences on Kerouac as a writer. Saroyan wrote about small towns and their inhabitants, subjects Kerouac related to. His first full-length book, *Atop an Underwood,* was in the Saroyan-Hemingway-Wolfe style. Saroyan died in 1981.

Marc D. Schleifer was the founder and editor of *Kulchur.* He did the first three issues and then went to Cuba. Schleifer was among the early *Village Voice* writers. He was born Jewish, later became a Moslem, changed his name to Suleiman Abdullah Schleifer, and moved to Cairo, Egypt. He later was chief of the NBC Bureau there and now teaches at the American University in Cairo.

Richard Seaver was an editor of *Merlin,* a literary magazine published in Paris during the early 1950s, which published the early works of Samuel Beckett, Jean Genet, and Eugene Ionesco, among others. In the 1960s he was managing editor of *Evergreen Review* and editorial director of Grove Press. During the 1970s he and his wife Jeannette founded Seaver Books, an imprint of the Viking Press which Mrs. Seaver still directs. Richard Seaver is currently president and publisher of the General Book Division of Holt, Rinehart and Winston.

Hubert Selby, Jr., was born and raised in Brooklyn. He went to sea as a Merchant Marine for several years before he contracted tuberculosis in Germany and spent three years in the hospital. He worked as a wire boy, clerk, secretary, and typist to support himself while writing. His work has appeared in *Black Mountain Review, Provincetown Review,* and *Kulchur,* in which he wrote a classic essay on brutality in mental hospitals, using the pseudonym Harry Black. His most famous and controversial novel, *Last Exit to Brooklyn,* was published by Grove Press in 1960 and is still in print. Selby now lives and works in Hollywood.

Shel Silverstein, author, cartoonist, composer, and folksinger, was born in Chicago. He was a correspondent for *Pacific Stars and Stripes* and achieved fame and fortune as a regular contributor to *Playboy* magazine. He has done about a dozen children's books and created the famous Uncle Shelby character. His recent books are *The Giving Tree, Where the Sidewalk Ends, A Light in the Attic,* and *Who Wants a Cheap Rhinoceros?*

Howard Smith has been a writer for the *Village Voice* since 1957, when, at age 20, his very first article (about Kerouac) was published. That piece was among the earliest to appear about the soon-to-be-famous author. Since 1966 Smith has penned "Scenes," the weekly *Voice* column. In addition, his work has appeared in many U.S. and foreign magazines. He's been a photojournalist, nationally syndicated radio talk show host, and cable television programming consultant, and has been producer/director of two feature documentaries, *Gizmo* and the Academy Award winner *Marjoe.*

William Lloyd Smith was a Chicago beatnik philosopher who ran for President in 1960. He ran as a "pacifist anarchist" who would abolish the government if he won and return the United States to a group of small primitive tribes. His campaign, although widely publicized, gained little support. He was an ideal oddball nominee, one who couldn't win, didn't want to win, and disapproved of winning on principle.

Gary Snyder, woodsman, linguist, anthropologist, and poet, was born in San Francisco, graduated from Reed College, and studied classical Chinese at Berkeley. In 1956 he went to Japan to study Zen Buddhism. He was the prototype for the Japhy Ryder fiction hero in Kerouac's *Dharma Bums.* He published his first book, *Riprap,* in 1959 and has since won a Bollingen fellowship and Guggenheim fellowship and a Pulitzer Prize in 1974 for his book *Turtle Island.*

Harriet Sohmers spent ten years in Paris writing, working for the *Herald Tribune,* and translating. Published in *Newstory, Swank, Nugget, Provincetown Review* (where she was also an editor), and *The Bold New Women,* she now teaches in Brooklyn. Her 20-year-old son Milo is a rock drummer.

Carl Solomon, born in the Bronx, was a child prodigy at seven. He went to CCNY, Brooklyn College, and the Sorbonne. Fascinated with Solomon's life, Allen Ginsberg, whom he had met in 1949, made him a legend by portraying him in *Howl.* An editor for his uncle's publishing house, Ace Books, Solomon published Burroughs's *Junkie* and in 1952 gave Kerouac a $250 advance for *On the Road,* but nothing materialized. Like Kerouac, Solomon was influenced by Saroyan. He still lives in the Bronx.

Susan Sontag earned a master's degree in philosophy from Harvard and began writing fiction and criticism in her late 20s. She has also written and directed films and is one of the most influential cultural critics in America. Her writings include *Notes on Camp, Styles of Radical Will, Illness as Metaphor,* and *On Photography.*

Gilbert Sorrentino was living in Brooklyn when he edited and published *Neon* from 1956 to 1960. He was also an editor at Grove Press. Sorrentino has written many poems and short stories and seven novels, including *Mulligan Stew, The Sky Changes, Aberration of Starlight, Steelwork,* and *Blue Pastoral.* He taught at the New School and now is full professor at Stanford University in Palo Alto, California.

William Styron was born in Virginia and went to Duke University. He wrote *Lie Down in Darkness* when he was 26. Among his best-known works are the Pulitzer Prize novel *The Confessions of Nat Turner* and *Sophie's Choice,* which was made into an Oscar-winning film. He has also been an editor at the *Paris Review* since 1953 and is on the editorial board of *American Scholar.* Styron lives and works in Connecticut.

Jerry Tallmer, a founding member of the *Village Voice,* was the associate editor and drama critic. He has been a reporter, critic, and feature writer for the *New York Post* since 1962. He was among the first to interview Kerouac when *On the Road* was published.

Sylvia Topp was born in Ottawa and has written for the *Village Voice, Mothering, Birth,* and *Swing* magazine. She was head of production at the *Soho Weekly News* for many years and has edited three books, all titled *As They Were,* containing writings and photos of well-known people as children. She lives in Greenwich Village with her husband Tuli Kupferberg.

Diana Trilling is a writer and editor on literary, social, and political subjects and is a contributor to *Partisan Review, Commentary, American Scholar, Harper's, Atlantic, Vanity Fair,* and the *Times* of London. Her most famous work is *Mrs. Harris—The Death of the Scarsdale Diet Doctor,* published by Harcourt Brace. Also to her credit is *Reviewing the Forties, We Must March My Darlings: A Critical Decade, D.H. Lawrence 1885–1930,* and *Claremont Essays,* a collection of her best work. The writer and teacher Lionel Trilling is her husband.

Stanley Twardowicz, painter and photographer, was Kerouac's neighbor in Northport, Long Island. Kerouac moved there in 1962 with his mother and gave the address only to trusted friends. He was the only one Twardowicz permitted in his studio, and it was where Kerouac did a painting of the "Pietà" and some drawings that Twardowicz has hanging on his wall. Their friendship was one of the most important in Kerouac's last years.

Jose Garcia Villa came from the Philippines, taught poetry at the New School for Social Research, and was a presidential adviser to the Philippine government on cultural affairs. His books of poems have been published widely, most notably *The Doveglion Book of Philippine Poetry, The Portable Villa,* and *The Essential Villa.*

Ronald Von Ehmsen was the quintessential bearded beatnik exhibitionist, media's darling, a ladies' man, a Christ figure to some, a legend in Greenwich Village. He modeled for fashion magazines, rented himself out as a beatnik, was taken to his gigs in a limousine, and ran the famous Café Rafio at 165 Bleecker Street until one day, wanting to enlarge the café, he served an eviction notice to the tenant who occupied the rear premises. But the angry 73-year-old occupant pulled out a .32 caliber revolver and shot Von Ehmsen three times, killing him right in the middle of Bleecker Street in front of the Café Rafio.

Dan Wakefield is a writer now living in Boston whose journalism has appeared in *The Nation, Atlantic Monthly, Esquire,* and many other publications. His novels include *Going All the Way, Starting Over,* and most recently *Under the Apple Tree.* Wakefield graduated from Columbia College and was a Neiman fellow at Harvard.

Bill Walker ran a famous coffeehouse in Washington, D.C., called Coffee and Confusion. He later became Norman Mailer's self-proclaimed bodyguard during his New York mayoralty campaign in 1969. Bill Walker died in a car crash in the 1970s.

William V. Ward, born in New York, has a political science degree from Boston University. He lived in Paris and also did a two-year research project in India. He is a poet and former editor of the famous *Provincetown Review.* Ward now lives in

Brooklyn Heights and works for the New York City Board of Education. He has a son, Sean Michelangelo.

Lew Welch was a high school track star who started out reading Joyce Kilmer and Robert Service. At Reed College he roomed with Philip Whalen and Gary Snyder. Welch, Kerouac, and Albert Saijo collaborated on the 1959 collection *Trip Trap, Haiku Along the Road from San Francisco to New York,* part of which was written on their visit with Fred and Gloria McDarrah in New York. Welch's collected works appeared in 1977, five years after his strange disappearance in the foothills of the Sierra Nevada, described in Aram Saroyan's definitive portrait, *Genesis Angels,* published by William Morrow in 1977.

Philip Whalen was born in Oregon, attended Reed College with Gary Snyder and Lew Welch, and was a leading figure of the San Francisco poetry renaissance. He first gained notoriety and a reputation at the Six Gallery reading on October 13, 1955. He has published over 20 books, including *Memoirs of an Interglacial Age* and *On Bear's Head: Selected Poems.*

John Wieners graduated from Boston College and attended Black Mountain College. He founded the magazine *Measure,* which published poets associated with Jesuit orders and with the San Francisco beat movement. He is the author of the dime-store opus *She's Turn on a Dime, The Hotel Wentley Poems, Behind the State Capitol,* and most recently *Dolores.*

Ted Wilentz was co-owner of the 8th Street Bookshop, a famous literary hangout in Greenwich Village. Wilentz was also the publisher with his wife Joan of Corinth Books, a small press that has produced 66 books since 1959, including Fred McDarrah's *The Beat Scene, Greenwich Village,* and *New York, New York* as well as books by Kerouac, Robert Creeley, Charles Olson, Frank O'Hara, Philip Whalen, LeRoi Jones, Gary Snyder, Barbara Guest, and Diane DiPrima.

Jonathan C. Williams, poet, publisher, essayist, photographer, and hiker, was born in Asheville, North Carolina, and educated at St. Albans School, Princeton, "Atelier 17," the Institute of Design in Chicago, and Black Mountain College. He is best known for his Jargon Society books, which include important texts by Charles Olson, Robert Duncan, Louis Zukofsky, Kenneth Patchen, Mina Loy, and others. Williams has won a Guggenheim fellowship and a National Endowment for the Arts grant. He divides his time between a farm in Highlands, North Carolina, and a stone cottage in Dentdale, Cumbria, England.

Daniel Wolf was educated mostly at the New School for Social Research and started his career writing sections of *The Columbia Encyclopedia* on Greek, Roman, and Arabic philosophy and psychology. He cofounded the *Village Voice* in 1955 and was editor for its first 19 years. He lives in Greenwich Village with his wife and two children and is now a nonpaid adviser to the mayor of New York.

Marian Zazeela majored in painting with Paul Feeley at Bennington College and graduated in 1960. She has presented light installations and conducted light performances throughout the United States and Europe and won both NEA and CAPS grants. She has collaborated with the avant-garde composer LaMonte Young and has been studying Indian classical vocal music with Pandit Pran Nath. Marian Zazeela currently holds a commission from Dia Art Foundation for research, design, and construction "of more permanent locations for extended duration installations and performances of her major works." She lives in New York.

BIBLIOGRAPHY

BOOKS

Allen, Donald M., ed. *The New American Poetry: 1945-1960*. New York: Grove, 1960.

Allen, Donald M., and Warren Tallman, eds. *Poetics of the New American Poetry*. New York: Grove, 1974.

Anderson, Elliot, ed. *TriQuarterly 43, The Little Magazine in America: A Modern Documentary History*. Evanston, Ill.: Northwestern University, 1978.

Bartlett, Lee, ed. *The Beats: Essays in Criticism*. Jefferson, N.C.: McFarland, 1981.

Beaulieu, Victor-Lévy. *Jack Kerouac: A Chicken-Essay*. Toronto: Coach House Press, 1975.

Berthoff, Warner. *A Literature Without Qualities: American Writing Since 1945*. Berkeley: University of California Press, 1979.

Charters, Ann, ed. *Dictionary of Literary Biography, The Beats: Literary Bohemians in Postwar America*. 2 vols. Detroit: Gale, 1983.

——. *Kerouac, a Biography*. San Francisco: Straight Arrow Books, 1973.

——. *Scenes Along the Road: Photographs of the Desolation Angels, 1944-1960*. New York: Portents/Gotham Book Mart, 1970.

Charters, Samuel. *Some Poems/Poets: Studies in American Underground Poetry Since 1945*. Berkeley: Oyez, 1971.

Clark, Tom. *Jack Kerouac*. San Diego: Harcourt Brace Jovanovich, 1984.

Cook, Bruce. *The Beat Generation*. New York: Scribner's, 1971.

Cook, Ralph T. *The City Lights Pocket Poets Series: A Descriptive Bibliography*. La Jolla, Cal.: McGilvery/Atticus Books, 1982.

DiPrima, Diane. *Memoirs of a Beatnik*. New York: Olympia, 1969.

Ehrlich, J. W., ed. *Howl of the Censor: The Four Letter Word on Trial*. San Carlos, Cal.: Nourse, 1961.

Faas, Ekbert. *Towards a New American Poetics: Essays and Interviews.* Santa Barbara: Black Sparrow Press, 1979.

Feied, Frederick. *No Pie in the Sky: The Hobo as American Cultural Hero in the Works of Jack London, John Dos Passos, and Jack Kerouac.* New York: Citadel, 1964.

Feldman, Gene, and Max Gartenberg, eds. *The Beat Generation and the Angry Young Men.* New York: Citadel, 1958.

Ferlinghetti, Lawrence, ed. *Beatitude Anthology.* San Francisco: City Lights Books, 1960.

————, and Nancy J. Peters. *Literary San Francisco: A Pictorial History from Its Beginnings to the Present.* San Francisco: City Lights Books/Harper & Row, 1980.

Gifford, Barry, and Lawrence Lee, eds. *Jack's Book.* New York: St. Martin's, 1978.

Ginsberg, Allen. *The Visions of the Great Remember.* Amherst, Mass.: Mulch Press, 1974.

Hipkiss, Robert A. *Jack Kerouac: Prophet of the New Romanticism.* Lawrence: Regents Press of Kansas, 1976.

Hoffman, Frederick J. *Marginal Manners: The Variants of Bohemia.* Evanston, Ill.: Row, Peterson, 1962.

Holmes, John Clellon. *Nothing More to Declare.* New York: Dutton, 1967.

Howard, Richard. *Alone with America: Essays on the Art of Poetry in the United States Since 1950.* New York: Atheneum, 1980.

Huebel, Harry Russell. *Jack Kerouac.* Boise, Idaho: Boise State University, 1979.

Hunt, Tim. *Kerouac's Crooked Road: Development of a Fiction.* Hamden, Conn.: Archon Books, 1981.

Johnson, Joyce. *Minor Characters.* Boston: Houghton Mifflin, 1983.

Jones, LeRoi, ed. *The Moderns: An Anthology of New Writing in America.* New York: Corinth, 1963.

Knight, Arthur Winfield, and Kit Knight. *Beat Angels.* California, Pa.: Unspeakable Visions of the Individual, 1982.

————. *The Beat Book.* California, Pa.: Unspeakable Visions of the Individual, 1974.

————. *The Beat Diary.* California, Pa.: Unspeakable Visions of the Individual, 1977.

————. *The Beat Journey.* California, Pa.: Unspeakable Visions of the Individual, 1978.

————. *The Unspeakable Visions of the Individual.* California, Pa.: Unspeakable Visions of the Individual, 1980.

Kostelanetz, Richard. *Master Minds.* New York: Macmillan, 1969.

Bibliography

————. *Twenties in the Sixties*. Westport, Conn.: Greenwood Press, 1979.

Krim, Seymour, ed. *The Beats*. New York: Fawcett, 1960.

Lepper, Gary M. *A Bibliographical Introduction to Seventy-five Modern American Authors*. Berkeley: Serendipity Books, 1976.

Lipton, Lawrence. *The Holy Barbarians*. New York: Messner, 1959.

McNally, Dennis. *Desolate Angel: Jack Kerouac, the Beats & America*. New York: Random House, 1979.

Meltzer, David, ed. *The San Francisco Poets*. New York: Ballantine, 1971.

Milewski, Robert J. *Jack Kerouac: An Annotated Bibliography of Secondary Sources, 1944-1979*. Metuchen, N.J.: Scarecrow Press, 1981.

Moore, Harry T., ed. *Contemporary American Novelists*. Carbondale: Southern Illinois University Press, 1964.

Nicosia, Gerald. *Memory Babe: A Critical Biography of Jack Kerouac*. New York: Grove, 1983.

Ossman, David. *The Sullen Art: Interviews by David Ossman with Modern American Poets*. New York: Corinth Books, 1963.

Parkinson, Thomas, ed. *A Casebook on the Beat*. New York: Thomas Y. Crowell, 1961.

Plummer, William. *The Holy Goof*. Englewood Cliffs, N.J.: Prentice-Hall, 1981.

Rexroth, Kenneth. *American Poetry in the Twentieth Century*. New York: Herder & Herder, 1971.

Rigney, Francis J., and L. Douglas Smith. *The Real Bohemia: A Sociological and Psychological Study of the Beats*. New York: Basic Books, 1961.

Sanders, Ed. *Tales of Beatnik Glory*. New York: Stonehill, 1975.

Saroyan, Aram. *Genesis Angels: The Saga of Lew Welch and the Beat Generation*. New York: Morrow, 1979.

Seaver, Richard, Terry Southern, and Alexander Trocchi, eds. *Writers in Revolt*. New York: Frederick Fell, 1963.

Tytell, John. *Naked Angels: The Lives and Literature of the Beat Generation*. New York: McGraw-Hill, 1977.

Waldmeir, Joseph J., ed. *Recent American Fiction: Some Critical Views*. Boston: Houghton Mifflin, 1963.

Wilentz, E., ed., with photographs by Fred W. McDarrah. *The Beat Scene*. New York: Corinth Books, 1960.

Wolf, Daniel, and Edwin Fancher. *The Village Voice Reader*. New York: Doubleday, 1962.

ARTICLES

Adams, J. D. "On Writers of Beat Generation," *New York Times Book Review,* VII (May 18, 1957), 2.

Adams, Phoebe. Book review of *Dharma Bums, Atlantic Monthly,* 202 (October 1958), 89.

———. Book review of *Holy Barbarians, Atlantic Monthly,* 204 (July 1959), 82.

———. Book review of *On the Road, Atlantic Monthly,* 200 (October 1957), 178.

Alden, Robert. "Police Pose as Beatniks in Narcotics Raid," *New York Times,* November 8, 1959, 1+.

Algren, Nelson. "Chicago Is a Wose," *Nation,* 188 (February 28, 1959), 191.

Allsop, Kenneth. "Beaten," *Spectator,* 202 (March 13, 1959), 350.

Amis, Kingsley. "The Delights of Literary Lecturing," *Harper's Magazine,* 219 (October 1959), 181–182.

Aronowitz, Alfred G. "The Beat Generation" (12-part series), *New York Post,* March 9–22, 1959.

———. Book review of *The Beats, Village Voice,* 5 (May 18, 1960), 7+.

———. "Portrait of a Beat," *Nugget,* October 1960, 15+.

Askew, M. W. "Quests, Cars and Kerouac," *University Kansas City Review,* 28 (March 1962), 231–240.

Baker, Carlos. "Itching Feet," *Saturday Review,* 40 (September 7, 1957), 19.

Baker, George. "Avant Garde at the Golden Gate," *Saturday Review,* 41 (August 3, 1957), 10.

"Bam; roll on with bam!" *Time,* 74 (September 14, 1959), 28.

"Bang bong bing," *Time,* 74 (September 7, 1959), 80.

Barbeau, C. C. "Plight of the Beat," *America,* 104 (November 12, 1960), 210–212.

Baro, Gene. "Beatniks Now and Then," *Nation,* 189 (September 5, 1959), 115–117.

———. Book review of *On the Road, New York Herald Tribune Book Review,* September 15, 1957, 4.

Bart, Peter. "Artists' Colony Fights for Life: Venice, Calif.," *New York Times,* March 14, 1966, 33.

Bartlett, Kay. "Where Have All the Beatniks Gone?" *New York Post,* January 10, 1970, 25.

"Beat Friar: Brother Antoninus," *Time,* 73 (May 25, 1959), 58.

"Beat Mystics," *Time,* 71 (February 3, 1958), 56.

Bibliography

"Beatniks' Friend: Proprietor of Chez Popoff," *Newsweek,* 66 (August 23, 1965), 36+.

"Beatniks just sick, sick, sick," *Science Digest,* 46 (July 1959), 25–26.

Beatty, J. "Trade Winds," *Saturday Review,* 40 (September 28, 1957), 6.

"Big Day for Bards at Bay: Trial over *Howl and Other Poems,*" *Life,* 43 (September 9, 1957), 105–108.

Bittner, William. Book review of *Dharma Bums, Saturday Review,* 41 (October 11, 1958), 36.

"Blazing and the Beat," *Time,* 71 (February 24, 1958), 104.

Bradbury, Malcolm. Book review of *Holy Barbarians, Reporter,* 21 (July 9, 1959), 40–42.

Breslin, James E. "The Beat Generation: A View from the Left," *Village Voice,* 3 (April 16, 1958), 3.

Broyard, Anatole. "Portrait of the Hipster," *Partisan Review,* 15, 6 (June 1948), 721–727.

Burdick, Eugene. "Innocent Nihilists Adrift in Squaresville," *Reporter,* 18 (April 3, 1958), 30–33.

――――. "Politics of the Beat Generation," *Western Political Quarterly,* 12 (June 1959), 553–555.

Butler, F. A. "On the Beat Nature of Beat," *American Scholar,* 30 (Winter, 1960–61), 79–92.

"Bye, Bye, Beatnik: Marriage of Gregory Corso," *Newsweek,* 62 (July 1, 1963), 65.

Carroll, Paul. "Interview: Allen Ginsberg," *Playboy,* 14 (April 1969), 81–92.

Chamberlain, J. "Kerouac Obituary," *National Review,* 21 (November 4, 1969), 1104.

Ciardi, John. "Book Burners and Sweet Sixteen," *Saturday Review,* 42 (June 27, 1959), 22.

――――. "In Loving Memory of Myself," *Saturday Review,* 42 (July 25, 1959), 22–23.

――――. "Epitaph for the Dead Beats," *Saturday Review,* 43 (February 6, 1960), 11–13.

Clay, George R. "A Sleepless Night with the Beat Generation," *Reporter,* 17 (October 17, 1957), 44.

"Confusion Conforms, Beat Generation in Washington," *Economist,* 192 (August 15, 1959), 432.

Conmy, P. T. "Literary Background of San Francisco Bay Area," *Wilson Library Bulletin,* 32 (June 5, 1958), 723.

Conrad, Barnaby. "Barefoot Boy with Dreams of Zen," *Saturday Review,* 42 (May 2, 1959), 23–24.

Cook, Bruce. Book review of *Desolate Angels, New Republic,* 181 (September 22, 1979), 51.

"Cool, Cool Bards," *Time,* 70 (December 2, 1957), 71.

Curley, Thomas F. "Everything Moves, But Nothing Is Alive," *Commonweal,* 66 (September 13, 1957), 595.

"Daddy-O," *New Yorker,* 34 (May 3, 1958), 29–30.

Daniels, Guy. "Post-Mortem on San Francisco," *Nation,* 237 (August 2, 1958), 3.

Davies, Lawrence E. "Beats in Middle of Coast Unrest," *New York Times,* January 31, 1960, 53.

———. "North Beach Center of Beat Generation," *New York Times,* June 14, 1959, 75.

Dempsey, David. Book review of *On the Road, New York Times Book Review,* VII (September 8, 1957), 4.

De Toledano, R. "Poetry of the Beats," *National Review,* 11 (November 18, 1961), 346+.

Dickey, James. "From Babel to Byzantium," *Sewanee Review,* 65 (Summer 1957), 508–530.

Dickstein, Morris. "Allen Ginsberg and the '60s," *Commentary,* 49 (January 1970), 64+.

"The Disorganization Man," *Time,* 72 (June 9, 1958), 98+.

Eberhart, Richard. "Young Poets on West Coast," *New York Times Book Review,* VII (September 2, 1956), 4.

Eberstadt, Isabel. "King of the East Village," *New York Herald Tribune Magazine,* December 13, 1964, 13.

"End of the Road," *Time,* 94 (October 31, 1969), 10.

"Endsville, Pull My Daisy," *Time,* 74 (December 14, 1959), 66.

"Every Man a Beatnik?" *Newsweek,* 53 (June 29, 1959), 83.

"Far-out Mission; Bread and Wine Mission," *Time,* 73 (June 29, 1959), 38.

Feldman, Irving. "Stuffed 'Dharma,'" *Commentary,* 26 (December 1958), 6.

Ferlinghetti, Lawrence, "Horn on *HOWL*," *Evergreen Review,* 4 (1957), 145–158.

Fischer, J. "Editor's Easy Chair: Old Original Beatnik," *Harper's Magazine,* 218 (April 1959), 14–16.

Fitelson, David. "The Beat Generation," *Partisan Review,* 25 (Summer 1958), 473–476.

Fleischmann, W. B. "Those Beat Writers," *America,* 101 (September 26, 1959), 766–768.

Fles, John. "The End of the Affair or Beyond the Beat Generation," *Village Voice,* 6 (December 15, 1960), 4+.

Bibliography

"For Hip Hosts," *Time*, 75 (February 15, 1960), 69.

Freedland, Nat. "Allen Ginsberg and the Law," *New York Herald Tribune Magazine*, May 24, 1964, 14.

Freud, Caroline. "Portrait of the Beatnik," *Encounter*, 12 (June 1959), 42–46.

"Fried Shoes: Beatniks," *Time*, 73 (February 9, 1959), 16.

Fuller, J. G. "Trade Winds: Ginsberg Trial," *Saturday Review*, 40 (October 5, 1957), 5–7.

"The Ganser Syndrome," *Time*, 70 (September 16, 1957), 120.

"Gaslight, Beatnik Spa, Extinguished Forever," *Village Voice*, 5 (July 11, 1960), 1.

Getlein, F. "Beatniks and Beaux," *New Republic*, 142 (January 11, 1960), 21–22.

Ginsberg, Allen. Book review of *Dharma Bums, Village Voice*, 4 (November 12, 1958), 3–5.

———. "The Great Remember," *Saturday Review*, 55 (December 2, 1972), 60–63.

Glaser, Alice. "Back on the Open Road for Boys, Ginsberg in India," *Esquire*, 60 (July 1963), 48–49 + .

Glauber, R. H. Book review of *The Holy Barbarians, New York Herald Tribune Book Review*, VI (May 24, 1959), 8.

Gleason, Ralph J. "Begone Dull Beats," *New Statesman*, 61 (June 2, 1961), 868.

———. "Kerouac's Beat Generation," *Saturday Review*, 41 (January 11, 1958), 75.

Goddard, Jack. R. "Lights Are Dimmed Along MacDougal Street," *Village Voice*, 5 (June 16, 1960), 1 + .

———. "Like Man, Where Do We Go from Here?" *Village Voice*, 5 (July 7, 1960), 3 + .

———. "MacDougal Street: Fruitcake Version of Inferno," *Village Voice*, 5 (June 23, 1960), 1 + .

———. "Run Beatnik, Run! to Mecca, 1960," *Village Voice*, 5 (June 30, 1960), 3 + .

Gold, Herbert. "The Beat Mystique," *Playboy*, 5 (February 1958), 20 + .

———. Book review of *Desolate Angels, New York Times Book Review*, VII (August 12, 1979), 3.

———. "Hip, Cool, Beat, and Frantic," *Nation*, 185 (November 16, 1957), 349–355.

———. "How to Tell the Beatniks from the Hipsters," *Noble Savage*, 1 (Spring 1960), 132–139.

Green, Mark. "A Kind of Beatness," *City of San Francisco*, July 27, 1975, 42 + .

————. "A One-Way Bore on the Road to Tragedy," *Village Voice,* 5 (February 3, 1960), 7+.

Hall, David. "It's Not Bohemia or the Beard That Makes the Poem, It's the Poet," *New York Times Book Review,* VII (May 3, 1959), 4.

Hazo, S. "Poets of Retreat," *Catholic World,* 198 (October 1963), 33–39.

"Heat on the Beatniks," *Newsweek,* 54 (August 17, 1959), 36.

Hecht, Anthony. "The Anguish of the Spirit and the Letter," *Hudson Review,* 12 (Winter 1959), 593–603.

Hines, L. J. "Stevenson and the Beats," *Commonweal,* 72 (September 9, 1960), 465–467.

Holmes, John Clellon. "This Is the Beat Generation," *New York Times Magazine,* VI (November 16, 1952), 10+.

————. "The Philosophy of the Beat Generation," *Esquire,* 49 (February 1958), 35.

"Hot Spot, Evicted Beats," *Newsweek,* 67 (February 7, 1966), 34.

Howe, Irving. "Mass Society and Post-Modern Fiction," *Partisan Review,* 36 (Summer 1959), 420–436.

Hynes, S. "Beat and the Angry," *Commonweal,* 68 (September 5, 1958), 559–561.

Jacobson, D. "America's Angry Young Men," *Commentary,* 24 (December 1957), 475–479.

Kastel, Warren. "Kerouac: The Road to Nowhere," *Rogue,* August 1959, 40.

Kempton, Sally. "Colder Children," *Esquire,* 61 (July 1965), 61+.

Kerouac, Jack. "Alone on a Mountaintop," *Holiday,* 24 (October 1958), 68+.

————. "Beatific: On the Origins of the Beat Generation," *Encounter,* 13 (August 1959), 57–61.

————. "Belief and Technique for Modern Prose," *Evergreen Review,* 8 (Spring 1959), 57.

————. "Essentials of Spontaneous Prose," *Evergreen Review,* 5 (Summer 1958), 72–73.

————. "The Last Word," *Escapade,* February 1960, 104.

————. "On the Road with Memere," *Holiday,* 37 (May 1965), 74–75.

————. "Roaming Beatniks," *Holiday,* 26 (October 1959), 82–87.

————. "Tangier to London," *Holiday,* 27 (February 1960), 88–89.

————. "Vanishing American Hobo," *Holiday,* 27 (March 1960), 60–61.

"King of the YADS," *Time,* 80 (November 30, 1962), 96.

Kiplinger, Suzanne. "This Hip-Historian Knows a Man's Pad Is His Castle," *Village Voice,* 4 (June 24, 1959), 7+.

Klein, Edward. "They Dig Booze, Jazz and Sex," *New York Daily News,* February 1958, 28.

Bibliography

———. "Wreckers Close In on the Last Bohemians," *New York Daily News,* February 20, 1959, 36.

Krim, Seymour. Book review of *The Holy Barbarians, Evergreen Review,* 3 (Summer 1959), 208–214.

———. "King of the Beats," *Commonweal,* 69 (January 2, 1959), 359–360.

Knight, Arthur Winfield. "Search for Jack Kerouac," *Review of Contemporary Fiction,* 3 (Summer 1983), 14–18.

Kostelanetz, Richard. "From Nightmare to Serendipity: A Retrospective Look at William Burroughs," *Twentieth Century Literature,* 2 (October 1965), 123–130.

———. "Ginsberg Makes the World Scene," *New York Times Magazine,* VI (July 11, 1965), 22–23 +.

Kramer, Jane. "Pater Familias," *New Yorker,* 44 (August 17 and August 24, 1968), 32–73; 38–91.

Laqueur, W. Z. "Moscow Makes the Scene," *Reporter,* 24 (January 5, 1961), 39 +.

Lelyveld, Joseph. "Kerouac Obituary," *New York Times,* October 22, 1969, 47.

Leogrande, Ernest. "The Beats: World Keystone Chase," *New York Sunday News,* May 29, 1966, 3 +.

Leonard, G. B., Jr. "Bored, the Bearded and the Beat," *Look,* 22 (August 19, 1958), 64–68.

Leonard, John. "Epitaph for the Beat Generation," *National Review,* 7 (September 12, 1959), 331.

Lipton, Lawrence. "Youth Will Serve Itself," *Nation,* 183 (November 10, 1956), 389–392.

Lottman, Herbert R. "A Baedeker of Beatnik Territory," *New York Times Magazine,* VI (August 7, 1966), 40.

Lyle, David. "Greenwich Village Poets Vs. Police," *New York Herald Tribune,* June 8, 1959, 1 +.

MacGregor-Hastie, Roy. "Waste Land in Russell Square," *Trace,* 32 (June–July 1959), 1–5.

Magid, M. "Death of Hip: The Changing Hipster," *Esquire,* 63 (June 1965), 89–103.

Mahoney, Stephen. "The Prevalence of Zen," *Nation,* 187 (November 1, 1958), 14.

Mailer, Norman. "The White Negro," *Dissent,* 4 (Summer 1957), 276–293.

Malcolm, Donald. Book review of *The Subterraneans, New Yorker,* 34 (April 5, 1958), 137.

Marowitz, Charles. "Rexroth and the Squares or Hipdom Hits London," *Village Voice,* 4 (July 8, 1959), 3.

May, James Boyer. "Flipping the Coin(age)," *Trace,* 34 (October–November 1959), 20–27.

McClintock, Jack. "This Is How the Ride Ends," *Esquire,* 73 (March 1970), 138+.

McDarrah, Fred W. "The Anatomy of a Beatnik," *Saga,* 20 (August 1960), 34+.

———. "Brooklyn's Angel Is MacDougal Street's 'Miss Beatnik,'" *Village Voice,* 4 (July 22, 1959), 1.

McFadden, J. P. "Howling in the Wilderness," *National Review,* 7 (September 12, 1959), 338–339.

McReynolds, David. "Hipsters Unleashed," *Liberation,* June 1959, 202.

———. "Youth 'Disaffilliated' from a Phony World," *Village Voice,* 4 (March 11, 1959), 1+.

"Mentholated Eggnog," *Time,* 73 (June 1, 1959), 88.

Millstein, Gilbert. Book review of *On the Road, New York Times,* September 5, 1957, 27.

———. "Rent a Beatnik and Swing," *New York Times Magazine,* VII (April 17, 1960), 26+.

"Minister for the Beatniks; Bread and Wine Mission," *Newsweek,* 53 (March 16, 1959), 88.

Montgomery, John. "Report from the Beat Generation," *Library Journal,* 84 (June 15, 1959), 1999–2000.

Moody, Howard R. "Reflections on the Beat Generation," *Religion in Life,* 28 (Summer 1959), 426–432.

Moore, Harry T. "Cool Cats Don't Dig the Squares," *New York Times Book Review,* VI (May 24, 1959), 1+.

Moore, Marianne. "The Ways Our Poets Have Taken in 15 Years Since the War," *New York Herald Tribune Book Review,* VI (June 26, 1960), 1+.

Moore, Rosalie. "The Beat and the Unbeat," *Poetry,* 93 (November 1958), 2.

Mottram, Eric. "Beat: Genesis and Writings," *Ark 33—Journal of the Royal College of Art,* 33 (Autumn 1962), 1–7.

"New Test for Obscenity," *Nation,* 185 (November 9, 1957), 314.

Nicosia, Gerald. "Focus: The Beats," *American Book Review,* 3 (May–June 1981), 7–9.

Oesterreicher, Arthur. Book review of *On the Road, Village Voice,* 2 (September 18, 1957), 5.

"Of Time and the Rebel," *Time,* 76 (December 5, 1960), 16–17.

O'Neil, Paul. "Only Rebellion Around," *Life,* 47 (November 30, 1959), 114–130.

Perlman, David. "How Captain Hanrahan Made *Howl* a Best-Seller," *Reporter,* 17 (December 12, 1957), 37–39.

Bibliography

Pinck, D. "Digging the San Franciscans," *New Republic,* 138 (March 3, 1958), 20.

Plummer, William. "Jack Kerouac: The Beat Goes On," *New York Times Magazine,* VI (December 30, 1979), 20–21+.

Podell, Albert N. "Censorship on the Campus: The Case of the *Chicago Review,*" *San Francisco Review,* I (Spring 1959), 71–89.

Podhoretz, Norman. "Howl of Protest in San Francisco," *New Republic,* 137 (September 16, 1957), 20.

———. "The Know-Nothing Bohemians," *Partisan Review,* 25 (Spring 1958), 305–311+.

———. "Where Is the Beat Generation Going?" *Esquire,* 50 (December 1958), 147+.

Pritchett, V. S. "The Beat Generation," *New Statesman,* August 23, 1958, 292, 294.

Rexroth, Kenneth. "Bearded Barbarians or Real Bards?" *New York Times Book Review,* VII (February 12, 1961), 1+.

———. Book review of *On the Road, San Francisco Chronicle,* September 1, 1957, 18.

———. "Dead as Davy Crockett Caps, Says Rexroth, Passing Through," *Village Voice,* 3 (April 23, 1958), 4+.

———. "Disengagement: The Art of the Beat Generation," *New World Writing,* 11 (May 1957), 28–41.

———. "Jazz and Poetry," *Esquire,* 49 (May 1958), 20.

———. "Jazz Poetry," *Nation,* 186 (March 29, 1958), 282–283.

———. "Revolt: True and False," *Nation,* 186 (April 26, 1958), 378–379.

———. "San Francisco Letter," *Evergreen Review,* I, 2 (1957), 5–14.

———. "San Francisco's Mature Bohemians," *Nation,* 184 (February 23, 1957), 159–162.

Rosenthal, M. L. "Naked and the Clad," *Nation,* 187 (October 11, 1958), 215.

———. "Poet of the New Violence," *Nation,* 184 (February 23, 1957), 162.

Roskolenko, Harry. "The Jazz-Poets," *Prairie Schooner,* 33 (Summer 1959), 148–153.

Ross, Basil. "California Young Writers, Angry and Otherwise," *Library Journal,* 83 (June 15, 1958), 12.

Ross, Don. "An Evening with the Beats: 'It's an Underground, Like,'" *New York Herald Tribune,* IV (July 19, 1959), 1–2.

Ross, Timothy A. "Rise and Fall of the Beats," *Nation,* 192 (May 27, 1961), 456–458.

Rubin, Louis D., Jr. "Two Gentlemen of San Francisco: Notes on Kerouac and Responsibility," *Western Review,* 23 (Spring 1959), 278–283.

Rumaker, Michael. "Allen Ginsberg's *Howl*," *Black Mountain Review*, 7 (Autumn 1957), 228–237.

"Sanity of Kerouac," *Time*, 92 (February 23, 1968), 96.

Schickel, Richard. "A Gone Group," *New York Times Book Review*," VI (May 15, 1960), 16+.

Schlamm, W. S. "Beauty and the Beatniks; Spanish Steps in Rome," *National Review*, 18 (January 11, 1966), 23–24.

Schleifer, Marc D. "Allen Ginsberg—Here to Save Us but Not Sure from What," *Village Voice*, 3 (October 15, 1958), 3+.

———. "The Beat Debated: Is It or Is It Not?" *Village Voice*, 4 (November 19, 1958), 1.

———. "Kenneth Patchen on the 'Brat' Generation," *Village Voice*, 4 (March 18, 1959), 1.

Schneider, P. E. "Rebellion Fades on the Left Bank," *New York Times Magazine*, VI (April 19, 1959), 37+.

Schumach, Murray. "Students Decry Corso Dismissal," *New York Times*, April 7, 1965, 9.

Scott, J. F. "Beat Literature and the American Teen Cult," *American Quarterly*, 1 (Summer 1962), 150–160.

Shapiro, Karl. "Poets of the Silent Generation," *Prairie Schooner*, 31 (Winter 1957), 298–299.

"Sickniks," *Newsweek*, 57 (May 22, 1961), 56.

Sigal, Clancy, "Nihilism's Organization Man," *Universities and Left Review*, 4 (Summer 1958), 59–65.

Sisk, J. P. "Beatniks and Tradition," *Commonweal*, 70 (April 17, 1959), 75–77.

Sitwell, Edith. "The Beat Rebellion" (letter to the editor), *Life*, 48 (February 8, 1960), 25.

Smith, Howard. "Fried Shoes," *Escapade*, 5 (February 1960), 9+.

———. "Off the Road, into the Vanguard, and Out," *Village Voice*, 3 (December 25, 1957), 1.

———. "A Time to Separate the Men and Boys," *Village Voice*, 4 (February 4, 1959), 4.

Squaresville U.S.A. vs. Beatsville," *Life*, 47 (September 21, 1959), 31–37.

Stanford, Derek. "Beatniks and Angry Young Men," *Meanjin*, 17 (Summer 1958), 413–419.

"Strange Taste," *Newsweek*, 61 (November 26, 1962), 94.

Talbot, Daniel. "Beat and Screaming," *New York Times Book Review*, VII (June 19, 1960), 5.

Tallman, Warren, "Kerouac's Sound," *Tamarack Review*, Spring 1959, 58–74.

Bibliography

Tallmer, Jerry. "Back to the Village but Still on the Road," *Village Voice*, 2 (September 18, 1957), 1+.

———. "What Ever Became of the Beat Generation?" *New York Post*, September 9, 1967, 31.

Treuhaft, Jessica Mitford. "The Indignant Generation," *Nation*, 192 (May 22, 1961), 451–456.

Trilling, Diana. "The Other Night at Columbia," *Partisan Review*, 26 (Spring 1959), 214–230.

Tynan, Kenneth. "San Francisco: The Rebels," *Holiday*, 29 (April 1961), 92–97.

Van Den Haag, Ernest. "Conspicuous Consumption of Self," *National Review*, 6 (April 11, 1959), 656–658.

Wakefield, Dan. "Kerouac Comes Home," *Atlantic Monthly*, 216 (July 1965), 69–72.

———. "Night Clubs," *Nation*, 186 (January 4, 1958), 19.

West, Anthony. Book review of *Dharma Bums*, *New Yorker*, 34 (November 1, 1958), 175.

Winn, J. "Capote, Mailer and Miss Parker," *New Republic*, 140 (February 9, 1959), 27–28.

Wolfe, B. "Angry at What?" *Nation*, 187 (November 1, 1958), 316.

"Zen-Hur, Pull My Daisy," *Time*, 74 (December 14, 1959), 66.

Zimpel, L. "Footnotes on the New Bohemia," *New Republic*, 143 (July 18, 1960), 16.

INDEX

Index

Index